# Stubborn Roots

# Stubborn Roots

*Race, Culture, and Inequality in U.S. and South African Schools*

━━●━━

## PRUDENCE L. CARTER

OXFORD
UNIVERSITY PRESS

# OXFORD
## UNIVERSITY PRESS

Oxford University Press, Inc., publishes works that further
Oxford University's objective of excellence
in research, scholarship, and education.

Oxford New York
Auckland   Cape Town   Dar es Salaam   Hong Kong   Karachi
Kuala Lumpur   Madrid   Melbourne   Mexico City   Nairobi
New Delhi   Shanghai   Taipei   Toronto

With offices in
Argentina   Austria   B razil   Chile   Czech Republic   France   Greece
Guatemala   Hungary   Italy   Japan   Poland   Portugal   Singapore
South Korea   Switzerland   Thailand   Turkey   Ukraine   Vietnam

Published by Oxford University Press, Inc.
198 Madison Avenue, New York, New York 10016
www.oup.com

Oxford is a registered trademark of Oxford University Press

Carter, Prudence L.
Stubborn roots : Race, Culture, and Inequality in U.S. and
South African Schools / Prudence L. Carter.
p. cm.
Includes bibliographical references and index.
ISBN 978-0-19-989963-0 (cloth : alk. paper) —
ISBN 978-0-19-989965-4 (pbk. : alk. paper)
1. Educational equalization—United States—Case studies.
2. Educational equalization—South Africa—Case studies.
3. Discrimination in education—United States—Case studies.
4. Discrimination in education—South Africa—Case studies.
5. Multiculturalism—United States—Case studies.
6. Multiculturalism—South Africa—Case studies.   I. Title.
LC213.2.C37 2012
379.2'6—dc23
2011039801


1 3 5 7 9 8 6 4 2

Printed in the United States of America
on acid-free paper

# *Contents*

# *Preface*

"2004" WAS A defining moment for two nations on different continents separated by thousands of miles of the Atlantic Ocean. Then, Americans commemorated the *fiftieth anniversary of the U.S. Supreme Court's ruling in Brown vs. the Topeka, KS Board of Education*.[1] South Africans celebrated *ten* years of its nascent democracy after nearly five decades of rigid racial exclusion under apartheid. Conferences and colloquia in these nations and abroad emphasized the shared and particular experiences of these societies, which had grappled with the inhumanity of racism, racial discrimination, and intolerance for far too long. Alas, the doors had "opened," and national leaders and policy makers in both places sought to equalize opportunity for historically disadvantaged racial, ethnic, and economic groups through schooling and education. At that celebratory "50–10" moment, the United States and South Africa had both undertaken school desegregation as a means to economic transformation and a more equitable society.

*Stubborn Roots* argues that although the two nations vary in their structure, discourse, and policy agendas, school practices in both countries converge when it comes to the incorporation of the previously disenfranchised racial and ethnic groups—Africans, Coloureds, and Indians (South Africa), and African Americans, Asian Americans, Latinos, and Native Americans (United States). On the ground, behind school walls, explicit codes and school-specific policies are strikingly "decoupled" from the national goals of equity, access, and equality in both countries.[2] How does this happen? And further, why do government initiatives and intentions fail to fully trickle down to the school level?

One morning, at a high-performing school in a southern U.S. state, an African American girl, "Tamara," lamented: "They don't really care about us when it comes to school; they [educators] just need us to perform well on these tests so that the school can look good, and they can keep their jobs," she said.[3] Obviously, not all students at this "good" school felt fully integrated in the academic culture. Tamara and about a dozen other students had been cast off to the school auditorium for in-school suspension, which lasted one to three days, because they had transgressed—mainly talking back to teachers or being repeatedly late for school. Sitting under the hawkish watch of a teacher supervisor, they feigned engagement with school work, although they declared utter boredom with school to me.

Sometimes, I am inclined to agree with Tamara. Indeed, all too many stakeholders in public education are concerned only with test scores and their international standing; there seems to be little interest in delving into the processes and mechanisms that produce deeply engaged citizens, critical thinkers, or future contributors to society. *Stubborn Roots* argues that because laws and policies are focused on the material redistribution of educational resources, they have not sufficiently tended to the social and cultural realms—which essentially engender relationships among school-based actors: educators, students, parents, and staff. What happens day-to-day in the interactions among the people inside of schools is largely absent from national debates and discussions on education reform. Many educators, policymakers, and researchers maintain a myopic stance about what it takes to properly educate children and ignore the messy social, cultural, and political issues that are both overt and latent in schools. A shifting of focus to the underlying processes by which schools either actively reproduce or diminish social and academic divisions among groups of students will shed greater light on the efficacy of specific educational policies and cultural codes and practices. From an outcomes perspective, such analyses reveal why similar groups of students may thrive in one educational context and not in another.

*Stubborn Roots* documents the social and cultural life within eight schools (four in the United States and four in South Africa) to help unpack the proverbial "black box" about specific mechanisms that produce differential educational well-beings among various racial and ethnic student groups. This book documents how schools' cultural environments cultivate boundaries that students and educators create to signify in-group and out-group status in academic, extracurricular, and other domains within the school. With the generous support of several funders, a team of research assistants and I spent hundreds of hours in the American and South African schools (which I introduce more fully in chapter 3), observing everyday activities, sounds, and practices and recording the social makeup of different academic classes, student social spaces, and extracurricular activities in order to develop "thick" descriptions of the sociocultural milieu of the schools.[4] We explored both similarities and differences between these schools in their sociocultural contexts. The narratives presented in the following pages are based on discussions and interviews with principals and teachers, classroom observations, and student surveys.

## Two Racialized Societies: Doing Cross-National, Comparative Schools Research

When a researcher typically conducts international, comparative studies, one common assumption is that the nations selected as cases are unique contexts whose own particular social conditions become the explanations for diverse outcomes. Thus, locating similarities or attributing related influences to certain outcomes in different societies might prove difficult. "We focus on context, on the one hand, and on the other, universal comparisons across [national] contexts," economist Martin Carnoy has stated. "Bringing this into the realm of practice, which is highly contextual, usually means decontextualizing our research—universalizing comparisons—just when contextual comparisons should be most important," Carnoy continued.[5] I agree with Carnoy on this point and have worked diligently to acknowledge the unique features of the two national cases, while recognizing noteworthy commonalities between them. For example, both countries have sought to transform their unequal educational systems through school desegregation.

Perhaps a greater challenge in comparative, international studies is attaining sufficient equivalence in each unit of analysis across array of variables on which the case studies are selected.[6] For example, with their own distinctive histories and national, state, and local structures of schooling, curriculum, and educational policy agendas, it could be difficult to argue that social systems work similarly in two diverse societies—one with a white and the other with a black majority. Yet, I write against convention and present findings that focus on several key similarities in various sociological conditions related to the social organization of students and student and teacher relationships in the United States and South Africa. That is, despite unique differences in their educational systems, some striking resemblances in the ways in which certain types of U.S. and South African schools operate *socially*—especially if they share certain dispositions—exist. *Stubborn Roots* documents both parallel and context-specific patterns of social and cultural dynamics in the focal U.S. and South African schools.

At first glance, three factors distinguish South Africa's school desegregation process from that of the United States. First, South Africa's experiment with racial mixing in schools rose out of the relatively liberal stage of the world polity in the 1990s, in contrast to the rigid, Jim-Crow context of pre-Civil Rights era that gave rise to the *Brown* decision. As a result, its progress with interracial schooling occurred more rapidly, within a matter of years. In comparison, desegregation efforts in the United States, in many cases, took a few more decades to come to fruition, and then only after years of protest and through additional legal action in the courts.

Second, South Africa shifted from a racist white regime of minority rule to a black-led democratic government, which claimed from the start to give full citizenship rights and access to its black majority. In the process, every major sector of society (with the exception of the private economic sector) received new leadership focused on the rights of Blacks, Coloureds, and Indians. New educational policies emerged immediately, charting a different course for African, Coloured, Indian, and White students. By all indicators, the African National Congress (ANC)-led government was not laissez-faire about its legislative and judicial mandates to integrate. The South African national government plays a prominent role in education and sustains a centralized and standardized system for learners across its nine provinces.

In contrast, the United States has historically supported a decentralized approach to education, according its fifty states with control and proprietary status over their respective systems, with some financial support provided through federal educational programs and funding for equalizing opportunities, like early childhood education (e.g., Headstart) and free and reduced lunch programs, available through means-tested programs. Ironically, the 2001 No Child Left Behind (NCLB) law introduced by the Republican administration of President George W. Bush—who worked in an alliance with then Democratic Senator Edward Kennedy of Massachusetts—has significantly expanded the role of the federal government in American public education by putting into place numerous metrics to determine school success and monitor progress on an annual basis.[7]

Third, the educational desegregation policies of both countries have focused on compensating for the economic disparities that resulted from their former racially exclusive practices and on leveling those differences through access to better schools. Yet in both practice and discourse, South Africa has made its commitment to racial and class equality more explicit. Its educational laws and policies signify the government's commitment to "radical inclusion"—which inheres in the nation's practices and policies to fully incorporate its diverse constituency by designating eleven official national languages and establishing, in August 2011, a new multicultural curricular policy. Further, upon gaining political control in 1994 after a successful movement to dismantle apartheid, leaders of the ANC sought to actively construct and sustain a nonracial democracy. Nonracialism, which prohibits the use of race as an operative category in myriad facets of South African society, has served as the basis of the ANC's reconciliatory actions toward the white minority in its attempts to create a strong national identity across all racial lines.[8] The nonracialist agenda in South Africa, nevertheless, remains challenged by attitudes and beliefs deeply entrenched in racist ideology maintained by segments of the population. While the South African Constitution renders race as an inoperative concept for the purposes of human, political, and economic rights, entrenched discriminatory practices pervade various aspects of society. Educational researchers, for example, find evidence of Black students' exposure to in-school racial tension and racist experiences.[9] Many South African schools promote an ethos of acculturation into whiteness where speaking either English or Afrikaans prevails[10] and where desegregation occurs only among students and not staff.[11]

Nevertheless, South Africa's commitment to equity is evident in policies that mandate equal teacher pay in poor, black, and coloured townships and wealthier, formerly white schools. Additionally, in 2008, the Ministry of Education disbanded a tracking system of "higher grade" exams—analogous to either honors or advanced placement in the United States—and "standard grade" exams, which disproportionately and adversely affected students of color, putting them on different trajectories for university admissions. (In the past, students had to obtain high pass marks on a requisite number of higher grade course exams—ranging from four to six exams, depending on their degree of concentration—in order to gain entry into one of South Africa's universities.) The minister also eradicated the fee requirements for students in extremely poor state schools.

If their systems are so different, then what makes the United States and South Africa comparable in terms of how they have addressed equal opportunity through schooling? Many public school students in both the United States and South Africa—especially those from middle-class and higher backgrounds—benefit from a wealth of academic resources in their schools. Yet, inequities endure even within these good quality schools. Administrators and teachers are often befuddled by the achievement disparities between white and nonwhite, middle-class and poor, students who attend such resource-rich schools. *Stubborn Roots* highlights the paradoxical relationship between historically disadvantaged students' access to resource-rich schools and the inequality embedded within the systems of cultural meanings in both the

American and South African contexts. On the one hand, many schools are considered "good" ones because they provide more rigorous academic training and resources, which enhance the chances of previously disadvantaged groups for greater development of their human capital, educational attainment, and economic mobility. Yet, in comparing and contrasting U.S and South African schools in their approaches to equity, *Stubborn Roots* spotlights an array of school-centered factors that weaken students' overall educational well-beings as they move across social and cultural contexts and boundaries to more well-off schools. What we found is that narrow definitions of equal opportunity—which mainly privilege the idea of access to schools with strong test-score or college-going rates—do not suffice to address the educational welfare of many students in these nations. Rather, how both U.S. and South African education produce practices of inclusion within the dual structures of their material *and* sociocultural contexts is critical to the attainment of equity.

How does obtain equity ? within schools / society?
- equal access to schools?
- inclusion?

# Acknowledgments

THIS BOOK WOULD not have been written without the support and insight of a great number of fabulous people. First, although they remain nameless for the sake of confidentiality, I am especially grateful to the students, educators, and other staff at the schools affiliated with my study. The seeds were planted for *Stubborn Roots* (pun intended) when I took my first study trip to South Africa with two colleagues. The assistance of Dr. Nelson Moloko, Dr. Dorothy Terry, and Trevor Van Louw—who, figuratively speaking, opened several doors—helped me to gain entrée to schools, not an easy task in itself.

Generous financial assistance from a National Academy of Education/ Spencer Foundation Postdoctoral Fellowship, the William F. Milton Fund at Harvard University, and a major grant from the William T. Grant Foundation paid for research expenses and provided opportunities to write. Thank you, especially, Robert Granger and Edward Seidman, for your support and attention. For their invaluable research, coding, transcribing, and/or editorial assistance, I owe deep thanks to Audrey Alforque Thomas, Grace Atukpawu, Adam Bad Wound, Jakeya Caruthers, Amanda Cox, Karen DeGannes, Lauren Ellison, Jessica Foster, Fagan Harris, Megan Holland, Rebecca Keegan, Rejoice Nsibande, Kathleen O'Connor, Erin Raab, Lazeena Rahman, Lauren Rivera, Carla Shalaby, Graziella da Silva, Dana Van Deman, Janet Vanides, Charnise Virgil, Joshua Wakeham, Bernita Washington, and Laura Wentworth.

Several incredible scholars took the time out of their busy schedules to read the entire manuscript—some even traveling halfway around the world—and to spend a day with me developing it: Drs. Jean Baxen, Amy Binder, Lori Hill, John L. Jackson, Roslyn Mickelson, Na'ilah Nasir, Mokubung Nkomo, sean f. reardon, and Karolyn Tyson—Thank you! Other colleagues around the nation and at my places of employment, Harvard and Stanford University, supported this project, my career, and me in some way: H. Samy Alim, James Banks, Richard Banks, Lawrence Bobo, Martin Carnoy, Linda Darling-Hammond, Jennifer

Eberhardt, Harry Elam, Michele Elam, Tyrone Forman, Patricia Gumport, MarYam Hamedani, Bruce Haynes, Allyson Hobbs, Janice Jackson, Nadia Kim, Michèle Lamont, Jennifer Lee, Amanda Lewis, Hazel Markus, Milbrey McLaughlin, Debra Meyerson, Mignon Moore, Marcyliena Morgan, Paula Moya, Carla O'Connor, Mica Pollock, Janelle Scott, Claude Steele, Deborah Stipek, Natasha Warikoo, Amy Stuart Wells, and William Julius Wilson. The project evolved even more, thanks to the numerous centers, sociology departments, and schools of education, which invited me to give a lecture at the following institutions: University of California-Berkeley, University of California-Davis, University of Chicago, Harvard University, Indiana University-Bloomington, New York University, Northwestern University, University of Massachusetts-Amherst, University of Notre Dame, University of Pennsylvania, University of Southern California, Stanford University, and University of Wisconsin-Madison. Professor Crain Soudien and the Education Department at the University of Cape Town and the Witwatersrand Institute for Social and Economic Research (WISER) kindly granted me visiting scholar status while in South Africa conducting field research.

A community of friends either read some drafts, discussed ideas, or made the arduous research and writing process more bearable by either imparting advice or encouraging perseverance: Sonya Anderson, Angela Counts, Eric Coburn, Douglas Brooks, Reena Karani, Martin McLee, Lebogang Montjane, Helen Schaub, Syma Solovitch, Dorothy Steele, Deborah Wafer, and Laura Wernick. There is only a partial list of those who offered support. I appreciate many others from various spheres of my life who have contributed to my intellectual growth. My editor at Oxford University Press, James Cook, the editorial and production team, Jaimee Biggins, Tina Hardy, and Molly Morrison, and the anonymous reviewers for the Press gave me great feedback and guidance as I labored to complete this book.

Finally, I acknowledge the love, continuous support, and encouragement of some very special friends and loved ones who have been there through thick and thin: Patricia E. Powell; my parents Clara Carter and William H. Carter, Sr., who paved the way; my siblings Melanie Carter, Camissica Carter-Hinton, and William H. Carter, Jr.; in-laws Kory Hinton and Tashana Carter; nieces and nephews Jameela Grace Ayoub, Maya Coleman, Jonathan Hinton, and William H. Carter, III; and my "PPP's"—Cassandra Davies, Marti Hunter, Priya and Francisca Friday-Pabros, Barbara Grimm, Nicole Troy, and precious Kily Tracy (GIGATT). Thank you for being love and light and for helping me to maintain a peace of mind and a balance of life.

September, 2011
Palo Alto, California

# List of Tables

# List of Figures

# *Introduction*

## DUAL STRUCTURES: WHY CULTURE MATTERS IN SCHOOLS

JUDAH HENDERSON, A fifteen-year-old civically engaged African American male, serves as North Village High School's student representative to the North Capital City's mayoral Youth Council. North Village High is an affluent and majority-white school that had been recruiting low-income and working-class Black and Latino students to its ranks for over four decades through the Voluntary Desegregation Program (VDP). Judah and I first met when I began research at the school. As adolescents are often wont to do, Judah made some incisive remarks about his school and about VDP in a casual conversation with me and one of his teachers that spring afternoon. I was so struck by his comments that I asked his permission to use them as a springboard for a larger conversation that I was to hold with Judah and a group of eight other boys several minutes later. Judah began:

> The school doesn't really appreciate us for our hardships, all the things that we go through. Nor do they appreciate us for our integrity or character, and I feel like it's unfair and that it needs to be changed, and I think that's part of the reason why a lot of us feel disconnected from the school. It's not because we left the school. It's because the school left us, and I feel like the school should really, you know, value us for what every individual is and what he has to offer to the school system, and I feel like this is an issue that affects the VDP program in particular because a lot of us do feel like this school does not want us here—at least I do, and so I feel like we need a lot of work, and we need to make

*the school doesn't appreciate them, doesn't want them, not seen as individuals* a lot of changes. We need to make a concentrated effort and demand some change. How do you guys feel?

*academics*

Derrick, another VDP participant who is also Black,[1] disagreed at once: "The teachers I have, they generally try to help me. We have to seek the help."

Yet, as I understood Judah, he was trying to articulate something different about the social and cultural dynamics of his schooling, and so I asked for clarification: "Is that what you were talking about, Judah, like getting help to develop academic skills, or are you talking about something else?" He responded immediately:

*inclusion*

> I'm referring to like the intangibles...not whether or not you can reiterate the facts that the teachers are teaching you. Not whether you can memorize like a math equation or a scientific formula. I'm talking about character, strength, and integrity and how we relate to other people, how we identify with other people and our creativity. Those are things that I feel are not being valued enough in the school system. I think that it's important to have those attributes if you want to make it far in life; but with the way the system is structured now, they solely focus on, you know, what grades you get, and I think that doesn't do us much justice.

Derrick chimed in again: "Isn't that what it's all about? Grades?"

Just as Judah starts to respond, "Well, it's not all about..." Jonathan, another student, jumps in to challenge Judah. "What is it about?"

Judah continued:

*Freire*

> It's about you being able to connect with other people. You being able to question what the teachers are teaching you.... You being able to take what they're teaching you and try to apply it to, you know, real-life scenarios but the problem is, the stuff they're teaching us, well, I'm not sure if I have the credentials to say this, but the stuff they're teaching us, I don't think does us much justice. I think that they should teach us more about, you know, morality, more about like the relationship with society. How we can change society?

As the debate unfolded, it was apparent that Judah was not alone in his assessment. "Are you feeling prepared for all of the purposes you think school is intended here at North Village?" I asked. There was a silent pause before Michael, a Latino boy, responded: "Not really. There's not much interaction because like the 'caf' [cafeteria] is split right down the middle...There's a space for you to walk. One side is all...basically all the VDP kids and the other side is the White kids. There's no interaction."

"Why not?" I asked "Can't you create that? Can't you guys create that interaction?" I looked around the room trying to get a handle on their perceived senses of agency, of what they believed they could control themselves. Michael continued: "We do individually like in classrooms. I don't know. It's like hi-and-bye relationship. You see them and you're like, 'What's up?' You know, 'What's up?'"

"But why do you think that happens in this school?" I press on. There is a pause, and then Judah begins again: "Because the system doesn't encourage us to interact. Think about it."

And I have been thinking about *it* ever since.

From a sociocultural and philosophical standpoint, the dialogue among Judah, Derrick, Michael, and Jonathan highlights a neglected dimension of schooling that is critical to their full engagement as students. For them, school officials need to pay more attention to not only emphasizing the essential goals of equal educational opportunities and outcomes—the most common way that public discourse frames educational equity—*but also* to what one scholar refers to as "substantive inclusion," having one group's affiliation fully acknowledged and equally valued as an active member of the community.[2] Both aspects are critical components of a fair and just education. By highlighting what he viewed as a lack of fulfillment in the contract between VDP and North Village, Judah argued: "The VDP is not just about [students of color] coming out to suburban schools, doing the homework and going back to our own homes. The VDP is about teaching suburban schools, suburban students what it's like to live in the inner city, what it feels like to be a person of color."

They do not all agree, however. Jonathan, who took an instrumentalist approach to his schooling, retorted, "I thought the VDP was to come out and get a good education." For Jonathan, a "good education" meant exposure to high quality teachers and educational resources that would put him and others on the track toward college preparation and ultimately a bachelor's degree. Two other boys, who had been quiet up until that point, agreed with Jonathan: "Yeah. Yeah." But Judah pushed his philosophical stance further: "No, it's not...it's the main purpose, but the other purpose is to teach each other what we have to offer."

Judah and Jonathan's debate is not unique. It mirrors an age-old one held among philosophers, sociologists, educational policy makers, and parents alike. Like these contemporary youth, prominent civil rights activists and

Black intellectuals argued over similar questions from 1932 to 1954, although this time explicitly about the role of education in ameliorating the "race problem."[3] What are the purposes of integrated schooling? Is school integration merely to provide proximity to better academic resources, or do moral and social imperatives mandate that educators in integrated schools foster educational environments of tolerance, respect for cultural differences, and the development of multiple ties across social lines?

The discussions among the North Village High students and mid-twentieth-century thinkers highlight an important sociological observation. Different camps of thinkers have chosen to place gravity on either the "material" advantage of desegregation *or* on what sociologist Charles Tilly referred to as the "dispositional aspect of attitudes and relations,"[4] but not both. Their arguments draw our attention to the fact that schools comprise at least two structures: the *resource* (or *material*) and *sociocultural*. The resource context comprises the durable and concrete inputs that a school possesses—including teacher quality, per pupil spending, average student family resources, level of academic rigor and preparation, book, curricular, and technological supplies, and achievement and attainment results. The resource context varies among schools, with studies finding that high rates of poverty, dropouts, and lower test-score performances characterize many urban, minority-dominant schools. Meanwhile greater wealth and improved conditions such as smaller teacher-student ratios, more experienced teachers, greater course offerings, more funds and diversity in extracurricular programs, and wider networks of information about college attainment are found in many middle-class, majority-white schools.[5]

The sociocultural context, in comparison, comprises the school's norms of academic achievement, its logic for student conduct and presentation of self, its pedagogical content and practices, and its climate of teacher-student, student-student, and other intergroup or intragroup dynamics. The school's cultural environment can also be characterized by the meanings students and educators attach to certain curricular patterns, such as which students belong in specific courses and who plays which sports or participates in particular school activities.[6] When Asian and White students are more likely to be enrolled in advanced placement and honors courses in a U.S. school, for example, while African American and Latino students are more likely to be found in the average, comprehensive classes, these various school settings acquire meanings as the specific "turfs" of one group or another.[7] That is, an implicit belief emerges that certain individuals or groups belong to a particular academic or extracurricular program. As a result, the school's sociocultural realm begins to constitute "a social structure with an underlying logic of its own."[8]

Conventionally, we do not often think of sociocultural spaces as "structure," as the "hard," "durable," and "material" aspects of social reality. Instead, "culture" in its varied forms is viewed secondarily as that "soft" and "mental" aspect of reality.[9] Yet, Anthony Giddens, William Sewell, and Sharon Hays have pointed to the inextricably linked material (resource) and cultural (ideology and codes) domains of a social setting such as a school. Giddens, one of the first to introduce the notion of the "duality of structure," has outlined how material resources shape social behaviors, and in tandem how individuals, as agents, use rules, codes, and other cultural tools to reproduce and legitimate the structures that govern their behaviors.[10] Similarly, Hays views structure as a product of two underlying and interconnected elements: systems of social relations and systems of meanings.[11] In refining Giddens's "structuration theory," Sewell has characterized structure as a dualism, resources that are simultaneously the enactment of cultural patterns or meaning-making processes. Structures may determine people's behaviors, how they interact, respond, and utilize resources; but in turn, people are the agents who make use of resources and carry out rules and codes that either keep structures in place or modify them.

Educational research often tends to focus only on schools as organizations, whose express aim is to cultivate students' human capital or rather their capacity to gain knowledge and to become productive economic actors. Hence, the focus is nearly always on outcomes pertaining to test scores, dropout or graduation or college-going rates. Questions about *how* schooling is organized disparately for students from different strata of society are often supplanted by these types of research inquiries. Without delving into the cultural structures of education, however, we undercut our ability to comprehend more fully what factors may very well disconnect a large body of students from schooling and from one another across myriad social lines.

The cultural logics of many schools can reinforce boundaries that adversely impact the academic incorporation of different groups.[12] Conventionally, we utilize the concepts of either school *engagement* or *involvement* to explore students' relationships within schools. "Academic incorporation" goes further than these concepts and captures how the school, as an organizational and cultural structure, moves myriad groups of historically disadvantaged students toward its center and away from its margins without forcing acculturation or loss of a group's cultural integrity, per se. Academic incorporation entails more than the degree of students' agency—that is, how they choose to participate in classes and activities—and it reaches beyond their propensity to either stay in school or drop out. Further, access to strong material resources does not necessarily beget many students' academic incorporation or gener-ate a stronger educational well-being overall in school. A gap in the current body of knowledge in the sociology of education pertains to how schools as cultural institutions impact the quality and depth of students' academic incorporation.

## Changing Schools, Shifting Identities

Socially and culturally, many Black, Coloured, and Indian learners in South Africa who now attend multiracial, former white-only schools are dubbed "Model C'ers," since they are enrolled at "ex-Model C" schools—the "Model C" refers to the funding classification of particular types of white public schools under apartheid. As "Model C'ers," these students are educated in set-tings where their racial groups frequently have less social and cultural power. That is, not only do they now cross spatial boundaries but also they must navi-gate and negotiate different social and cultural norms and practices. The first time I visited Williston High School, a middle-class ex-Model C school, I sat around with a multiracial group of learners at one of the outdoor plazas. This gregarious group of South African youth spoke about their likes and dislikes in the "new" South Africa; they were pioneers forging ahead in the experi-ment of racial integration postapartheid. They understood how the resource contexts differed drastically between the segregated township schools and the former white-only schools. "Those schools in the township are not good, and we come here to get a better education and to move up in life," declared Mokubung, a matric (twelfth grader) at Williston. Mokubung's approach to Williston was similar to Jonathan's at North Village High in the United States, even though both boys lived thousands of miles apart.

Like the VDP students, many of their Black, Coloured, and Indian peers in the Republic of South Africa also traverse neighborhood boundaries daily to attend better schools. Although Mokubung and his peers' schools differ in significant ways from American schools, similarly, they face social and cul-tural issues that arise as they became boundary-crossers in schools where more than 90 percent of the teachers are White. Commuting daily from Letisi's black townships, they especially grapple with the notion of being a part of these schools and what that signifies about their identities. Mokubung and his schoolmate, Mpiko, another African boy with bright eyes and a frank manner, described their interactions with other Black youths who were schooled in the townships: "Miss, they call us 'coconuts'; they think we are 'acting white.'" Mpiko described how Black youth back in the townships perceive the "Model

C'ers." After spending eight hours a school day with students from different racial backgrounds in an English-medium school, Mpiko and Mokubung return to the townships speaking mainly English, not one of the African languages. For this reason, students from the township schools perceive them as cultural "sell-outs," Mpiko said. Even fellow Model C'ers refer to classmates as "coconuts" because the latter allegedly take up other perceived "white" styles. That group includes Cindy, a Black middle-class eleventh grader, whose friends are mostly White and Indian. Explaining why some of the Black kids call her a "coconut," Cindy said the following: "I'll wear, like, big shoes, which only the *White* [Cindy's emphasis] kids wear, you know. I'll wear the labels Billabong where others will be wearing pantsula culture and stuff,[13] where I wear all the surfer labels, so it's, like, a big issue as well. I mean, [my friends] even call me a 'coconut,' but then, when they call me a 'coconut,' you know, it's, like, all right, because, you know, to them it's not such a big thing, because they're actually playing, whereas some people actually mean it."

Cindy was right; some people do mean it. Mmabathu, another middle-class Black student, but one who lives in a township, attached very different meanings to being "Black" in a white school, and she was critical of Cindy and others for allegedly "acting white" or being "coconuts." Earlier Mmabathu had given a speech in her class, revealing how she felt. Telling me about the speech, Mmabathu shared the following:

Mainly [my speech] was about that I am very, very irritated by Blacks. A "coconut" being a person that's black on the outside and is white in the inside, like the things that they do ... about people's styles. Because I grew up in a multiracial school ... I've never been to a township school but I can still, when I go, I can still relate to the people in the township. But it really, really bugs me, the "coconut" in that they feel that they can't relate to like, what happens in black culture and everything, just because they're living somewhere in larney [South African slang for "fancy"] places, and they feel ... It's not nice, because some people are underprivileged, they can't afford to go to a multiracial school, and I feel that we that are privileged, [and we] shouldn't like make them feel that they don't exist, or feel that they're just low class. I think that a Black person should just remain a Black person, no matter what.

PRUDENCE: What's a Black person? Give me your definition.
MMABATHU: A Black person is a person that knows where they come from. That you stand up for what you've been taught, you know.

Because our parents really struggled for us to be where we are today. So I feel that that shouldn't be forgotten, just because times have changed and apartheid is.... I feel that we should keep that in mind, whatever you do and wherever you go.

The universality of the coconut (or acting white) phenomenon signifies an enduring tension in the upward mobility narratives of historically disadvantaged (racial and class) groups. On the one hand, members of subordinate (racial or class) groups make strategic choices to acquire resources, both material and cultural. Some members of the historically subordinated groups, like Cindy, may even embrace without reserve many of the dominant group's perceived cultural practices. Yet, internal cultural conflicts may arise that compel other group members like Mmabathu to reinscribe (narrow) boundaries around identity and insist upon the usage of different ethnocentric, cultural forms to signify one's commitment to the group's collective identity.[14] For people like Mmabathu, the issue per se is not so much that Cindy and others would emulate "white" culture as they became more upwardly mobile, but rather that they would "forget" their own cultural heritages and social histories in the process of embracing so-called white cultural tastes.

This tension between Mmabathu and Cindy is not unlike the dynamics that ensue among American Black students who also negotiate crossing ethnoracial and social boundaries at school and maintaining the sanctity of their own cultural identities. And of course, the "coconut" phenomenon was not new to me. Just a few years prior, I had completed a study of low-income youth in New York, in which I found a similar pattern: African American and Latino youth challenged peers who had traversed ethnoracial boundaries and chose to emulate White peers' styles of interaction, slang, music, and clothing tastes instead of embracing the constructed cultural practices, which, for them, symbolized their own ethnic group identity.[15] I did not expect to confront this issue to the same extent in South Africa, but I did.

Indeed, the aforementioned exchanges are what motivated me to think comparatively, to explore both the universal and particular ways in which race, ethnicity, and class operate across varied school contexts in both the United States and South Africa. I wondered how particular cultural codes and their meanings would change when historically disadvantaged groups' numerical, political, and economic standings shifted from one school context to another. Therefore, I designed this study to explore how cultural and social dynamics influence intragroup and intergroup relations in schools with differing demographic profiles—specifically among Black, Coloured, Indian, and

White students and educators in South Africa and among African American, Asian American, Latino, and White students in the United States. I wanted to understand how schools' cultural and organizational environments contribute to students' perceived cultural *flexibility*—their propensity to expand, to move across myriad social and cultural boundaries, and to embrace multiple cultural codes, practices, or currencies. I learned that students' cultural flexibility has much to do with the schools' own organizational and cultural flexibility. That is, students from similar racial, ethnic, and socioeconomic backgrounds but who attend *different* schools—with varying organizational climates and boundary maintenance—can attain significantly different levels of cultural flexibility.

## *From Boundaries to Cultural Flexibility*

Most studies, with a few exceptions, have investigated the impact of mixed-race schooling on short- and long-term gains in achievement and attainment, as opposed to its impact on intergroup relations.[16] Indeed, improved academic resources are critical for the economic mobility or higher attainment of those members of society historically denied full access to equal educational and economic opportunity. A school's sociocultural context, nonetheless, fosters a system of meanings in which students and educators create and reproduce in-group/out-group boundaries, which are likely to be associated with the degrees to which all students are fully incorporated into the academic setting. Social boundaries in schools have consequences for the web of social relations and the distribution of resources. In fact, to ignore how boundaries impact the sociocultural well-being of historically disadvantaged students in well-off schools is to fuel more educational and social inequality.

In theory, one key aspect of attendance at a socially diverse, resource-rich school is its capacity to develop culturally flexible students who over the course of their social development effectively navigate diverse social environs such as the workplace, communities, and neighborhoods. By "flexibility," I mean the extent to which students, as well as school officials, engage in practices and behaviors that diminish academic, attitudinal, and social barriers. Sociologist Eviatar Zerubavel argues that there is no reason why entities should have only one fixed meaning and that the world can be much richer when individuals possess "flexible" minds, are willing to "step out of their skins," notice certain structures and choose to destroy them from time to time, and even retain their selfhood when they choose.[17] At the individual level, educators and students need be neither too rigid nor too malleable culturally. To be cognitively "rigid-minded" (that is, having an unyielding commitment to the mutual exclusivity of outsiders) or "fuzzy-minded" (unfocused with no attention to structure, appropriate resources, and boundaries among the in-groups and out-groups) stunts the well-being of many individuals and organizations.[18] While Zerubavel's social psychological work focuses primarily on the individual level, I consider cultural flexibility a multidimensional concept whose scope spans from the organizational (school) to the group level (for example, social class or ethnicity) to the individual (student and educator).

Cultural flexibility, like another of its twin concepts, "cosmopolitanism,"[19] constitutes the behavioral or human practices embraced by an individual in his or her cross-cultural participation.[20] Whereas cosmopolitanism focuses intently on international experiences in terms of cross-cultural participation, I use the concept of cultural flexibility here to highlight the local social and cultural practices of high school adolescents. Few scholars have written explicitly about cultural flexibility, specifically as it pertains to social behaviors in schools. Cultural flexibility, I argue, enables educators and learners to cognitively commit themselves to an altogether different mindset and foster an academic environment that allows for both social change and academic rigor.

Promoting cultural flexibility also encourages the diminution of social and symbolic boundaries in school.[21] What do I mean by "boundaries"? Sociologists Michèle Lamont and Virág Molnar have written the following: "Social boundaries are objectified forms of social differences manifested in unequal access to and unequal distribution of resources (material and nonmaterial) and social opportunities."[22] As social actors, human beings continuously draw markers around who constitutes "us" versus "them." Race, ethnicity, class, and gender are a few of the social categories through which we construct boundaries. Other school-related categories include the "gifted" versus the "nongifted," "advanced placement/international baccalaureate/honors" versus the "regular" (the colloquial term among adolescents for the non-advanced placement students), or the "neighborhood/local" students versus the "bused-in" kids. Social boundaries are also apparent in patterns of residential and labor market segregation, the nature of white, male-dominant leadership in Fortune 500 companies, the affluent student population of elite colleges and universities, or even the student makeup of selective classes and extracurricular activities within high schools. Couple these classifications with power relations and enduring struggles over resources throughout humankind and then we experience how boundaries (both intangible and tangible) mark who is in and who is out, who is on top and who is at the bottom.

In comparison, "symbolic boundaries are conceptual distinctions made by social actors to categorize objects, people, practices, and even time and space."[23] Symbolic boundaries are the cultural tools that individuals and groups struggle over and come to agree upon definitions of reality. They are used to demarcate class distinctions[24] or even differences in the professions.[25] Symbolic boundaries are reinforced when cultural gatekeepers use specific metrics or sociocultural indicators to denote an "intelligent" versus an "unintelligent" student, a "respectful" versus a "disrespectful" pupil, a "worthy" versus "unworthy" learner. While symbolic boundaries often reinforce social divisions, sometimes they can be permeable and facilitate some diffusion of cultural practices across social lines so that different groups begin to share certain tastes or interests.[26] That way, out-group members can gain entry and acquire status within in-groups, taste cultures, or organizations by acquiring the latter's cultural resources, knowledge, and capital.[27]  *→ however, other out-group members could see this as abandoning the "other"*

When geographic movement across school boundaries occurs, we can refer to this characteristic of the school's social boundary as permeable.[28] Some examples of both the strength and permeability of social and symbolic boundaries were mentioned earlier as Cindy, Mmabathu, and Mokubung in South Africa, grappled with tensions between social and economic mobility and their own and "white" South African cultural practices. Some researchers have identified challenges that ensue from students migrating across schools, and they have critically documented what appears to have become a conventional expectation of school boundary-crossing—that the "newcomer" students are required to acculturate and assimilate before they can be perceived as worthwhile or fully included members of the school community.[29] Some would refer to this latter aspect of the boundary as "tilted" or asymmetric.[30] This imbalance illuminates what Pierre Bourdieu has labeled as "symbolic violence"[31]—the persistence of the system of cultural meanings embedded in some "good" schools to exclude, minimize, and render invisible the experiences of students from nondominant groups.[32]

In the everyday life of many schools, symbolic boundaries buttress the social distance among students of different backgrounds or abilities attending school together. The school's norms of academic achievement, its rules for student conduct and presentations of self, its disparate curricular and pedagogical content in classes set apart by ability grouping, and group dynamics between teachers and students—all components of the sociocultural domain of schooling—can reinforce symbolic boundaries. For example, as Ann Ferguson has found, cultural modes of students' emotional and physical presentations of self become significant factors in decisions by adults about their academic potential, and they influence decisions teachers make about the kinds of academic programs in which students will be placed.[33] Further, schools can either overtly or covertly reproduce racial meanings and inequality in their day-to-day activities, by mapping particular racial identities onto knowledge and intelligence,[34] and respectability and competence.

## Organizational Habitus and Boundaries

Lamont and Molnar have argued that we know very little about the specific characteristics of boundaries in everyday life.[35] Generally, the basis of comparison in the boundaries research, which has been conducted predominantly through interview research, has been on individuals of a particular social standing who interact with broad cultural ideas. Less is written about these individuals' behaviors and interactions within specific organizations.[36] Moreover, research on boundaries has rarely linked individuals to any particular institutional arrangements—such as having focal social actors come from the same workplace or voluntary association or school.[37] Certainly, we have paid very little attention to the nature of symbolic and social boundaries among students in schools.

Boundaries as group- and organization-level phenomena are reproduced in schools, which maintain a specific cultural habitus. "Habitus," another concept that French sociologist Pierre Bourdieu popularized, refers to the set of entrenched cultural dispositions—habits, views, or styles, for instance—that individuals, families, and communities hold, based on differences in their socioeconomic positions in society.[38] Sociologist Patricia McDonough has applied Bourdieu's "habitus" concept to capture how organizations act in systemic ways and use policies, practices, symbols, and codes to either enhance or diminish the outcomes of the individuals who operate within them.[39] "Organizational habitus," according to McDonough, differs from what we consider "organizational culture," because it goes beyond an understanding of the meaning-making processes conferred on practices by individuals in the organization and instead encompasses how these practices affect the lives and welfare of those participating in it.[40]

To capture the processes of boundary making at an organizational level, often one has to be situated in the setting, witnessing how these boundaries are reproduced. Much of what we know about social boundaries, however, comes from interview studies, as individuals draw lines and make meaning of tangible and intangible differences between them and others about various aspects of society. *Stubborn Roots*, in contrast, focuses on specific school practices that either weaken or strengthen the academic and social boundaries among students.

From a study of the reproduction of boundaries within schools, we can also gather that identity is multidimensional, that individuals do not simply embody one self. Rather, they can choose to define themselves from multiple standpoints. Their markers of identity include a range from ascribed ones like race, ethnicity, class, and gender to cultural tastes to philosophical differences, to name a few. The differences in attitudes, opinions, and cultural tastes among the students introduced so far provide a hint of the multidimensionality of their identities, despite their hailing from similar class and ethnic or racial backgrounds in their respective societies.

We can also gather that both individual and collective identities are neither stable nor fixed across different school contexts. People's ways of thinking about themselves are different depending on the context in which they find themselves.[41] Therefore, we might find that students who share a certain social identity and are located in one type of school environment with one type of cultural ethos may make sense of a particular educational practice differently from students who share a similar identity but attend a school with sharply different cultural ethos. The differences in how students behave or make sense of themselves and their overall educational welfare correspond to the variation in schools' sociocultural and ideological climates.

Ordinarily, cultural practices deemed appropriate and effective within schools are either controlled by those with the power in that context or by a wider social logic that privileges the cultural repertoires of the dominant social class in the society.[42] Consequently, school officials may either establish school rules or implicitly enforce racial, ethnic, and class segregation within schools (and even curricula) that limit or deny students the opportunities to acquire awareness and share some of the cultural tastes and historical sensibilities of their non-White peers. Such practices signify an aspect of organizational (in) flexibility that bars reciprocity in cultural exchanges among students within schools.[4] Increased social interactions among different groups of students, across social identities, and across social boundaries should, in theory, compel them to expose each other to "new" cultural practices and tastes and thus become more culturally flexible.

From an academic standpoint, the habits of educators and school organizations in limiting reciprocity of cultural exchange—or two-way cultural exchanges among students—may play a huge role in the extent to which master narratives about groups influence their collective and individual senses of self and educational well-being. Research by psychologists Claude Steele,

Gregory Walton, and Geoffrey Cohen of stereotype threat and belonging, respectively, finds strong, experimental effects of how racial and ethnic minority students perform based on their perceptions of how the dominant group feels about them and welcomes them into the folds of the community.[44] In addition, a study based on a nationally representative sample by sociologist Robert Crosnoe shows that the stronger the social isolation of poorer students from middle and upper-class students, the more adverse the impact on various social psychological outcomes such as self-esteem and depression.[45]

In sum, "cultural flexibility," "organizational habitus," and "boundaries" are highly interconnected concepts discussed in what follows, and their relationships become apparent as I move from different units of analyses from chapter to chapter, ranging from the school (or organization) to the group to the student levels. What the reader will glean from the following chapters is that the schools' organizational habitus has some association with its students' levels of cultural flexibility. The school's sociocultural climate—specifically certain policies, practices, codes, and pervasive ideas and meanings—indicate something about the school community's actual approaches to equity and inclusion. Observations reveal that the provision of access to resourceful schools alone does not necessarily blur social and symbolic boundaries. The findings here indicate that the degree of social and cultural *flexibility* of both the school organization and of its students is critical to not only the diminution of boundaries but also the educational well-being of students, as well.

By drawing the reader's attention to both the school's resource and cultural contexts that impact the academic incorporation of historically disadvantaged and marginalized students, this book aims to broaden the discussion of what equity and educational opportunity really mean. Because of national differences in institutional policies between the nations—such as tracking, bilingualism, and mandatory student uniforms—the nature of organizational and cultural flexibility within schools in South Africa and the United States expresses itself differently. Nonetheless, a comparative study of their educational landscapes offers significant insights about opportunity and schooling for historically disadvantaged or unequal groups.

## Chapter Snapshots

The chapters in this volume detail comparisons among cultural, institutional, and group dynamics in schools whose aims (at least on the surface) were to create educational equality within the United States and South Africa. Yet, inequalities are sustained by boundary-making processes that influence the cultural flexibility of myriad individuals and groups. Deep-rooted boundaries stem from the social, economic, and political histories of both South Africa and the United States. Chapter 1 situates this study and provides an overview of comparative racial and ethnic formations that distinguish the two countries. It also provides an overview of how desegregation practices have developed in the United States and South Africa, highlighting cross-national similarities and differences in race relations and inequality in schools and society. In addition to describing the general methods used to conduct the study discussed in this text, chapter 2 introduces the eight schools that participated in the research study.

The main empirical chapters focus on different levels of analysis among the following: 1) nations, 2) school organizations, 3) individuals, 4) groups, and 5) some combination of them all. Chapter 3 compares and contrasts the different cultural practices within schools, the structural factors that shape them, and the ways that students and teachers either reinforce or diminish social boundaries, which influence cultural and organizational flexibility. Drawing on multiple data sources, the chapter argues that schools with strong resource contexts must be aware of latent social and cultural inequalities and how they affect historically and socially disadvantaged students, who now attend these "good" schools.

Using mixed methods, chapter 4 examines differences in cultural flexibility among students enrolled in either majority-minority or white-dominant schools. This chapter shares findings about the association between students' self-reported levels of cultural flexibility and their social and academic placement in schools. Expanding the conceptualization of cultural flexibility at a group level, chapter 5 examines the racial attitudes of White students, who are in the "minority" position in both the U.S. and South African schools in the study, but who live within societies where their racial groups maintain economic (and political—in the case of the United States) dominance. Comparatively, it offers some insight into the anxieties and fears of these students, who grapple with their beliefs in equality and their disagreement with specific equity-oriented educational practices. This chapter asks pressing philosophical and social questions about the functions of education and the tensions between institutional and collective wills in regard to the matters of educational equity and equality of opportunity for all members of a society.

Drawing from organizational, group-, and individual-level data presented in the prior chapters, chapter 6 offers a typology that emerges from this study about the multiple dimensions of mixed-race schooling to which educators must be attuned to optimize the academic incorporation of their students across all groups and to avoid the glaring racial, ethnic, and class patterning that currently loom large within education. Finally, chapter 7 summarizes the findings and arguments, ranging from cross-national to interorganizational to between group comparisons. Also, this chapter offers some ideas for educators to consider as we attempt to uproot the weeds of educational inequality that have long vexed these two national systems. Overall, the research highlights areas where educators, parents, policy makers, and students can staunch the invasion of both overt and latent practices that stifle educational equity in democratic, multiethnic societies.

# I

## *Distinctions and Convergences*

### A BRIEF HISTORY OF RACE AND EDUCATION IN
### THE UNITED STATES AND SOUTH AFRICA

AN ADEQUATE REVIEW of how history unfolded to allow students of different racial backgrounds to move across previously exclusive school boundaries merits an entire book itself. And in fact, others with significantly more expertise than I have written about the historical forces of slavery, apartheid, and racial oppression in each of their respective national contexts.[1] Nonetheless, the arguments that unfold in the subsequent pages require some overview of the two focal societies in this book. The sociology of mixed-race schools in the United States and South Africa is directly related to their histories of geographic and social separation. Historian George Fredrickson's seminal work, entitled *White Supremacy: A Comparative Study in American and South African History*, provides one of the most comprehensive comparisons of the convergences between two nations' histories, steeped in palpably racist pasts, and in terms of my own knowledge base about South African history, so does Bernard Magubane's *The Political Economy of Race and Class in South Africa.*[2]

The origins of racial stratification in South Africa began around the time colonizer) Dutch explorers colonized and established a permanent settlement in the Cape Colony in the mid-seventeenth century. Initially, the Dutch landed at the tip of South Africa, looking for a way station, a stopping point along the trade route between Asia and Europe. They encountered the indigenous Khoikoi and San peoples—pastoral and hunter-gathering groups, respectively—upon reaching the windy shores of the very southern tip of the massive African continent. Other major African groups they encountered were the Zulus in the northeast, the Xhosa in the southeast, and the Sotho, Pedi, and Tswana groups in the interior. As the Dutch came and went, they built their ports throughout what eventually became known as the Western Cape, bringing indentured servants and slaves from East Africa, Madagascar, Mozambique and other regions along the Indian Ocean basin, including Indonesia, India, Sri Lanka, and Malaysia. As the eighteenth century came to a close and Dutch mercantile power began to wane, the British arrived. They, too, initially stopped along the tip of South Africa looking for a stop-over point as they sailed the trade routes. But eventually, the British began to lay economic and political claims to the settlement that they found, and the initial settlers enticed more British persons to immigrate and settle in South Africa. As some forms of human interactions would have it, the European settlers, Khoikoi, San, imported workers, and slaves (sons and daughters of various parts of Asia) interacted and engaged in sexual relations, creating a population of multiracial persons who were the progenitors of those who later became officially referred to as "Coloureds" by the South African colonial and apartheid state.

Like imported African slaves in the United States, African and Coloured slaves provided through their labor the very foundations of economic production in South Africa; they tilled the soil, hoisted up buildings and houses, and produced the crops and textiles that served as the bases of exchange and profit in this society. Fredrickson and Magubane also inform us of how the native Khoikoi and San, like the natives of North American soil, knew the land well, and further how White colonists depended on them as trade partners for livestock and food and thus found it more difficult to commit the natives to bondage in slavery. Eventually, Dutch settlers—whose descendants referred to themselves as "Afrikaners"—and British colonists fought with native Africans, engaging in a string of imperialist wars throughout the nineteenth century to amass and proclaim ownership of their cattle, land, numerous territories, some brimming with profitable minerals and ores such as gold and diamonds.

Moreover, Afrikaners and the British did not coexist peaceably; they fought, too. Increasing British presence and domination evoked interethnic competition and conflict; they spoke different languages, maintained dissimilar religious dogma and practices, and even held divergent ideas about slavery. Afrikaners subscribed to notions of ethnic purity and superiority. Thus, tensions fomented as these two groups struggled over power, politics, and land. Between 1824 and the early 1840s, fed-up Afrikaners (farmers or "Boers" mainly) began the Great Trek, a long migration inland and up toward the northern hinterlands of South Africa. Although the bases of fighting differed in the United States, students of early South African and American history cannot help but notice some similarities between the Afrikaner-British struggles in the South African War from 1899–1902, also known as the Anglo-Boer War, and the Union-Confederate struggles in the American Civil War. On the other hand, ethnic and national origin differences existed between the former, while in the United States kin members very easily fought against one another if they lived in different regions over matters of states' rights and the "peculiar institution"—namely, the right to maintain the selling and holding of African slaves. Divisive tensions fomented bloodshed among Whites in both countries, and usually the bitter conflicts evolved around the question of land, political power, and the issues relating to what to do with the subordinated black and brown populations that had been stripped of their human rights.

South African slavery ended earlier than in the United States by three decades in 1833. The British empire forbade the trading and selling of slaves in 1807, while the United States's slave trade officially ended in 1808, though slavery would continue until President Abraham Lincoln signed the Emancipation Proclamation in 1863, which was officially reinforced by constitutional sanction in 1865. An end to slavery is not a sufficient condition for an end to black disenfranchisement, however, and in both the United States and South Africa, white political and economic power ensured that people of color would be positioned as second-class residents, limiting their citizenship rights.

Throughout the twentieth century, laws and practices outlawing Blacks' access to public places and accommodations, schools, neighborhoods, voting rights, and economic opportunity marked one of the crudest dehumanizing periods in American history. The Jim Crow era had a fraternal twin in South Africa, and its name was "apartheid"—an Afrikaans word meaning "separate development." As Afrikaners amassed political power and negotiated with Whites of British origin for how to control Blacks, Coloureds, and Indians, they, too, implemented numerous policies to keep these groups spatially, culturally, economically, and politically isolated. In 1948, the National Party, led by of Daniel François (D. F.) Malan, cemented the divide among the groups, officially recognizing them as racial others. The National Party's political agenda involved a renewed and more rigid commitment to white supremacy in South Africa, calling for programs that spawned and promoted separatism. A bevy of laws was designed to monitor and control the placement and distribution of African labor, including the Population Registration Act and the Group Areas Act of 1950. Along with the Immorality Act of 1950, these laws, respectively, controlled the identities, residency, movement, and sexual relations between racial groups. Consequently, today a new democratic South Africa faces institutionalized inequalities that are deeply rooted, where Africans are among the poorest people in the world compared to the white population of the country.[3] As Magubane stated, "Apartheid did not just mean political exclusion; it was also an economic system of extreme economic exploitation."[4]

A visit to the highly informative and visually rich Apartheid Museum, nestled behind a seemingly nondescript building near Gold Reef City, a few kilometers outside of the center of Johannesburg, brings to life the experience of what these legal acts entailed. Blacks, Coloured, and Indians had to carry passes that bore their official racial categories and signified where they could live, work, and be present at particular times of day and night. Interracial sexual relations and marriage were outlawed, and families were physically torn apart when it was discovered that a spouse and child were actually Coloured and not White, although they could pass at their own risk.

"Chameleons"—people who changed their racial statuses or passed as a racial "other"—existed. Though a highly risky and personally dangerous act when committed for either social gain or political resistance, it was not uncommon for South African citizens to petition the state during the apartheid era to move from one racial category to another: from Coloured to White, Indian to Coloured and sometimes White, African to Coloured and sometimes White, and even White to Coloured if, for example, one were a political resistor of the representation of whiteness in the twentieth-century South African state. However, as archived articles from the *Johannesburg Star* revealed, never did a person petition to move from White to Black, the lowest and largest rung of the racial hierarchy.[5] The National Party's institutionalization of these group classifications exemplifies what sociologists regard as the social construction of race. In the South African context, race was somewhat malleable or changeable for those who could document the reasons why they belonged to one group versus another.

Further, racial classifications in South Africa differ from the racial nomenclature of the United States. Under the apartheid state, there were four institutionalized racial groupings: "Asians," "Africans" (or Blacks), "Coloureds," and "Whites." Many mixed-race peoples in South Africa are classified as "Coloured," and this racial categorization encompasses a number of combinations of ethnic and racial heritages, including Malaysian, Chinese, Dutch, English, and African. Under apartheid, Coloureds were not only prohibited from attending school with Whites but also with Blacks, who were lower down on the rungs of the racial hierarchy, and with Asians. This latter group included mainly the descendants of Indians—who arrived first as migrant workers in the late nineteenth and early twentieth centuries—and a small group of Chinese. Thus, school desegregation in the opening of South African society meant not only the mixing of White and non-White students but also the mixing of Coloureds with Blacks, Asians with Blacks, and Asians with Coloureds.

What makes South Africa's racial taxonomy more complex and nuanced is the fact that "Black" has multiple meanings. On the one hand, it denotes a constructed racial category for those with indigenous and African origins, the descendants of the multiple ethnic or population groups, including the Zulus, Xhosas, Ndibeles, Pedis, Sothos, Swazis, Tswanas, and Vendas. Yet, during the anti-apartheid resistance era, in progressive political circles the concept of "black" became inclusive, comprising all of the economically and politically disenfranchised groups—Africans, Coloureds, and Indians. Throughout this text, unless I specify otherwise and for the sake of analysis, when I use "Black" in the South African context, I am referring primarily to the group commonly known as "African" and even "native," to those of native descent.

Meanwhile, black-coloured social relations, especially within the Western Cape Province, are complicated by the latter's close ties to the Afrikaans language and Afrikaner culture, although many members of both groups share some common heritage. Historically, Coloureds have been accorded an "in-between" status in South Africa's racial hierarchy. Though not formally recognized as White, both Coloureds (and Indians) were given formal hiring preferences and other rights over Africans during the apartheid era. In the postapartheid era, some Coloureds' former and relatively more privileged status among Whites, as well as their collective support of the National Party during the democratic transition, have complicated their relationships with Blacks, who control the government and constitute the majority of the national population. Because of this history and the differentiated nonwhite statuses between Africans and Coloureds, the two largest historically unequal groups in South Africa, I included in the study a coloured-majority school, which has been desegregated to include Africans.[6]

Comparatively, in the United States, the hypodescent rule that rendered any individual with one drop of "black" blood or other nonwhite heritage "soiled," precluded the same person's eligibility for whiteness.[7] That is, thicker and less permeable racial boundaries exist(ed) in the United States, and strikingly, a fair-skinned American with black heritage would be perceived as a different racial character in South Africa, where multiracialism and even whiteness are relatively more attainable based on skin color.[8] In short, the social rule of hypo descent—or being defined with the race of lowest status (i.e., Black) if a person has some of that heritage in his or her biological line—is not one that defined South Africa's racialization process, but it did in the United States.

## Desegregating Schools in the Twentieth Century
### American School Desegregation

The educational systems of both the United States and South Africa mirrored their predominant racial and ethnic orders in the twentieth century. In the United States, it was illegal for Blacks to even learn to read and write until the end of slavery. While some educational opportunities presented themselves during the Reconstruction era and even later during the regressive Jim Crow period, generally Blacks and other non-Whites confronted substandard schooling conditions.[9] People like my maternal grandparents, who were Mississippi sharecroppers, often acquired no more than the equivalent of a second- or third-grade education in one-room rural schools that hosted students of various ages and levels. But the basic survival needs of their families and a forced reliance on the exploitative cotton economy yanked them from the classrooms to seed, cultivate, and plant many months of the year, extremely limiting what little educational exposure they received. Their children, my parents, raised in the 1940s and 1950s, had a relatively better time of it, but the conditions were still grossly disparate from their white counterparts. Undereducated, too, they walked to schools, while White children rode by on buses, and they relied on hand-me-down books with torn pages that the white schools no longer needed. In comparison, Blacks in the northern cities faced relatively better educational conditions, and in some instances attended schools with Whites.[10] Yet, the majority of Blacks was concentrated in the former slave states of the South, and though many moved to the northern cities during the Great Migration of the twentieth century, they arrived with very low literacy and numeracy skills.[11] Separate, substandard education was the rule of the times for many Blacks, and thus, it is no wonder they pushed for more integrated schooling with Whites as they pressed for civil rights. They expected that the resources would be significantly better.

An obvious starting point for a consideration of the significance of school desegregation in the United States is the 1954 *Brown v. Board of Education* decision that was heard before the highest court in the land and argued by a young lawyer, Thurgood Marshall, whose destiny would ultimately include a seat on that very court. Historian Richard Kluger's *Simple Justice* provides a thorough and comprehensive telling of U.S. school desegregation—a long journey full of toil for civil rights activists and lawyers such as Marshall and Robert Carter.[12] Having been denied admission to law school at the University of Maryland in 1930, Marshall was determined that equal educational opportunity would one day be given not only to African Americans but also to other racial and ethnic minorities. Yet, Marshall quickly learned that the struggle for educational opportunity had to be fought systematically. The *Brown* case comprised several individual cases that challenged the separate but equal ideology of the *Plessy v. Ferguson* ruling. The first of these five initiatives to the *Plessy* ruling was a case evolving in Clarendon County, South Carolina, where segregated schools abounded. In December 1952, lawyers for the National Association for the Advancement of Colored People (NAACP) argued that school desegregation itself was a violation of the equal protection clause of the Fourteenth Amendment. And so as an attorney for the NAACP, Marshall began fighting discrimination cases in a number of venues, including schools in Texas and South Carolina and ultimately the *Brown* case in Topeka, Kansas, which the U. S. Supreme Court ruled on May 17, 1954. The *Brown I* Court declared that "separate educational facilities are inherently unequal," explicitly overturning *Plessy v. Ferguson 163 U.S. 537* (May 18, 1896), the landmark case that established the separate but equal doctrine. Some localities openly resisted the Supreme Court's ruling, like Prince Edward County, Virginia, where public schools were closed from 1957 to 1964. This Supreme Court's phrase, according to the NAACP, pleased neither proponents nor opponents of public school integration and may have unintentionally opened the door for subsequent strategies to resist both *Brown* decisions.[13]

Simply because the demands of justice and equality in a democracy call for educational access does not mean that those historically advantaged and privileged by a more closed system gravitate to unequivocal openness immediately. In the aftermath of the Supreme Court's *Brown v. Board of Education* decision, American citizens witnessed a rejection of the court order, outright defiance, and resistance to the call for school desegregation. And often, once students of color entered these mixed-race schools, the reach of court-ordered and constitutional demands encountered a "ceiling" or "threshold"—a decoupling of institutional will and group and individual interests.

Social science studies have shown that attitudes have changed; polls show that Americans profess to have a strong taste for racial integration.[14] However, an attitude-behavioral paradox exists. Residential and educational behaviors of American families do not correspond to their avowed acceptance of and

taste for integration. According to a 2004 report by the Civil Rights Project by
Gary Orfield and his associates, U.S. schools have shown movement toward a
regressive period of resegregation where, except for the South and Southwest,
most White students have little contact with minority students.[15] Rural and
small-town school districts are, on average, the nation's most integrated for
African Americans and Latinos. Central cities of large metropolitan areas are
the epicenter of segregation; and further, segregation is severe in smaller central cities and in the suburban rings of large metropolitan areas, attributable
mainly to out-migration by Whites and even some middle-class individuals of
color.[16] While it has been over five decades since the landmark judicial decision of *Brown v. Board of Education*, the United States has still not succeeded
in equalizing educational outcomes and life chances for its Black populace
and various other racial and ethnic minorities.

## School Desegregation in South Africa

As it has been in the United States, the task of redefining schools as particular
resources for the social and economic advancement of historically unequal
groups is a key aspect of the social transformation that is now underway in
postapartheid South Africa. From an economic standpoint, some scholars
argue that in the late nineteenth century, mineral discoveries of diamonds
and gold on the Witwatersrand, the geographical terrain that encompasses
Johannesburg and surrounding towns, required the development of bipartite
labor segmentation of black and white worker pools, as business magnates
dealt with the requisite technologies and mechanisms for mining in that era.
Michael Cross and Linda Chisholm argue that previously unskilled and rural
Whites were trained, educated, and skilled to manage and oversee the mines,
while largely Black migrant workers were exploited for cheap labor to ensure
good profit and consequently, were left with little to no formal education.[17]
Social and economic policies were subsequently developed to cement this
racially stratified system of labor.

South African educational policy between 1945 and 1976 related to economic and political changes, too, playing out the primary forms of control of
the increasing urban Black youth populations.[18] Though mass schooling for
African students was not mandated until the advent of democracy in 1994,
some form of mass schooling began earlier, as proponents of apartheid sought
to stabilize the urban population, produce a semiskilled workforce in the post–
World War II era of industrialization, and mitigate the potential for juvenile
delinquency and political militancy among urban working-class youth.[19] As

the decades progressed, several enactments forced schools to comply with the norms of separate development and segregation. The Bantu Education Act of 1953, the Coloured Persons Education Act of 1963, the Indian Education Act of 1965, and the National Education Act of 1967 laid the foundation for the implementation of nineteen different and separate departments of education for African (Black), Afrikaner, Anglo White, Coloured, and Indian students in each of South Africa's provinces.[20] Signifying the principle of inegalitarian pluralism (or rather "separate but [un]equal"), the numerous departments concretized where the lines were drawn in the racial hierarchy.

While Coloureds, Indians, and Whites were given the control to operate their separate educational departments, African education and its allocation of meager resources fell under the auspices of a central cabinet.[21] The national government spent mere pittances on the education of African youth, however. "At the height of apartheid, per pupil spending in white schools was ten times that in the African schools. Even after a significant increase in spending on behalf of Black learners during the waning years of apartheid, spending on White learners remained two and a half times that of African learners in urban areas and three and a half that of African learners in most of the homelands."[22]

Government intervention in African education ensured some form of hegemonic control, by incorporating an ideology that entrenched a sense of national consciousness and a right to self-determination through the establishment of separate black homelands.[23] Moreover, national policies enacted Afrikaner principles pertaining to the maintenance of Christian National Education, the "purity" of Afrikaner culture and the perceived inferiority of Blacks, whereby peoples of different ethnic cultures would have separate and culturally divided systems—though national laws intended this in a unidirectional and lopsided way favoring its White students. It would take more than four decades for the African resistance movement—embodied most visibly internationally in the work of the African National Congress led by political activists such as Nelson Mandela, Walter Sisulu, and Oliver Tambo—to chisel away at the laws that kept the majority of South Africa's residents from realizing the fullest meanings of citizenship and rights to a quality education. Schools and universities often served as sites of resistance to the powerful and deeply entrenched barriers of apartheid, as the 1976 Soweto student protests and later student-led resistances indicated. African youth were forced to accept Afrikaner culture and domination in their schooling. Yet, they struggled against the imposition of their oppressors' culture and language on them in school by boycotting and marching in the streets in protest.[24]

International pressure to repeal its supremacist policies and the dogged but incrementally successful resistance movement compelled the South African government to begin a reexamination of its practices. In late 1990, the South African minister of "white education," Piet Clase, announced new models for limited school desegregation, which gave white schools the power to decide their own admission policies. Clase's plan included the "Model C" school, which permitted white schools to convert to a semiprivate status and forced them to comply with a 50 percent plus one white enrollment policy.

When the African National Congress (ANC) gained political control and power in 1994 and during the implementation of the South Africa Schools Act (SASA) of 1996, formerly all-white schools experienced an influx of Black, Coloured, and Indian learners, which consequently led to a proliferation of multiracial schools in South Africa. Now, because of a financing structure that relies heavily on fees paid by learners and their families, ex-Model C schools are mainly accessible to the middle class, who can afford the ex-Model C's better educational resources and academic results. Unlike the general practice in the United States where schools tend to be zoned by neighborhood, students in South Africa who attend public schools commonly move across neighborhood boundaries and travel for distances to a school beyond their local zone, if they can afford the opportunity. As is the case in the United States, segregated schooling (namely, black, coloured, and Indian township schools) is related to segregated neighborhoods (poor black, coloured, and Indian neighborhoods), while desegregation requires Black, Coloured and Indian learners to engage in neighborhood boundary crossing, often traveling via car, taxi, or on foot (unless their parents have the means to live in the proximate neighborhood) to former all-white neighborhoods where the ex-Model C's reside. Furthermore, the teaching force in the "opened" (South African parlance for desegregation) or ex-Model C schools remains over 90 percent White, despite the relatively rapid student desegregation of these schools by race.[25]

As sociologist Gay Seidman has stated, "With the end of legal apartheid, South Africa is poised to move into a new position in the annals of social science...it is increasingly used as an exemplar, in discussions of democratic transitions, development strategies and globalization, and post-colonial transformations."[26] As the nation constructs a new nonracial democracy, comparative studies that draw on insights from other parts of the world to reexamine aspects of South African society, including racial identities and changing patterns of cultural, social, and racial relations, are needed.[27]

## Desegregation in South Africa and the United States

What makes South Africa a striking comparative case to the United States is the twist that in the former, the majority of the nation's population (more than 80 percent) is seeking academic and economic advancement after decades of educational segregation, discrimination, and economic exploitation, while in the United States, minority groups, which constitute less than a third of the population collectively, have suffered these inequities for over a century. In addition, South Africa aims to transform its society via the opening up of education in a relatively more progressive era—the late twentieth century—than that of the United States, which began its own unfinished experimentation with integration in the middle part of the century.

A few factors distinguish South Africa from the United States with regard to its orientation toward the creation of "opportunity-to-learn" contexts.[28] First, the United States, a wealthier nation, is decades ahead in terms of equalizing the resource context of its schools across the fifty states. Township schools in South Africa in the current era are quite reminiscent of the grossly underresourced schools that civil rights activists fought against in the 1950s. Youth educated in the Jim Crow South encountered ragged and outdated textbooks in the classroom, some insufficiently trained teachers, limited extracurricular opportunities, and deteriorating physical structures, which belied the separate but equal doctrine of the day. Although I am mindful of the gross inequities that American educators like Jonathan Kozol[29] have documented, which continue to besiege many of America's inner-city schools today, these conditions remain for many South African township schools, where even some of the poorest U.S. schools may appear to be "rich," in relative terms. For example, rarely, if ever, would an American teacher have to hold classes outside in wet, cold weather because there is no classroom space for all teachers and students— something that I witnessed repeatedly at the black township school, Montjane Secondary School. And in the United States, teachers are more likely to be guaranteed basics like chalk for writing on the board, paper, textbooks for each student, and various teaching aids, or schoolwide heating in winter, while it is not uncommon to find these basics lacking in township (and rural) schools.

Although the resource contexts of South African and U.S. schools differ in significant ways across the board, a second distinction that matters to the projects of desegregation and integration is the moral and legal state of implementation in both countries. After completing a study of both public and private schools in South Africa and a meta-analysis of historical documents outlining the evolution of desegregation in the United States, Krisztina

Tihanyi argued that the rationale for desegregation in South Africa is predicated on a moral argument, while that of the United States is based on the legal protection of material interests of previously marginalized racial and class groups.[30] In the former, some white schools began to desegregate well before the change of political regimes from the rigid racial exclusivity of the Nationalist Party to the radically inclusive (at least, discursively so) ANC. Some white schools desegregated prior to 1994, in response to protest movements aimed at allowing Black students to fill empty places in schools left behind by the declining population and the out-migration of South African Whites.[31] Moreover, some private and religious schools in South Africa began to spearhead the movement of opening the schools to Black, Coloured, and Indian students as early as the 1970s,[32] although most white state schools did not open their doors to these groups until two decades later. In short, select school communities utilized their own local control to respond to the rising tide of demand for racial, ethnic, and economic equality in South Africa.

Furthermore, the South African Schools Act saw an integrated educational system as addressing the collective needs of a fledgling democracy. Given that the apartheid government had used inequitable educational policies to sustain racial stratification, the SASA called for a deracialized and unified national system of education. The act states the following:

> WHEREAS this country requires a new national system for schools which will redress past injustices in educational provision, provide an education of progressively high quality for all learners and in so doing lay a strong foundation for the development of all our people's talents and capabilities, advance the democratic transformation of society, combat racism and sexism and all other forms of unfair discrimination and intolerance, contribute to the eradication of poverty and the economic well-being of society, protect and advance our diverse cultures and languages, uphold the rights of all learners, parents and educators, and promote their acceptance of responsibility for the organisation, governance and funding of schools in partnership with the State.[33]

South Africa's national approach to school desegregation has differed from the United States because it explicitly considers education as a social institution requisite to the national project of "transformation," to fundamentally rescue its society from the rigid claws of apartheid and its consequent social, economic, and political harms to unifying its people and redistributing resources more equitably, as opposed to simply providing equal opportunities to marginalized groups. The SASA used inclusive language, such as "all learners" and "all our people's talents and capabilities," which signaled the government's recognition that the foundation of a strong democracy is social unification.

South Africa's 1997 Language in Education Policy relied on this notion that the people of society have an inherent value. The document states, "The new Constitution of the Republic of South Africa, the government, and thus the Department of Education, recognises that *our cultural diversity is a valuable national asset* and hence is tasked, amongst other things, to promote multilingualism."[34] (This policy, which supports the instruction of the nation's eleven official languages, addressed segregation from a linguistic standpoint and continued a trend of inclusivity found throughout postapartheid legislation.

A curriculum reformation began with the introduction of Curriculum 2005 (C2005) in 1997, which was predicated on the principles of outcomes-based education—a student-centered and group learning approach—that had been popularized in some developed nations such as Canada, New Zealand, Australia, Scotland, and parts of the United States. C2005 was revised in 2002, reincarnating as the Revised National Curriculum Statement (or RNCS). According to the Ministry of Education, the RNCS is based on the following principles: social transformation; outcomes-based education (OBE); high knowledge and high skills; integration and applied competence; progression; articulation and portability; human rights, inclusivity, environmental and social justice; valuing indigenous knowledge systems; and credibility, quality, and efficiency.[35] In addition, the RNCS derived its critical and developmental outcomes from the country's constitution, highly acclaimed for its moral foundation of radical inclusion, describing the kind of citizen the education and training system should aim to create to equip the nation's students with adequate skills for participation in the global knowledge-based economy. As of 2008, not only were learners from grades R–12 (or pre-K through 12) following the same national and standardized curriculum, but that year, the senior "Class of 2008" became the first to participate in the new National Senior Certificate (NSC) examination, the largest public examination ever to be given in South Africa.

In short, South African government policies aimed to concretize the moral precepts that no government institution such as formal education could collude in any form of "dehumanizing" bias or discrimination and that schools serve the purpose, too, of promoting respect and understanding of people's diverse cultural, religious, and language traditions. Through the media and various other outlets, the first democratic South African government strongly encouraged an acceptance of nonracialism and racial reconciliation that would enable the society to approximate the ideals of a "rainbow nation." The promotion of these ideas, which permeate South Africa's educational policy and presumably its school contexts, however, has occurred in a relatively more modern and liberal historical and cultural moment, at the close of the twentieth century.

By comparison, the U.S. Supreme Court ordered the dismantling of segregated schools in a period of intense interracial conflict, and by some accounts, the desegregation mandates of the Supreme Court themselves appeared to further stir and inflame those social conflicts. American schools were forced open as a matter of judicial remedy, and historians of the period and various records show that Whites resisted for many years after the *Brown I* decision. Not until the 1960s did significant waves of desegregation actually begin to occur across the United States. Tihanyi attributes the poor U.S. experience with integration to the constricted moral context in which it was legally mandated; and consequently, white attitudes were slow to change in favor of an educational condition imposed upon them. However, if desegregation were allowed to occur more organically, at the local level, Tihanyi argues, perhaps then the outcome would have been different.[36]

Although the United States is decades ahead of South Africa in terms of its advanced industrial and economic development, many of the former's schools have moved in a direction opposite of the intentions of the original *Brown* decision, and in the wake of the U.S. Supreme Court's 2007 rulings for the parent petitioners of the Louisville, Kentucky, and Seattle, Washington, school districts, the ideals and practices of racial integration in American society could ultimately dissipate, unless we can learn from both past and present experiments with mixed-race schooling and desegregation about what will work best. Certainly, some American school districts remain committed to the goals of integration, by either participating in voluntary desegregation programs[37] or existing as educational spaces where diverse racial groups gravitate and remain because of these schools' academic reputations and/or geographic locations, in addition to a culture that supports and encourages diversity.

The differences in nation building have resulted in different legal and policy structures in the United States and South Africa regarding school desegregation. In the former, more local control has been given to U. S. school districts as they deal with the question of school integration, particularly as the federal courts' roles have diminished. This has created some variation across the fifty states. In South Africa, in contrast, the legal scaffolding for integrated education is built intrinsically into the national constitution, leaving provinces and local municipalities little to no room to dissent or vary their practices.

Still, there are key similarities between the two nations that make a comparative schools study viable: 1) both societies deal now with the legacy of racial oppression and inequality; 2) both lean on the educational system as a means to create an equitably society; 3) both have confronted a persistent achievement gap, marked by significant racial differences; and 4) in both countries, one of the most vexing and biggest preoccupations are gross achievement disparities among ethnoracial groups in terms of test-score performances and high school graduation and college matriculation rates. Dismal achievement and attainment results belie any declarations that equity has been attained. It is clear after fifty-five years that the goal of *Brown* has yet to be fully realized in the United States, and even though South Africa's desegregation efforts span less than two decades, integration also is far from being achieved.

So, where do we go from here? Let me be clear: The subsequent arguments in no way question the venerable goals of school integration. Rather, my goal is to offer insight into *why* it is necessary that the matters of multisocial schooling (in terms of race, ethnicity, class, culture, gender, and so forth) must be addressed holistically, so that we truly realize the goals of integration. As difficult as the process of desegregation has been within the two wider societies of the United States and South Africa, we should not abandon the struggle toward integration, but rather consider both the sociocultural and material aspects of dismantling educational inequity.

## 2

# *Selecting "Good" Schools in the United States and South Africa*

THIS BOOK DESCRIBES research gathered from purposive case studies of eight schools located in four different cities. In January 2004, I landed in Coast City, South Africa, to spend the first quarter of a new academic year in two high schools (grades eight through twelve): one a predominantly coloured high school (Groveland Secondary School) of 1,400 learners, situated in Wilson Heights, one of Coast City's populous Coloured communities; the other a multiracial, former white high school with 1,000 learners (Palmer High School), located in a middle-class neighborhood, Woodside. South African schools run during the calendar year from January to December and are broken up into quarters with two-week breaks interspersed. After three months in Coast City, I moved north to Johannesburg, the expansive business and cultural center of South Africa. Not far from its corporate limits is a municipality called Letisi. For the next quarter, I visited daily Montjane High School, an all-black township school of approximately 1,400 learners, with an all-black teaching staff. Every other day, I alternated visits between Montjane and Williston, a multiracial, ex-Model C high school of approximately 980 learners, over half of which were racially identified as Black. I returned to all four South African schools in 2008 for follow-up interviews and to revisit those learners who had been in eighth grade when I first met them. By then, they were twelfth graders ("matrics").

With a major grant in hand and time off on a research sabbatical, I began the companion American study in 2007. The four U.S. public high schools are located in the southern and northeastern sections of the country: two each in a southern and a northeastern locale—South Capital City and

North Capital City, respectively. One school in each city is identified as minority dominant (predominantly Black and/or Latino) and the other is multiracial with a significant percentage of White students. Over time these two cities experienced racial and ethnic strife during civil rights battles. Yet, they also represent different regions in the country where the degrees of interracial and interethnic contact and permeability of group boundaries vary.[1]

South Capital City and North Capital City are comparable to the two South African cities, Letisi and Coast City, respectively, on a few key dimensions. South Capital City (USA) and Letisi (RSA) are both relatively medium-sized urban locales abutting rural areas and have a significantly large percentage of Black residents from mixed socioeconomic backgrounds. In comparison, North Capital City and Coast City, both coastal settings, are large cities with significant percentages of Blacks and Whites, as well as sizable percentages of other racial-ethnic groups. Almost one-third of the students in the North Capital City public schools identify as Latino or Hispanic, while Coast City boasts a sizable percentage of Coloured students in its schools.

In each, I gathered a list of all the high schools and divided them into categories according to their sociodemographic profiles. Then, I intentionally chose schools that are considered typical and solidly performing in their respective local contexts. The U.S. schools profiled here share one main criterion with the South African schools: they are all mixed race in terms of student composition, with one exception; and half have a significant white student presence while the other half have a majority of students of color.

The key difference in the selections between the United States and South Africa is that the average academic orientation of the schools is held constant in the former. American schools are quite varied in terms of many factors—from social makeup, budget, average teacher quality and experience, organizational type, curricula, location, and a host of other factors—with all of these possibly influencing a multitude of students' educational well-being. Thus, I consciously decided to choose four U.S. schools similar in their academic performance profiles so that I could investigate the sociocultural spheres of the schools better with minimal "contamination" of those other possible social factors. Each of the American schools is considered a relatively high performing school in its respective local contexts, scoring repeatedly in the highest two status categories in its state's Annual Yearly Progress report required by the federal No Child Left Behind law. This option was not readily available to me in South Africa, given the stark dissimilarity between poor township schools and mixed-race, white-dominant schools whose educational outcomes tend to be significantly and highly correlated with their respective resource contexts. Furthermore, as far as I know, there are no instances of schools in majority-black or coloured South African townships or communities where significant numbers of White students are in attendance.

In the forthcoming empirical chapters, the bulk of the analyses relies mainly on five of the school case studies—particularly the mixed-race schools, which are considered either "desegregated" (noting that in South Africa desegregation is not merely a black-white issue) or "mixed-race" (namely, schools that include a critical mass of students of color and Whites). I focus on the latter schools mainly because the organizational and sociocultural issues that I discuss are more germane to these schooling contexts. In some instances, however, I utilize data from all eight schools, and will discuss when and why I choose to do so. In the remainder of the chapter, I provide brief introductions of each school and then lay out more details as I move through the ethnographic, survey, and interview findings.

## *The Four South African Schools*

### Groveland Secondary School (Coast City)[2]

Just months shy of the tenth anniversary of democracy's advent in the Republic of South Africa, I made my first visit to Groveland Secondary School accompanied by a provincial school official, Thomas Van Maanan, a charming caramel brown-skinned Coloured man who had acquired some education in the United States and now supervised curricular programs in Groveland's regional district. Mr. Van Maanan had assisted me in making contact with Groveland and its leadership, and he accompanied me to the school on that first day. As we drove along the highway toward Groveland, I looked out over the plain, observing a sea of tin shacks covered with newspaper and held together with nails and screws that seemed barely able to keep out the blustery Coast City winds blowing off the Atlantic or the monsoon-like rains that would shower the metropolitan area during the wet winters in July and August. The shacks lined the major thoroughfare that led us into Wilson Heights, the home community of Groveland. Analogously, the "flats" are to Coloureds what the "townships" are to Blacks, spatially bounded, racially coded, and residentially segregated spaces distinguished by the dominant racial or population group that lives within them.

As we approach Groveland, the architecture of the houses changes to more sturdy, square wooden homes, some painted brightly and seemingly more tolerant of the winds and rains. We drove up to the gates of the school where a short, Coloured man wearing a cap guarded a conglomeration of rectangular, redbrick buildings behind tall fences wrapped in electric barbed wire meant to deter a burglar. Each time a car pulled up to the school, he would check the car's passenger contents for recognition, and once satisfied that the visitors were legitimate, he would pull out the keys from his pocket to open the door, through which he allowed us to enter.

Mr. Van Maanan and I headed immediately to the office of the vice principal, Donald Gaines, a brown-skinned Coloured man with a big smile, who warmly welcomed us and shared much about the history of Groveland Secondary School. It opened in 1983, the year Mr. Gaines arrived, two years prior to the 1985 desegregation attempts of the apartheid resistance movement. Groveland, as Mr. Gaines told it, was the first Coloured school to admit Black learners, and the first ones came from hundreds of kilometers north because the police violence there was so severe that many schools had to be closed down. Under apartheid, the state demanded separate departments of education for each of its classified racial groups; Coloureds and Africans had not been schooled together, just as these two groups were segregated from Whites. Consequently, at that time, Groveland was taking a risk by admitting these students.

"Well, what about the Blacks in this area? Did they not come, too?" I asked Mr. Gaines. He responded that when local Black families found out about the Soweto learners' admission to the school, they began to seek admission for their children, too. Principal Arum Naipal, a tall man, brown-skinned man with broad shoulders of Indian descent whom I met next, elaborated on Groveland's history. Under his predecessor's leadership, Groveland's enrollment had plummeted. "The conservative Coloured community did not favor Groveland for its role in the [apartheid resistance] movement and avoided sending their kids there," Mr. Naipal said. In the past, Coloureds were accorded an "in-between" status in South Africa's racial hierarchy. Though not formally recognized as White, they were given preferential treatment over Africans. In 1955, the Coloured Labor Preference Policy (CLPP) forced a divide between the two groups by giving Coloureds priority for employment in designated areas near Coast City. The policy's main objective was to protect Coloured workers from competition from Blacks in the labor market. It set quotas for the number of Blacks who could be employed in the region and required Labor Department certification that no Coloured applicants were available for the job before an employer could hire a Black applicant. Hence, black-coloured relations are complicated by the manipulation of the National Party to maintain a wedge among non-Whites by implementing a social hierarchy favoring lighter-skinned and mix-raced Coloureds over Africans.

So, when Coloureds withdrew from a school that had opened its doors to Blacks, "the school had to do something to keep from closing," Mr. Naipal explained. A local man approached the existing school leaders and asked them to consider offering admission to Black students from Soweto, a well-known township of Johannesburg, where many schools had been shut down because of the severe hostility between the government and student activists.[3] Groveland received some financial compensation for educating these students, who lived in a hostel and "paid lots of money" to attend the school. As a result, not only did Groveland expand its student population to keep its doors open, but also it became the first coloured school in the Coast City area to enroll African students.

Social protest is no stranger to Groveland's learners and educators. "This is a school with a political history," Vice-Principal Gaines later commented. "The students of the struggle differ from those of this generation. Those of the struggle had responsibility, and I can probably guarantee you that all of the learners from 1983 to about 1990 have jobs because they picked up skills from the struggle. They learned how to speak and write and organize," he continued. Groveland was often sanctioned for being one of the few to resist the apartheid laws and to protest them. "We were closed all the time [because students and educators were protesting]," Mr. Gaines said. Even the school's former principal had been targeted by the government for his anti-apartheid resistance activity, and later he self-exiled to the West.

Today, in terms of numbers, Groveland is still overwhelmingly Coloured, with a student body of 1,400. About 25 percent, or 350, of its learners are identified as Black, primarily of ethnic Xhosa origins. I included it in the study to examine the complexity of African-Coloured student and teacher relationships. "We're a working class school," Mr. Gaines told me, even though the statistics belie this. Sixty-five percent of the learners' parents were unemployed, which made me wonder how many of them could really afford the R350 (approximately $51 in 2004) school fees a year. Meanwhile, Groveland had a 35 percent pass rate at the matriculant level (twelfth graders seeking the equivalent of a high school diploma), and like those at many poor schools, many of the tenth-grade students failed their final exams, which are standardized and set by the South African Ministry of Education. That explains why, out of a school of 1,400 learners, there were less than one hundred matrics. Of that number, Gaines said that only about two would probably get jobs immediately after completing grade twelve, and maybe one or two would head to university.

Indeed, Groveland is a poor school. It runs on a shoestring budget. Meanwhile, many of its teachers seek to help their students in the ways that they can. Some had met earlier on the morning of my first visit to discuss assisting one of their graduates from the year prior. The student had done well on the matric exam and gained admission to the University of Stellenbosch where he earned decent grades in his mechanical engineering program (A's, B's, and a C or two), but he could not afford to return in the second year. His mother was unemployed and his father deceased. The teachers had discussed setting up a small "corporation" to sell things to raise funds. To get him through the university would cost about R5000 per year (approximately $694 in 2004).

Ironically, like many educators I met in South African townships (or flats), these teachers and principals did not tend to send their own children to the schools where they worked. Mr. Gaines's three daughters, for example, attended a wealthier school near his home about "two minutes away." Still, he shared that although one of his oldest daughters had finished at a technikons (a vocational college) in clothing manufacturing, she had to return to school because she could not find a job with that degree. Subsequently, his daughter returned to school to study chemistry and mathematics to become a teacher. Given the high unemployment rate in South Africa, I wondered how South African educators grappled with the disjuncture between educational and job attainment. "How do you continue to instill in students the value of an education when the opportunity constraints appear so tight?" I asked. Mr. Gaines grimaced and admitted that it is the most difficult part of his job, getting up daily in front of very poor township students to motivate them, and yet knowing that once they leave high school, very few job opportunities await them without a university degree. Still, Gaines and his colleagues persisted to keep these learners from succumbing to pessimism and hopelessness and sought to help them build initial sources of human capital through literacy and numeracy skills.

Students, at least, would learn to read and write. And further, they would be bilingual, at least minimally so. Groveland is a dual-language medium school offering all major subject classes in both Afrikaans (the home language of the majority of the Coloured students) and English. In addition, it offers language classes in IsiXhosa (the home language of most of its Black students), taught by the only Black teacher on the staff, who is also ethnically Xhosa.[4] As I made my way across the country later, Mr. Gaines informed me, I would observe a big linguistic difference between Black learners living north in Johannesburg compared to those living in the townships of Coast City.

why have schools chosen English?

Mr. Gaines taught in Afrikaans and English, and sometimes he would have a student translate the lessons for the Xhosa learners, or he would have the IsiXhosa teacher to translate. "Learners in Johannesburg will have a better grasp of the English language," he said, suggesting that living in a larger, cosmopolitan city is a big contributor to learning English. In my observations, Mr. Gaines was only partially correct. Noticeably, the black population in Johannesburg spans a wider socioeconomic spectrum with a greater representation in the middle and upper classes than Blacks in the Coast City area. Indeed, the correlation between blackness and poverty is significantly more conspicuous in Coast City than in Johannesburg. Yet, in the Letisi townships not far from Johannesburg, I encountered many poor Black learners who appeared to be about as facile with English as those attending Groveland. Nonetheless, overall, these language challenges, as well as poverty and other ecological factors such high parental unemployment challenged the educational pathways of Groveland's learners.

## Palmer High School (Coast City)

On another point on the socioeconomic spectrum of South African high schools, Palmer is a solidly middle-class school located only about ten miles away from Groveland. Approximately one-third of its 1,000 students are White and over 60 percent are Black, Coloured, and Indian.[5] The main language spoken at Palmer is English, and either Afrikaans or IsiXhosa is the second language that most students take to fulfill the second language requirements.

Situated in a predominantly white suburb, with a white principal and mostly white teaching staff, Palmer possesses facilities of all sorts, including a ceramics studio with kilns, two large networked computer labs, art studios, home economics and woodworking shops, a library decked out with a metal detector so that learners would not take out books without checking them out, music rooms for the band and piano, a theater, and an assembly hall. The lawns are meticulously manicured and are not fenced like Groveland's, an all too-familiar image at schools in the townships and flats.

Arriving at Palmer that first morning was like entering a familiar space, relatively speaking, like many of the affluent (and suburban) high schools with which I am familiar in the United States. I drove into the gate and entered the circular driveway of this red-bricked school fashioned on the British-style school architecture, with its open plazas here and there. As I entered the white façade archway, to the left there was a reception window and across from it was a waiting lounge. The female attendant at the front office directed me to a couch in the waiting area to await the principal. A jovial, attractive, thirty-something principal, John Dalton arrived and escorted me to his cavernous suite down a hallway lined with portraits of the school's former principals—all dignified looking White men. The anteroom to Dalton's office was where his executive assistant sat (a White female immigrant from Zimbabwe). Behind her were a number of stainless steel file cabinets and French-style (multipaned) windows looking out toward the side of the school compound. Dalton's office was open and airy, twice the size of Vice Principal Gaines's office at Groveland and outfitted with a stylishly upholstered couch and chairs, unlike the plastic ones sitting in Gaines's office. A grand wooden desk outfitted with a full computer setup, bookshelves, and open windows stood at the back of this executive office.

Across from the reception area was the faculty room, filled with round tables, a kitchenette, couches, a bulletin board with announcements and provincial test results. Unlike the township schools, learners at Palmer High School did not have to sweep floors and empty the trash. Palmer had a team of Black housekeepers and groundsmen who kept the school immaculate. The women mopped and swept and provided coffee and tea, often taking my tea-cup and washing it immediately after I finished. At Palmer, I got a glimpse of what things looked like under apartheid (and other, perhaps, neocolonial societies). With females wearing bright blue maids' outfits and males dressed in khaki worker pants and shirts, Black workers continue to serve in manual and low-skilled positions, mainly as helpers and cleaners, while White female office assistants greet visitors to the school in the front office or at the bursar's window where parents pay their children's school fees, due quarterly.

On my first day, Principal Dalton introduced me to the teachers at the staff meeting, and they welcomed me warmly with applause. I was also introduced to Jennifer Benson, a middle-aged woman with a wry sense of humor who was the guidance counselor (a post that I did not encounter at Groveland). Jennifer would be my go-to person as I oriented myself to Palmer, and she gave me a tour of the campus. Jennifer also runs the "Diversity Trippers," a program that she and another teacher designed and implemented in 1999 to bring together learners of different social backgrounds to discuss diversity issues while on a mountain retreat. Learners are handpicked after they apply, stating why they feel they should be accepted to the program. From Jennifer, I learned that Palmer was one of the first ex-Model C, formerly all-white schools to open its doors to Coloured and Black learners. Students here come from the sur-rounding tony neighborhood (where a number of faculty members from a flagship university live), a contiguous township, and the city center. Jennifer told me about her commitment to "diversity" and how she was influenced by her membership in a group called "Black Sash," middle-class White women who were part of the anti-apartheid resistance struggle.

Most of the Palmer teachers whom I met were relatively "new"—that is, hired post-1994. Palmer had only a few Black teachers, the eighth-grade IsiXhosa teacher named Mr. Ernest Zulani was from the Eastern Cape and was, at the time, studying via a distance-based program at the University of South Africa (UNISA) to be a lawyer. He had come to Palmer only a couple of years before. I sat in on his IsiXhosa class (where the learners are taught in English, which I discovered is the case for most "foreign" language courses).[6] Mr. Zulani gave me a copy of the learners' "textbook," a compendium of photocopied pages that listed grammatical rules, vocabulary, and basic phrases.

Also, on that first day, Principal Dalton introduced me to the entire school at a weekly assembly program. Students gathered in the hall and sat on the floor, all adorned in their navy blazers with khaki pants for the boys and blue skirts and white shirts for the girls, though a few girls wore pants, too. Teachers marched into the assembly hall and sat on the stage followed by me, the prefects (head boys and girls), and the principal, who sat closest to the lectern. I was offered an opportunity to address the student body and explain my presence, and I chose this time to entice potential survey and interview participants with offerings of free pizza, pens, and t-shirts, if they participated in the study. This was the how my first day began, and in the days to come, I would visit and observe classes, speak informally to learners and educators during breaks, survey students, and navigate the entire school terrain for as long as I was allowed.

## Montjane Secondary School (Letisi)

After a ten-day quarter break in April, I returned to South Africa, although this time I headed to the Letisi. As I turned off the main road on my first morning to Montjane Secondary School, I had to inch my car down the road leading to the school, brimming with impatience and couched between kombi taxis that made stops at every block and corner. I drove toward the school through the township of Lighttown and observed many unemployed men standing on the local street corners. Once I entered the school grounds and parked in the small lot where teachers and administrators sometimes had to double park to fit all of the cars, I met with Mr. Jonah Nkomo, Montjane's principal, whom I had met three years prior during my first visit to South Africa.

Located adjacent to a field and stadium in Lighttown, Montjane's new school building was "secured" behind green gates bound by barbed wire and had a security guard sitting in a small booth at the entrance. The security guard swung open the gate to allow me to enter the small parking lot where educators' cars were double, and in places triple, parked. As I entered the gates, three small, white trailers stood before me and to the right lay an open plaza within the brick school structure.

Mr. Nkomo greeted me in the parking lot and escorted me to his office. Inside the school, learners moved about in their uniforms of brown skirts or trousers with bee-gold shirts. The staff room, bleak and barren, was located at the opposite end of the hallway from Mr. Nkomo's office. It was filled with a few long tables and folding chairs for the educators; there was a striking absence of bulletin boards, books, or posters. Mr. Nkomo and I chatted in his office, which was equally as modest as the staff room, although he proudly displayed the school's trophies and certificates for their good exam results. He had a few assistants, including Lloyd, a Black man in his twenties; Lillian, a thirty-something Black female receptionist; and some Black female housekeeping staff members who would bring tea in white tea cups. Next door to Mr. Nkomo's office was that of the female vice principal, Mrs. Gloria Nala, a forty-something Black woman with a pleasant smile, who had been teaching and working at Montjane for several years. A very hospitable Mrs. Nala would often welcome me into her office, where I sat occasionally when it was too cold to sit elsewhere in the building during breaks or at moments when I needed to record field notes or make arrangements for the learner surveys.

Montjane's student body comprises approximately 1,430 students with thirty-six teachers, and school fees are approximately R250 per year (approximately $36 in 2004). Many of these learners are ethnically Sotho, Zulu, Pedi, and Tswana, and all of the teachers are Black, mainly Sotho and Zulu. That year, there were seventy-eight matrics at Montjane. Physically, the school is not large enough for the student body. Every morning a teacher leads a pep rally commencing with a Christian prayer and song in the outdoor plaza. Some classes are held in the plaza, even when it is cold, due to the lack of sufficient space for the full enrollment. Learners are required to either stand or sit directly on the ground during either these assemblies or classes because no seating is available.

Mr. Nkomo is proud of his school, established in 1994, and its opening is commemorated with a plaque at the school's entrance, mentioning the attendance of then minister of education, Kadar Asmal, and other dignitaries. On my first tour of Montjane's premises with Mr. Nkomo, I observed crowded classrooms of children and noticed teacher absenteeism immediately, as talkative children sat bustling with rowdy chatter in teacher-less classrooms. On the top floor of the building, opposite the principal's and main offices, stood a new computer lab enshrouded in iron bars. Each of the approximately twenty-five computers had its own plastic, hard case to protect it from burglars. There was a special security system in this room, and it had not been used until I offered a one-hour lab one day to a group of matrics. Despite having a new school building, Montjane lacked many of the amenities, even the basics. Often there was neither toilet paper nor paper towels in the faculty restrooms, for example. The small kitchenette outside the staff room had a malfunctioning oven. A local woman from the township, who was the lone janitor, cleaned the school, and she was assisted by the female students who had to sweep, empty trash cans, and clean the classrooms. Montjane's learners, unlike those at Palmer and Williston, had no gym or auditorium. In fact, the class schedule ensured that most teachers had to shift from room to room to teach the next class, since many did not have their own classrooms.

While a critical mass of South Africa's Black learners will attend underresourced high schools, if they are lucky, they may find themselves in a place like Montjane Secondary School. It is dubbed an "ex-Model C of the townships" because, in many of its previous years, over 90 percent of its twelfth graders passed the National Senior Certificate or matric exam—the South African equivalent of a high school diploma. Montjane had been recognized and lauded several times by the provincial education department for its dedication, commitment, and delivery of high pass rates on the senior certificate exams.

## Williston High School (Letisi)

Each week I alternated daylong visits between Montjane and the mixed-race, white-dominant Williston High School. Entering Williston's campus entails ringing the bell at the gate, which opens onto manicured lawns surrounded by red-bricked buildings with ivy-covered walls, various open-faced plazas, and colorful flowers tended by Black men wearing blue laborer jackets and pants. Williston desegregated in the early 1990s and now welcomes many lower middle- to middle-class African, Coloured, and Indian students to its rolls. Before school began, boys of all races would run around an outdoor basketball court in white shirts, striped brown ties, and brown pants, competing against one another. Later, they would put on their school jacket adorned in Williston's school colors of brown, yellow, and white. Williston is visibly a middle-class school and has a prominent brick façade entrance with white shingles.

Wood paneling covers the walls of the reception area and the anteroom to the principal's office. That first day, I introduced myself to the secretary, a middle-aged White woman named Joan Pringle, who greeted me warmly and welcomed me back to Williston High school. They had been expecting me. Caryn Billups, the principal, stood at the photocopy machine, completing her task before greeting me with a hug, stating that, of course, she had remembered me from years prior when I was first at Williston as a visitor on a tour of a few South African schools. Mrs. Billups was too busy to meet at that time, and she seemed hurried, almost frenetic about her multiple tasks for the day. She asked Joan to usher me into the faculty lounge, where I was introduced to Helen Anthony, one of the two vice principals, who then invited me to tea. Our chat presented me with an opportunity to get an update on the school.

Williston has about 1,000 students, half of which are racially identified as Black; 38 percent are White, 5 percent are Indian, and 6 percent are Coloured. Ninety-eight percent of the thirty-eight teachers are White and 2 percent are Black and Coloured.[7] There are a few more Black teachers at Williston than when I first visited, but I later learned that they were student teacher apprentices from one of South Africa's flagship universities. Similar to Palmer, Williston High School teaches primarily in English; Afrikaans is offered as the primary second language, although the former is the first language for most students there. Unlike Palmer, Williston does not offer instruction in either of the native languages of its majority-Black student population.

Down the corridor from the faculty lounge is the bursar's office, enclosed behind a gate and doors. One has to be buzzed in to enter; this is, presumably, for security purposes. Here I learned that school fees are greater than R3500 (approximately $504 in 2004), over ten times the amount paid by pupils at Montjane. Further down this corridor on the right is a well-stocked library with a few computers. On an adjacent corridor leading back to the principal's office is a suite of offices for the department heads. Across the plaza and to the back is a full-fledged, operative computer lab staffed by a teacher. At lunch time students are free to come and go from the lab, although mostly boys appeared to hang out there.

Williston also has an art classroom where students' work covers the walls. More advanced art students attend extra sessions after school. There is an auditorium, too, where I attended several performances, as well as a full assembly that included government dignitaries. A tuck (or snack) shop is located on the school grounds. Students also have access to vending machines selling crisps (potato chips), cookies, candy, and gum. Funds from the machines are

used to extend the school's coffers. Out back, there is a large field for sports
activities such as soccer and rugby.

The black attendance and admission to Williston has increased over the
years, and Vice Principal Anthony mentioned that Black and Coloured students were more acculturated than they had been in the early 1990s when the
school first "opened." Then, language issues emerged, since many were not
proficient in English, but now, "they have fewer issues with language," she
commented. Mrs. Anthony also told me that many of the Black parents did
not participate in their children's education and schooling as much as parents
in other groups. When I asked her why, she stated, "I think that some parents
may be insecure about their educational backgrounds." "But what about all
of those wealthy Black parents who drive the fancy cars that you mentioned
earlier?" I asked. "Oh, they work such long hours; they don't have time to
come," she said.

While I was never able to verify Mrs. Anthony's claims about Black
parents' participation, I do know that not many are active in the parents'
association, which I discovered when I attended the school's annual parent
fundraiser one evening, a gala event featuring an all-white cast of three men
and two women singing show tunes and interjecting humorous comments
with political and racial overtones. Notably, my good friend Lebogang,
whom I persuaded to attend with me, was the only South African Black person in the audience. At our table sat an Indian parent, who was a school principal in Lighttown; the remainder of the audience was White. As I explored
reasons for the audience makeup, Principal Billups told me that there was
only one Black parent in the Parent Teacher Fund (PTF), a mostly "social
organization," as she described it, which holds at least one function per term.
The PTF differs from the school governing body, which sets policy and manages the school budget. When I inquired whether every student was asked to
sell a ticket to parents to attend the function, Billups said that only parents
who were members of the PTF had tickets to sell. No wonder, then, that
there were no Black or Coloured and only a few Indian parents in the organization; these communities would not have access to tickets and/or would
not have an awareness that the event was occurring. Despite the conspicuous
racial distances (more on this later), Williston is a thriving school that offers
many, if not all, of the amenities that middle-class parents seek for their children, and it can continue to do this as South African socioeconomic stratification insures that its significantly higher school fees can only be afforded by
families from a particular economic class.

## Brief Recap of South African Schools

High rates of poverty and other disadvantaged socioeconomic conditions characterize many of the township and rural schools to which much of South Africa's majority non-White population was confined until the 1990s. Desegregated, ex-Model C schools, on the other hand, are now highly regarded for their larger budgets, smaller educator-learner ratios, more experienced faculty, greater course offerings, more funds and diversity in extracurricular programs, and wider networks of information about college attainment. Groups previously excluded now attend these schools, seek better educational resources, and have chances for greater academic attainment.

Palmer High in Coast City and Williston in Letisi, both multiracial and white dominant, are considered open public schools because of the diversity of their students. The apparent changes in the racial demographics of Palmer and Williston result from South Africa's burgeoning middle class of African, Coloured, and Indian families, in the more open opportunity structure, and from the exodus of middle-class families from the segregated townships throughout the country.[8] Even when these families do not relocate their residences geographically, they may choose to send their kids away from the township schools. Thus, school desegregation primarily benefits the lower middle and middle classes in South Africa, not the poor. Like their private school counterparts, Palmer and Williston charge relatively high fees, so the poor are less likely to avail of this experience. Palmer and Williston also have smaller learner-educator ratios, more amenities and space resources, and a significantly higher percentage of their matrics passing the senior certificate exams at a level sufficient to enter any South African university.

Montjane (Black) and Groveland (Coloured and Black), in contrast, would be considered segregated schools because of their concentration of student poverty in conjunction with their ethnic and racial composition. In stark comparison, they face a long recovery period from the legacy and residual effects of the apartheid system, which proactively sought to keep non-Whites from becoming equipped with the critical thinking and technical skills requisite for participation in the national and global economies of the twentieth and twenty-first centuries.[9] In terms of their resource contexts, these two groups of schools reflect much of the variation in the resource contexts of public schools in the post-apartheid democratic era (see Table 2.1).

**Table 2.1 Descriptive traits of South African schools**

| Indicators | Groveland (Coloured) | Montjane (African/black) | Palmer (ex-Model C) | Williston (ex-Model C) |
|---|---|---|---|---|
| 1. Library, textbook and computing resources | Library-limited / No open computer lab / Auditorium / No fields | Library-limited / Computers, no instruction / No auditorium / Playing fields | Library / Open computer lab / Auditorium/gym / Playing fields, tennis courts, pool, pottery/ceramics studio, theater, band hall, home economics lab | Library / Open computer lab / Auditorium / Playing fields, home economics lab, art room |
| 2. Learner-Educator ratio | 34:1 | 40:1 | 19:1 | 26:1 |
| Learner racial diversity* | 25% Black / 75% Coloured | 100% Black | 29% Black / 36% Coloured / 2% Indian / 33% White | 50% Black / 6% Coloured / 5% Indian / 38% White |
| Educator racial diversity* | 2% Black / 93% Coloured / 5% White | 100% Black | 6% Black / 13% Coloured / 81% White | 5% Black / 3% Coloured / 92% White |
| School fees (in 2004 U.S. dollars) | $51 | $36 | $1050 | $550 |
| Number of students | 1,400 | 1,400 | 1,000 | 980 |

*Note: Author tabulated based on principals' reports and faculty and student rosters

# A Nation Apart: Introduction of the U.S. Schools

## South County Prep (South Capital City)

In January 2007, I was welcomed at South County Prep High School, a school of grades nine through twelve, comprised of 1,389 students, located at the fringe of a medium-sized, urban city in the American South. According to the year 2000 Census, there were 497,197 people residing within South Capital City's metropolitan statistical area (MSA). The racial makeup of the MSA is 53 percent White, 45 percent African American, 0.7 percent Asian, and one percent Hispanic or Latino of any race. At South County Prep High School, about 77 percent of the students are racially classified as White, 21 percent Black, and 1 percent Asian and 1 percent Hispanic.[10] South County Prep's student-teacher ratio is 17.3 to 1, and with the exception of three, all of the teachers and staff are White. Most of the African American and White students at South County will tell the curious visitor that they attended nearby elementary and middle schools together. In doing so, they alternate between personal accounts of tolerance and interracial friendships and macro-level and school-level narratives of racial inequity and division. Students at South County Prep also span the socioeconomic spectrum across both races; here one can find poor, working-class, though mainly middle-class African American and White students.

Its campus is a sprawling complex within the boundaries of multiple affluent subdivisions of massive single-level and multilevel brick homes with two- to three-car garages. Driving along the main road leading to the school, one cannot help but notice the many megachurches and new malls occupied by designer stores that have cropped up in the area over the last few years. Outfitted with modern brick buildings, a large baseball field marked by the colorful logo of an area bank that sponsors the sport's program, a wide football field surrounded by a freshly paved track many yards away, and a newly built arts and theater complex, where some school assemblies are held. South County Prep is clearly a resource-rich school.

*environment*

Mary Jennings, a White female in her fifties, who has served in some capacity at South County Prep for twenty-nine years, is the school principal, a position she has held for more than a decade. Having taught a range of students with varying abilities including those with special needs, Jennings is especially sensitive to the differences in how students learn and advocates schools' getting away from conventional report cards. "We've got to get away from kids working for a grade," she says. Rather, Jennings stresses her goals of preparing students to think conceptually and to teach analytical and critical thinking skills requisite for socioeconomic mobility in the twenty-first century. "We have to get to where kids are working for meeting a standard. And, it doesn't matter if it takes you five times to do it or you do it the first time. If you meet the standards, you've met the standard. What difference does it make how long it takes you to get there?" Jennings continues. Elaborating on her point, Jennings declares the following:

> If we just get rid of these grades and teach objectives and standards, I think our kids would be better off. Your child has met this objective. They're ready to move on. And if you can meet them in half a year, then move on to the next set of objectives. Some kids could do it in a half a year; some can do it in a year. What is to say that just because it takes me a year to make those Algebra I standards that it's more important that you're a better person cause you met them in a half a year? We both met the same standards. Maybe you can do it better than I can, but we both got the standards to move on to Algebra I.

Jennings, like many principals beholden to the mandates of the No Child Left Behind (NCLB) educational legislation, works continually with her curriculum planners to insure that her school meets the state accountability standards, but she is aware that the state's standards are significantly lower than the national ones.

South County Prep runs on an AB schedule, which means it rotates classes every day. Mondays, Wednesdays, and Fridays are A days; Tuesdays and Thursdays are B days. On "A" and "B" days, students attend different sets of classes. Students also enroll in a core class, whose focus is on a specific career option or job sector that meets every day for thirty minutes. Furthermore, students meet with the same group of students and instructor for the entire four years that they attend South County Prep. For example, a select group of students interested in business would meet with one teacher for thirty minutes and with the same group of fellow learners interested in business for all four years of their high school experience. For the last several years, South County Prep has met its achievement goals, scoring an "exemplary" rating by state NCLB standards and making it one of the best performing schools in its state.

## South City Honors (South Capital City)

Ten miles west of South County Prep sits South City Honors High School, an urban, comprehensive high school of grades nine through twelve with a notable advanced placement program, one of the most productive in the state. South City Honors has 1,333 students, 93 percent of whom are racially classified as Black and 6 percent as White. With a student-teacher ratio of 19.6 to 1, it is led by a multiracial staff of sixty-eight teachers. Prior to the 1980s, South City Honors was an all white high school with a strong academic reputation, but white flight from the surrounding neighborhoods led to the gradual browning of the school, although the legacy of a strong academic community endures. South City Honors' gray, drab-looking physical plant shows signs of wear and tear, and students complain of the leaky roofs and cracked paint in walls, among other things. Teachers, such as like the advanced placement physics teacher, Mr. Alejandro Jimenez, a Cuban émigré, lament the fact that students in an advanced science subjects must work without a lab. "This is a physics class!" he proclaims. "How can they expect me to teach without a lab? This is the United States!" Mr. Jimenez exclaims.

Today, many of the school's students come from humble socioeconomic backgrounds, if the percentage of those eligible for free or reduced lunch— nearly 64 percent—is any indication. The school, nevertheless, forges ahead with its academic programs, particularly its advanced placement and honors curriculum and a special program "APEX" (Academic Performance of Excellence)—which has been in existence for more than two decades. APEX is a demanding and competitive academic and artistic program to which not only South City Honors students but also others from around the metropolitan area of South Capital may apply. Many argue that it is APEX that has kept the minority of White families at South City Honors invested in the school. Given its competitive nature, generally APEX students are quite gifted and academically outstanding, and consequently their status at the school is quite high. Frequently, one witnesses and hears about the social and symbolic boundaries drawn between the APEX and non-APEX students. Some members of the latter group sense that students in APEX are those who keep South City Honors on the map as a "Level 5" (or top-performing) school in the state's accountability system.

The leader of South City Honors is a former military man, whom the teachers, staff, and students refer to as "Admiral," although his given name is Dr. Bradley Raymond. Admiral runs a tight ship, figuratively speaking. The disciplinary climate at the school is one of its most striking features to the casual observer, and on any given day, about thirty to forty students spend some time in ISS (in-school suspension), on lockdown in the school's auditorium for an infraction, for anything, from boys wearing their pants hanging too low or a tenth-grade girl wearing an airbrushed t-shirt—both violations of the school's

dress code—to talking back or swearing at a teacher in class. The Admiral has
a zero-tolerance policy for student "misbehavior," and he informs his teachers
during a faculty meeting not to waste precious curricular time on dealing with
behavioral issues. Rather, he directs them to send students to ISS or to the
main office so that either he or his vice principals can deal with the matter. The
top priority of his teachers is to insure that as many students as possible score at
or above the proficiency level on the state tests at the end of the year. After all,
South City Honors has a reputation to uphold, and the educators insure that
their students know that this is the school's main mission.

## North City Tech (North Capital City)

North City Tech School is one of several competitive public schools in
North Capital City—where students have to score above a certain threshold
on a common examination given in middle school in order to be admitted
and where more than 80 percent of its 1,190 students can be categorized as
"minority" or students of color. Although many of these students performed
better than the majority of North Capital City students on the requisite
entrance tests, most North City Tech students do not score high enough to be
accepted to the two other exam schools that are considered more elite and are
ranked higher. Some students at North City Tech rather self-deprecatingly
refer to themselves as the "leftovers," meaning that they were the ones who
lost out on admissions to the other two more prestigious exam schools. Still,
the school is respected for its math and science focus, and it delivers some of
the highest test scores in the state.

Out of the four U.S. schools in this study, North City Tech is the most
balanced in terms of race and ethnicity of the student body, with about
45 percent Black, 23 percent Asian, 20 percent Hispanic, and 11 percent
White.[11] North City Tech's student-teacher ratio is 18.3 to 1, and like South
City Honors in South Capital City, it maintains a multiracial teaching staff
and an administration of about sixty-five. Students hail from various neighborhoods and corners of Northern Capital City, taking various transportation modes, including trains, cars, and buses, to get to school.

North City Tech's principal, Sam Jemison, is a White male in his midthir-
ties who has a master's degree from Northwestern University. At first encounter, he comes across as a casual and affable man who seemingly understands
the complexity of the racial, ethnic, and class dynamics that permeate the
student-teacher relations in his school. Jemison is the fourth principal that
North City Tech has had in five years, and this turnover, he explained, has led

to conditions in which parents have become antagonistic toward the administration. He is also up front about the tensions between him and some of his older, mainly African American teachers. Some of the African American faculty, particularly a handful of women and a highly student-favored male history teacher named Allan Ford, see Jemison as someone who favors the young White teachers, whom they perceive as having been hired to displace them—in terms of power and access—from the more high-status positions in the school, including those teaching the advanced courses.

North City Tech is not a resource-rich school. Jemison confided that the parent committee had been unable to get together and create a successful fundraiser necessary to raise additional and greatly needed money for the school because of a small cohort. Jemison also made the hiring of teachers a priority, so he and his leadership team had decided to spend money marked for supplies on a teacher's salary. This meant that school supplies—books, technology, and paper—were often in short supply and that teachers often had to purchase their own materials.

Physically, North City Tech is located in a stretch of long, interconnected, sparsely decorated, rectangular, industrial buildings of mostly painted cinder blocks and steel, with few windows. One enters the school through an inconspicuous door near the rear faculty parking lot. The windowless hallway is lit with only fluorescent light, but a large, colorful mural painted on the wall makes it seem brighter. The hallways are relatively quiet, though on any given day, there are a few girls and boys passing through; a few parents and students shuffle in and out as the school secretaries attend to them. We were surprised to walk by a Chinese language class, filled with students of many different racial and ethnic backgrounds. We also observed, with significantly more frequency, multicultural and multiethnic history displays at North City Tech than at the other three U.S. schools.

## North Village Prep (North Capital City)

To find a comparative, majority-white school with a critical mass of Black and Latino students, I had to look in a suburban, upper middle-class school district that participates in North Capital City's metropolitan voluntary desegregation program (VDP).[12] North Village Prep High School is located twenty-three miles northwest of North City Tech High School. Since 1967, it has participated in the VDP to attract African American or Black and Hispanic students, most of whom entered a lottery to attend affluent suburban schools like this one.

The VDP youth, perhaps, arise earlier than other students in their neighborhoods to attend schools in the suburbs, leaving home as early as 5:30 a.m. to catch a bus leaving at 6:00. Daily there are three return buses to their communities, one that returns to Northern Capital City immediately after school lets out at 2:45 p.m., one at 3:30 p.m., and one at 5 p.m. The school also schedules transportation for students when there are after-school dances and other extracurricular activities on the weekends and evenings.

Of North Village Prep's student population of 1,242, White students make up 84 percent, while 6 percent are Black, 5 percent Asian, and 3 percent Latino. With the exception of one African American and one Asian American teacher, all of North Village Prep High School's eighty-eight teachers are White, and its student-teacher ratio is 14.1 to 1. The lone African American teacher of history was due to retire by the end of the school year. Meanwhile, a staff of three has oversight of the participation of Black and Latino students in the VDP and their parents, and it includes a local director, a middle-aged Black woman named Diane Newsome, her staff assistant and receptionist, a Latina named Gladys Portrero, and Beverly Kite, a twenty-something African American woman hired to tutor, mentor, and provide some remedial services for the VDP students. A graduate of and participant in the VDP at another school years earlier, Beverly also oversees the room (the "VDP" room) next door to the band and orchestra hall. The students from North Capital City tend to congregate there during study breaks or free time, some leisurely surfing the Internet on one of the four Apple computers in the room, or simply hanging out with one another, while Beverly provides either individualized attention or supports a group with homework at the conference table planted in the middle of the room.

The differences in resources between North City Tech and North Village Prep High School are significant. Like South County High down in South Capital City, North Village Prep has most of its classrooms outfitted with smart boards, sophisticated electronic equipment that allows teachers and students to interact with information and material from the Internet that is projected onto the bulletin board at the front of the class. In addition, teachers have usage of televisions, DVD players, slide and PowerPoint projectors, along with a host of other amenities. There are no paper or supply shortages here. North Village Prep also has its own student radio station, which transmits shows throughout the local area, along with a three-floor library with an airy and open floor plan and fully stocked shelves, books on CD, puzzles, games for students, magazines, comfy chairs, and numerous computers. There are a lot of tables and small study carrels where one could often sight students wearing MIT and Harvard sweatshirts, for example, or listening to their iPods or completing an assignment on an Apple iMac laptop. On the school grounds is a new athletic facility, the Granite Center, which houses what appears to be an Olympic-size swimming pool with lanes and diving boards, a whirlpool, a child's pool, a weight room, and a cardio room. North Village Prep's teachers are contracted to instruct only four classes and a maximum of ninety students total per day, compared to teacher contact hours based upon six and seven classes and over a hundred students per day at other schools. At the time of our visits, North Village Prep was in the midst of a hiring frenzy because a number of young female teachers who had become new mothers were choosing to work part time. And parents had become concerned about the quality of the applicant pool for new teachers. Stuart Beckham, the white-haired sixty-something principal at North Village Prep meets the first Monday of each month with parents, allowing them to address whatever issues or concerns they have about the school. Most in attendance are White mothers, and Mr. Beckham had to assure them that the teacher applicants were "amazing." They were getting teachers who were leaving a rival high school in a nearby community, and the biology teacher they planned to hire had a PhD, while the math teacher they were getting had written a math book, which would be available for students who needed extra help in trigonometry.

North Village Prep parents are also quite concerned with college admissions, particularly at the selective, elite universities and colleges. Often Principal Beckman—an educator with thirty-seven years of experience under his belt, although he had been in principal leadership roles for only the last decade—has to assure them of how well their students are achieving, compared to rival, affluent communities. The number of schools to which North Village Prep students apply has risen. One student had applied to twenty colleges, and in a previous year, another had applied to twenty-four. But that was nothing compared to the thirty-two to which a student in a neighboring community had applied, which was the most that Mr. Beckman had heard of.

## Brief Recap of U.S. Schools

In summary, South City Honors (majority African American) and South County Prep High School (majority-white) in South Capital City and North City Tech (majority-minority: African American, Latino, and Asian) and North Village Prep High School (majority-white) in North Capital City varied in their sociodemographic profiles, in their overall school resources, and in the cultural ethos (more on this later) that permeated throughout their organizations. Table 2.2 provides some general descriptive details about these four U.S. schools. I should note that I use a different nomenclature for the U.S. schools. The reader will note that I signify the regional locale of the school first by using either "North" or "South." I also utilize spatial terms such as "City" to denote the majority-minority, urban public schools and "County" and "Village" to denote the two majority-white, suburban public schools. This is my attempt to 1) differentiate the American schools from the South African schools and 2) to conform somewhat to the convention that local school districts in the United States utilize to signify both symbolic and spatial markers of urban (generally coded as majority racial and ethnic minority) and suburban (generally coded as white majority) schools. I hope that this rubric does not prove to be too confusing as the reader follows the analyses; my intent is to make it easier to follow.

## Levels of Analyses: Comparing Schools in the "Rainbow Nation" and the "Land of Opportunity"

At first glance, a comparison of U.S. and South African schools from a material standpoint may appear to be equivalent to a comparison of apples and oranges. The majority of schools in the United States have significantly more resources than the majority of South African schools. Moreover, having experienced some modicum of a racial democracy for a longer period than South Africa, the United States produces more high school and college graduates from its various racial and ethnic groups. According to 2007 Census surveys in both countries, the percentage of students completing some degree beyond high school is nearly three times higher in the United States than in South Africa, with 29 percent of adults aged 25 and over possessing a college degree, compared to 10 percent in South Africa.[13] Eighty-six percent of U.S. adults hold high school diplomas compared to 28 percent of adults over 20 years of age in South Africa. In economic terms, the United States is a rich country with a gross domestic product (GDP) of 13.81 trillion dollars in 2007 compared to 277.58 billion in South Africa; the former is an economic superpower while the latter is classified by the World Bank as an upper middle-income nation, the wealthiest country on the African continent.[14]

Notwithstanding the significant national socioeconomic differences, this book does not aspire to compare two different national educational systems, and I would be remiss if I did not acknowledge that the eight school cases

**Table 2.2** Demographic traits of the U.S. schools

| | North Capital City | | South Capital City | |
|---|---|---|---|---|
| | North City Tech (majority-minority) | North Village Prep (majority-white) | South City Honors (majority-minority) | South County Prep (majority-white) |
| Total number of students | 1,190 | 1,242 | 1,333 | 1,389 |
| Racial diversity of students (%) | | | | |
| Asian | 23 | 5 | 0 | 1 |
| Black | 45 | 6 | 93 | 21 |
| Latino | 20 | 3 | 0 | 1 |
| White | 11 | 84 | 6 | 77 |
| Percentage of students on free or reduced lunch | 63 | 2 | 64 | 16 |
| Student-Teacher ratio | 18.3 | 14.1 | 19.6 | 17.3 |
| Percentage performing passing, basic or above, proficient or above on 2007 grade ten state English accountability test: | | | | |
| Asian | 100 100 79 | 95 95 90 | — | — |
| Black | 100 100 93 | 100 100 86 | 85 74 39 | 76 59 28 |
| Latino | 100 100 99 | 100 100 90 | — | — |
| White | 100 100 100 | 99 99 97 | 92 92 83 | 93 82 53 |

Table 2.2  (Continued)

| | North Capital City | | South Capital City | |
|---|---|---|---|---|
| | North City Tech (majority-minority) | North Village Prep (majority-white) | South City Honors (majority-minority) | South County Prep (majority-white) |
| Percentage performing passing, basic or above, proficient or above on 2007 grade ten state math/science accountability test: | | | | |
| Asian | 100 100 96 | 95 95 90 | — | — |
| Black | 100 100 96 | 100 100 72 | 96[a] 92 80 | 88 82 59 |
| Latino | 100 100 98 | 100 100 80 | — | — |
| White | 100 100 100 | 98 98 90 | 96 96 96 | 96 96 85 |
| School NCLB accountability performance rating | Very high** | Very high** | Exemplary (4) | Superior (5)** |
| Number of students in survey sample | 207 | 146 | 102 | 197 |

*Author Tabulated; Sources:* National Center for Education Statistics, 2007-2008 Data (retrieved online 2 February 2010); Assessment & Accountability Reports from Respective States (Retrieved online 15 April 2008); ** Denotes highest performance ranking for the state; [a] For South City Honors & South County Prep, the science scores are reported instead since math scores were unavailable for White students at the former in 2007 (due to low numbers having taken the test).

that constitute the focus of the research described herewith do not represent the entire landscape of schools in both nations. The study was designed in a manner that would demonstrate the most variation with eight schools in four different locales between the two countries.

The central link among these schools is that more than half of them have experimented with desegregation and mixed-race schooling in the aftermath of rigid and historic racial discrimination. Furthermore, two of the desegregated South African schools can compete with many U.S. high schools in terms of annual budget (adjusted for cost of living), course offerings, facilities, and graduation output. Palmer and Williston in South Africa are schools that are affordable mainly to middle-class students and families and that maintain annual multimillion rand budgets, just as North Village Prep and South County Prep in the United States primarily cater to middle- and upper middle-class American students and families. In the empirical chapters that follow, much of the discussion focuses on five schools (including Coast City's Groveland), although occasionally they will be compared to the three other schools—schools mainly comprising students of color—when appropriate.

# The Paradoxes of Opportunity

## RESOURCES, BOUNDARIES, AND
## ORGANIZATIONAL-RACIAL HABITUS

WALK INTO ANY socially diverse high school in various parts of the United States and South Africa today and you are likely to find some evidence of racial and ethnic separation among its students. Sure, students may share classroom spaces. Still, when it comes to their friendships and with whom they hang out during lunch breaks, students often organize themselves in same-race or ethnic groups.[1] Ask students about why their peers tend to gravitate to their own racial or ethnic groups, and you might generally hear a matter-of-fact response that it is not about "race" or "class" but common, shared interests. To them, an affinity to one's own racial or ethnic group members is as a "natural" social condition, the result of shared histories and cultural narratives and social and economic locations. Henry, an Asian American boy, at North City Tech High School (a high-performing majority-minority school), mentioned that our social preferences stem from our social backgrounds, our families and communities, and then we arrive at school with social boundaries already in place:

> Well, things like when [students] first come to the school, they really don't open up much, so they just stay with their own group. You're used to people you are already accustomed to [be]cause people who share the same beliefs and whatever... it's easier to get along with people.

Henry's belief just might be a universal one. After my first day at Coast City's Palmer High School, I learned that I had to be strategic in where I sat in the teachers' lounge before school began. In South Africa, students, like their teachers, do not casually or naturally sit next to each other in class and faculty lounges, respectively. Whether intentional or not, the teachers at Palmer were seated by ethnicity: Afrikaner teachers sat at the round table near the bulletin board; Anglo teachers sat at an adjacent table; the Coloured teachers (mostly men) sat nearer to the entrance door; and a few faculty, including the lone Black (West African) teacher, lined the wall along the back window.

Similarly, on my second day at Williston a few months later, I shadowed a soft-spoken, tenth grader named Reema who allowed me to hang out with her and her friends at break time. Reema is a member of South Africa's modest-sized Indian population, and on this particular sunny afternoon during one of the two daily school breaks, we met up with other Indian learners, all girls, at the back of the school. As many teenagers looked curiously at me, the foreign stranger, I took note of their social arrangements. Overt social boundaries endured. Groups of Black, Indian, Coloured, and White boys and girls—the former decked out in brown and gold school blazers, the latter in short brown skirts and brown v-neck sweaters—milled about separately from one another. They ranged in size and gender composition. At one point I excused myself from Reema and her friends and made my way toward a group of African female students seated at a table in the middle of the school plaza, and I heard them speaking another language, Sesotho. Once I greeted them, they switched to English and indulged this inquisitive researcher with answers to the questions about their names, grades, and whether they study Sesotho at Williston. The answer was "no."

Occasionally I voiced aloud my observations of students' and educators' tendencies to self-segregate into ethnoracial, and even gender, groups. Matter-of-factly, some would respond that it had nothing to do with race but rather "tastes," "interests," and "activities." Noma, an eleventh grade, Black female at Williston, told me that the practice of in-school social segregation in her group was because she and her African friends share the same customs. Similarly, two of her White male classmates, Will and Thomas, agreed by chiming in that it is standard for learners to hang out with those whom they consider friends and who speak their language. "It's not like we're racist or anything," Will said. "It's just that we respect *their* differences, and they respect what *we* do." Here, Will used language as one of the symbolic boundaries that both normalize and perpetuate racial boundaries among his schoolmates.

Psychologists offer that self-segregation plays a protective role for students, especially those in the numerical minority who feel either isolated or margin-alized and not really included in their school environment.[2] Understandably, students attending mixed-race schools like Palmer and Williston here have sought out social spaces where they feel what some psychologists refer to as "identity safe" in their schools.[3] At the same time, if educators do not actively encourage social interaction across racial lines outside of the classroom, then the social boundaries that integrated schooling is meant to diminish will endure, as is the case for students like Mmabathu at Williston High School. I mentioned my observation that students tend to separate into their respective ethnic and racial groups during the break times, and she responded as follows:

**PRUDENCE**: Do the different groups here get along? The different racial and ethnic groups, do they get along with each other?
**MMABATHU**: Yes, they do. But it's only up to a certain limit.
**PRUDENCE**: I notice that you guys spend a lot of time in your own groups. What is that about?
**MMABATHU**: I don't know, I really don't. I just don't see myself during break with White people. I just don't.
**PRUDENCE**: But you go to school with White people.
**MMABATHU**: Yes, but break, it's all about talking about what happened during the weekend and such things.

Mmabathu declared that racial groups in her school got along only up to a certain limit and that the social and cultural interests that she shares with Black schoolmates trump any tendency to hang out with fellow White students at break time. When you ask other groups of students, they say the same thing. These youth, as well as scholars, tend to supplant the racial overtones of their school's social organization with the idea that shared cultural interests really dictate intimate social network choices. Tastes and participation in school activities are not independent from the influences of social forces such as segregation, however. If we continue to ignore that tastes, like social capital—the resources embedded in social connections or ties—are linked to the racial logic in which our societies operate, then we ignore another manner in which racial boundaries that facilitate exclusion are continually maintained.

Based on her ethnographic work of a high school in Durban, South Africa, Nadine Dolby might agree with Mmabathu's, Noma's, Will's, and Thomas' assessments that racial identities are about taste and that youth carve out their identities along the lines of shared tastes and cultural expressions.[4] Dolby has argued that globalization and the diffusion of youth culture across national borders facilitate the shifting notions of "Black," "Coloured" "Indian," or "White." She wrote the following: "Interpreting 'race' as taste does not diminish its force…[Instead] it points to the ever-changing dynamics of race and highlights the potentially potent configuration of race that responds to a changing global situation."[5] Tastes, in the case of the students in this study, however, generally tend to be associated with ascribed racial identity and do not appear to correspond to the expansion of specific identities based on the diffusion of youth culture from around the globe.

Some perceptive students recognized the inflexible boundaries in place at their schools and believed that opening (integrating) their schools meant more than merely sharing classroom space. John, a White male in the twelfth grade at Palmer High School in Coast City, was one of several to make this point:

> You'll see that all the White people are together, all the Coloured people are together, and all the Black people are together. So I think integration is not only just coming together to the same school, I mean, we've still got our own racial groups that you're speaking to. I think integration is actually seeing groups of separate races together, regardless of their race where as individuals together for things you have in common, besides the race, besides the gender…your likes and dislikes, interests and hobbies…So I think integration is part of [more than] saying that segregation is over, people have to get together and be willing to be together, more comfortable with each other.

I asked John if he witnessed segregation within his school. "Ja [yes], definitely," he responded. "But how? In what ways?" I inquired. "I think in sports teams, actually. I think races generally are sticking to separate sports. If you look at hockey, I think people playing hockey are White people. And netball…" Jean, a Coloured female twelfth grader, interjected: "Netball is mostly [played by those who are] Coloured." Amanda, a White twelfth-grade female, declared the following: "That's one of the reasons I didn't play netball because I thought I was going to be the only White person in the team. It was back in standard six [grade eight]."

For these Coast City Palmer students, an awareness of how social and symbolic boundaries exist to undermine real integrative practices was beginning to sprout, nonetheless. John and Amanda were two of about forty students who had participated in an overnight retreat program, the Diversity Trippers, whose mission was to get these youths to think and reach out beyond their social differences. Though a start, many rigid boundaries, the stubborn roots of a racist apartheid history, still endure. For now, Amanda's and John's extracurricular preferences still tend to reinforce boundaries and create racial "turfs" out of certain school activities. Palmer's students, like others elsewhere, have not uprooted all of the troublesome social weeds of their society's past.

In our schools, like in our families and communities, we actively reproduce the social boundaries that continually remind us of who "they" versus "we" are. Whether students ignore and cross the lines of those boundaries often depends on the social and cultural ethos that is fostered by adults who lead their schools. That is, both the strength and diminution of boundaries among students are influenced by the signals that educators and other critical adults in their lives either consciously or unconsciously transmit through their own personal behaviors, as well as the organizational policies and practices that they implement in the schools. Thus, students are more likely to boundary cross in schools where educators noticeably model socially or culturally flexible practices. For some reason, intergroup relations appeared to be the most difficult in terms of flexibility for both students and teachers in nearly all of my schools.

### Survey Says...Examining Racial Patterns in Academic and Nonacademic Participation

Survey data confirm John's, Jean's, and Amanda's claims that racial differences existed in terms of actual extracurricular participation. Among the 917 South African learners surveyed, White learners in the two desegregated schools, Palmer and Williston, reported participating more in extracurricular activities than the other groups—86 percent compared to 72 percent, 69 percent, and 53 percent of Black, Coloured, and Indian students, respectively. Also, White learners had the highest participation in sports (67 percent), followed by Coloureds (59 percent), Blacks (54 percent), and Indians (36 percent).

While desegregation facilitates the permeability of previously exclusive schools, other social and symbolic boundaries can persist in them. The racial differences in who participated in extracurricular activities and the higher tracked classes highlighted just where they existed organizationally. Within South African high schools in 2004, learners could choose to either enroll in "standard grade" or "higher grade" courses, provided that their schools offer the latter. Standard grade courses were the equivalent of conventional, comprehensive high school courses, while "higher grade" courses were more advanced classes in various subjects used to ascertain eligibility for entrance into university degree programs. If a school offered higher grade courses, which at the time were more readily available in the more economically advantaged schools like the ex-Model C's, then students might have used their earlier grade performances in a subject to determine whether to enroll in one. Or rather, teachers might encourage particular students to enroll.

Indian, Coloured, and Black students (in that order) in the ex-Model C schools aspired to attend university at significantly higher rates than Whites: 75 percent, 69 percent, 64 percent, and 55 percent, respectively. However, although Black and Coloured learners at Williston and Palmer High Schools were more likely than their counterparts in the segregated township schools to be enrolled in the "higher grade" courses—these learners were still enrolled in significantly fewer higher grade courses than their White peers in these schools.[6] At Williston High School, White and Indian learners were almost three times as likely to take a higher grade course in the four major subject areas (language, math, science, history) than their fellow Black and Coloured learners—40 percent and 36 percent versus 14 percent and 0 percent, respectively. At Palmer, on the other hand, where the administration proactively sought to equalize opportunity (see more below), no significant differences were found among students.

To ascertain whether there were significant racial differences in performance, I examined the (self-reported) grades of all of the surveyed students at Williston enrolled in standard grade math—which the majority of students enrolled in math classes took. In this representative sample of the student body,[7] thirty-eight out of sixty-seven (or 57 percent) Black students, twenty-three out of twenty-six (or 88 percent) Indian students, and fifty-two out of seventy (or 74 percent) White students enrolled in any math course at all in the tenth through twelfth grades. Among those in standard grade math, I found no statistically significant racial differences in self-reported student grades. That is, the proportion of A's through F's of students in standard grade math was similar for Blacks ($N = 27$); Indians ($N = 12$); and Whites ($N = 30$).

Student choice, prior performance, and teacher encouragement/selection are three main determinants of placement of students in the higher grades. And if we presume a similar distribution of ability based on the self-reported math grades, then it is striking that half as many (or less) Black students (16 percent) as White (31 percent) or Indian (42 percent) students enrolled in higher grade math. Instead, more of Williston's Black students appeared to take higher grade courses in accounting—a modal aspiration for many South African students of all races in the study. Students were particularly aware of accounting as one of the most lucrative and fastest-growing fields in the country. It is a math-intensive profession, nonetheless, and the level of difficulty of the certified public accountant exams precludes an easily obtainable credential. Yet, significantly more Black (16 percent) and Indian (17 percent) than White (6 percent) students aspired to become accountants at Williston. Yet, more than 40 percent of the Black students had not enrolled in any type of math course, whether by choice or other factors.

But things change. During a follow-up visit to the study schools in August 2008, four years after the bulk of the data was collected, the National Ministry of Education dismantled the system of standard and higher grade examinations, one of the final pieces in a curricular policy focused on equalizing educational opportunity to students in schools across the socioeconomic spectrum. That year, for the first time, learners across South Africa were exposed to the same national curriculum, marking the implementation of the final phase of a radical curriculum change in the postapartheid era. Notably, the Ministry of Education mirrored the national government's aims to eradicate any school practices that threatened the inclusion or well-being of any learner. Although the Ministry of Education has faced some outcry and objection to its "policy borrowing" of curricular guides from other industrialized nations, its emphasis and focus on building a citizenship inculcated with ideas and skills to promote human rights, equity, social justice, and nation building are what distinguish its approach from those elsewhere.[8]

Speculation abounded about what the outcome of ridding the schools of higher and standard grade courses would be, now that expectations are elevated so that all students are, in theory, to be exposed to the demands of higher grade courses. The first set of results revealed in early 2009 shows that the relatively resource-rich and former white and Indian schools have managed the curricular transition well, while the pass rates in poor and disadvantaged black and coloured township schools have declined.[9] The main point here, however, is that the national government has chosen to be vigilant about how even curricular boundaries could augment its already palpable issues with the residual effects of racial apartheid. Mandating access to the same curriculum for all students across all subjects is a radically inclusive tactic that does not exist in most school districts in the United States, even as its policy makers and educators profess aspirations for equity for their students.

### Beyond the One-Drop Rule: Boundaries among South African "Blacks" and "Coloureds"

Salient social boundaries exist among non-Whites, too, as relations between Black and Coloured learners at Groveland showed. Racial antipathy in South Africa is not just a white/nonwhite matter; and historically, social divisions have existed between Coloureds and Africans, creating a quadripartite racial system (with the inclusion of Indians) as early as the nineteenth century.[10] While later the apartheid state mandated a distinction between descendants of the mixed-race slaves and free men and women ("Coloureds") and indigenous Africans ("Blacks"), in the anti-apartheid resistance movement the term "black" was used as an all-encompassing term to refer to all groups who shared the common experiences of marginalization, racism, and discrimination. Today, various fissures render the political concept of blackness as fragmented and variegated, breathing new life into the apartheid-sanctioned classifications of those defined as either "Black" or "Coloured." [11]

Sitting with five ninth-grade Coloured students one morning, I asked them to describe the relationships among students at the school, and Alicia, a girl with a honey-colored skin tone who was the most outspoken in the group, said the following: "It's like it was under apartheid. The Africans don't like us. They speak Xhosa all the time, which we can't understand, and they don't want to be with us." Miranda, another Coloured girl, chimed in and said that the Africans were the majority of the school, while others in the group nodded in agreement. Knowing that out of a student body of approximately 1,400, only 350 learners were African, incredulously, I asked them what gave them that impression, and Alicia responded, "The Africans have taken over this school." Though Groveland's student population was one quarter African students, Alicia had reached her "tipping point," perceiving that they were the majority.

Meanwhile, African students felt that Coloured students disliked them, too. Days after my talk with Alicia, Miranda, and the others, I chose to sit in on an eleventh-grade Xhosa language class of about thirty-five learners, and unexpectedly, the teacher, Ursula Dziba, told me that the students wanted to ask me, the foreign visitor, some questions. The first question was a big one: "Does racism exist in the United States?" And although I could have spent the entire class speaking about this condition, I answered briefly, albeit affirmatively, and then asked the class why they wanted to know. Ms. Dziba informed me that the students were shy but wanted to talk to me about the racial dynamics in their school, and once I assured them I would protect their privacy, they shared first that the Coloured students would either move or shoo them away when they tried to sit next to them in class and how the principal had different disciplinary policies for Black and Coloured learners. One very upset and angry female learner described how, whenever a Black and a Coloured student would fight, the Black student would be expelled, while the Coloured student would be merely reprimanded. I asked her what happens when a Black student fights another Black student, and the students responded that the police would be called in to take them away. They said, and the class got noisy as many tried to explain this, if the situation were Coloured and Coloured, the principal might call the police, but usually the police would walk away and not take the students.

As I sat in classes, I noticed how Coloured and Black students conspicuously chose not to sit next to each other in class or talk to each other; it was only when a teacher made them work on assignments with random partners that I observed some interaction, often with hesitance. And because of the language tracks, many Coloured students chose Afrikaans-speaking courses (a second or third language for the Black students), while the Black students chose either Xhosa or English. However, if both Black and Coloured students enrolled in classes taught in English, they were likely to meet in the classroom. Real and unavoidable language differences existed among students, however, and while Groveland schooled learners in their home languages, this particular organizational practice reinforced social boundaries. Attending to cultural (linguistic) differences pedagogically did little to defuse the ethnoracial divide between the school's African and Coloured students.

The intergroup dynamics that I witnessed at Groveland stem from the historical baggage of racial division. Social distances between the two groups are attributable to a number of factors, including the past preferential treatment of the mixed-raced population, skin colorism (or favored treatment based on lighter skin), and contemporary divergences in political ideology, alliances, and voting patterns that sustain social distances between Black Africans and Coloureds. Although Groveland outpaced the other schools in the study by allowing access to African students much earlier (even in the face of legal sanctions by the apartheid regime), the school's leadership and organization did little over time to dissolve the palpable racial and ethnic boundaries, which were maintained by students and intensified by hurt feelings and other potentially explosive emotions for which there was no clear, organized outlet for resolution. Coloured students believed that Groveland was first and foremost a coloured school, and African students perceived that they were tolerated mostly to maintain the school's economic viability.

One main observation was clear: racial proximity in schools, paradoxically, can easily sustain social separation. On any given day, at any of the three aforementioned South African schools, the casual observer would note that during the two, thirty-minute breaks built into the schools' schedule, learners would immediately disperse from their multiracial classroom settings and separate into conspicuously homogeneous racial groups, in some instances coed; in others, not. Sociologist William Trent once commented, " 'Desegregation' is about demographic changes [in schools], and 'integration' is about normative change," about a shift in the collective hearts and minds of the people.[12] Once groupness was no longer determined by racial identity, and once learners interacted and participated in activities with one another across these lines, then some semblance of integration might be achieved. Many of these everyday social dynamics among learners begged for proactive attention and guidance by school leaders.

## Social Boundaries and Schooling in the United States

On a spring day at South City Honors High School in South Capital City, I sat in on the advanced placement English class of a 2007 ACT (American College Test) star teacher, Cate Gilman, a tall, slender, thirty-something White female with fine, medium-length brown hair and fair skin. Her classroom walls were lined with sketches of the faces of famous literary characters, including Jane Austin, D. H. Lawrence, and George Orwell. Gilman had also posted a picture of Toni Morrison in a collage of other writers' pictures on the bulletin board to the right of the door; Morrison was the only writer of color in the mix. Her second-period class has twenty-two students: fourteen Black females, three Black males, two White females, and three White males. I was familiar with some of the faces, including Xavier, the African American male who was one of the two National Achievement semifinalists in this year's senior class. Also, there was Benson, a White male who was the high school valedictorian and had obtained a perfect score on the ACT.

Gilman had asked her students to complete an advanced placement practice test exercise, and they worked for about twenty minutes on a difficult prose passage excerpted from a literary work written about two virtues—charity and humility —and how a nineteenth-century aristocracy dealt with these virtues. As they worked, Williams walked around and passed out cards marked with the number of a particular question. As students answered the questions correctly, she handed them a card with remarks such as "You got #1 correct; you're a genius!"

Nearly 1,500 miles away at North City Tech, similar diverse classrooms and student and teacher dynamics were witnessed. In an advanced placement physics class with Edgar Martinez, a young, thirty-something Latino man sporting a closely-shorn haircut and wire-rimmed eye glasses, and a well-worn University of North Capital City sweatshirt embossed with a logo promoting a local youth program at the university. The class was large (around thirty kids), interactive, and lively. It was also racially mixed and fairly balanced in terms of gender. Mr. Martinez' classroom had the feel of a physics lab with the entire back wall lined with multiple kinds and sizes of gears, pulleys, and levers and with student-made physics-themed mobiles hanging from the ceiling.

Students sat together at tables, interacting across race and gender. On this particular day, a Black male, upon entering the room, gave pounds and handshakes to a group of very diverse boys. As they worked, the students shared ideas and answers, supporting one another in solving the assigned problems. They moved freely from table to table to help one another, and all conversations between them appeared to be physics-related.

The two observations made at South City Honors and North City Tech High Schools, respectively, are fairly representative of many of the courses at these schools, especially the ones for high-achieving students. While not all of their classes can be depicted as engaging as these, the main point is the contrast between these two schools—whose predominant groups are characterized as racial and ethnic minorities in the U.S. context—and the two other American schools in the study.

In comparison, students at North Village Prep and South County High Schools, the two multiracial, white-dominant schools in the United States, grappled with their emotions and the social and symbolic boundaries they endured behind school walls. A stroll into North Village Prep's school cafeteria on any given day reveals some of them. The large cafeteria vibrantly filled with chatter is a sociological laboratory for the study of adolescent group relations. The most noticeable and immediate observation is the sight of the VDP students—almost all of North Village Prep's African American and Latino students—sitting on the right-hand side near the back door entrance, while the White and Asian students sit on the left-hand side in duos and groups according to clique preferences. Like their South African peers at Williston and Palmer High Schools, North Village Prep students expressed their racial separation as a matter of "interests" and shared understandings, too. Vonda, an African American sophomore, explicitly likened "why all the Black kids sit together" to common interests:[13]

I think that people just notice that we sit together because we're a different race or we're different…we're like…most obviously different from outside than everybody else, but I think like either Mr. Donaldson or Ms. Perry said, [the VDP kids] may very well be a group of basketball players, a group of nerds, a group of hockey players, a group of, you know, ballets or a group of like musical. You know what I mean? In the cafeteria they all sit with each other and have cliques, but you can't tell because they all look similar and then we are in the corner over there (laughs). Like obviously different so people are just like, "Oh, they don't like us." But it's not that. It's just we find just like human race…like human, I don't even know the word I'm using but like just in general people find similarities with other people, and they relate to them and be friends with them and we all understand each other, so we end up doing that. It's the same thing with all the hockey players who understand each other and talk about hockey all day or all the like (pause) you know, singers will all sit with each other and sing with each other all day…

Vonda tried to convince this interviewer why racial, ethnic, and ostensibly class division led to a sense of shared interests and a social cohesion that presumably would lead any group of humans with something in common to create groupings and to distinguish themselves from others spatially in the cafeteria. Unlike their White schoolmates, however, Vonda and her peers did not have the luxury to break down by specific social, extracurricular, academic, or hobby interests. Their small numbers and high visibility prevented that sort of social organization among the VDP kids. Still, the more conspicuous and critical issues are why the other interest groups did not enfold some of these students, since presumably they had tastes for music, sports, language, academics, and other interests, too.

The answer seems to lay with the nature of the sociocultural and sociopolitical contexts at the type of schools that Vonda and her peers attended. A survey question—using a Likert-type response categories with 1 being "strongly agree" and 4 being "strongly disagree"—asked a random sample of 647 students attending the four American high schools to respond to the following statement: "I feel like I am a part of this school." Ninety percent of White students at North Village Prep agreed with this statement, compared to 38 percent, 84 percent, and 74 percent of North Village Prep's African American, Asian American, and Latino students, respectively. The difference was not as wide between the two racial groups represented at South County Prep as at North Village High but noticeable and significant, nonetheless. Sixty-seven percent of South County Prep's White students agreed with this statement compared to 59 percent of African American students.[14] In contrast, sixty-six percent of White students at North City Tech felt a part of their school, compared to 83 percent, 62 percent, and 69 percent African American, Asian American, and Latino students, respectively. At South City Honors, White and African American students felt a part of their school to nearly equal degrees—76 and 72 percent, respectively.

The most striking finding here is that African American students in the majority-minority schools (North City Tech and South City Honors) had significantly different educational experiences in terms of their attachment to school than their African American peers in the majority-white schools

(South County Prep and North Village Prep).[15] For Latino students—who were represented only in North Capital City—the pattern was similar to the African American students; they felt significantly more attached at North City Tech. For Asian students, the reverse was true; they felt more attached at North Village Prep than at North City Tech. Further, the pattern was not the same for White students when they were in the minority. Indeed, those attending North City Tech felt significantly less a part of their school than the African American students, though similar in attachment to Asian American and Latino students. In contrast, Black and White students at South City Honors felt equally a part of their school.

Exposure and social contact with one another compel students of different social backgrounds to deal with the racial, ethnic, and class baggage and emotions that historically fraught race relations have bred. In actuality, North Village Prep and South County Prep provided a better resource context than either North City Tech or South City Honors. Yet, access to academic opportunities varied at the better resourced high schools for Black and Latino students. In addition, the schools' resource contexts did not appear to have a positive association with students' propensity to cross social boundaries. How did schools maintain an ethos that reinforced social boundaries such that nondominant groups of students participated significantly lesser or greater in certain aspects of schooling than in others?

## Equity Is as Equity Does: Variation in Organizational and Ideological Approaches to Inclusion

A group of African girls approached me the first time I visited Williston High in Letisi during one of the school's two breaks to express their dismay at the perceived unfair and stringent policies that forbade them to wear their hair in braids and twists—traditional hairstyles for African women. Naomi, an eleventh grader, said the following: "[S]ome of us like dreadlocks, some of us have extensions, otherwise it just—it looks neat but then they [the school administration] won't allow it." I asked, "Why won't they allow it?" She responded, "I don't know. Maybe it's because—they made a comment that, you know, for Black people we do extensions. There are already some White people who want to do extensions, but then it doesn't look that nice on them, so they've restricted it to nothing at all." Naomi believed that her school officials encouraged symbolic boundaries through the designation of certain hair styles as "black," and further, she perceived that the fear of tastes for "black" hairstyles being spread (or diffused) to White learners compelled them to prohibit any learners from wearing them.

Fast forward three years, and the same issue emerged again when I arrived at Williston for in-depth research. After several students raised issues with the school policy that prescribed how hair should worn, forbidding certain ethnic hairstyles among girls and closely-shaved heads among boys, and specifying a limited number of plaits that could be worn, I decided to ask Principal Billups about it directly. "Hair must be neat and tidy; it can't be too long, no fancy hairstyles. And that's about all. We don't allow dyed and coloured hair, dreadlocks, braiding and all of those things; those are regarded as fancy hairstyles," Mrs. Billups said. "Why is that 'fancy'?" I asked. Mrs. Billups responded as follows:

> Well, because it's just not normal, and short back and sides… They [must] keep it neat. I mean if you look at them, they kind of have varying in that. So they can keep it really short if they want to. But they mustn't let it get too unruly. If it starts getting too long, then the girls plait it in neat little plaits, but then it's not all this fancy—because I mean they all have hairpieces and all of that, they can do that after school.

At Williston, I learned firsthand how school officials maintained symbolic boundaries through the exclusion of "ethnic" hairstyles—a rather unexpected discovery. Mrs. Billups took a tough-line approach and refused to allow "fancy" heads in her school, disregarding 1) the disproportionate cultural burden placed on Black learners and 2) the racialized overtone this policy had taken in a school whose objective was to provide equal educational opportunity in a non-racial manner. Although Black students had approached their elected student representatives annually since my first visit, the school governing body (SGB)—comprising parents, teachers, and the principal, Mrs. Billups and her faculty had structured their hard-line policy such that no learner would be allowed to present "fancy" hairstyles, which were outlined in the school handbook, and thereby had avoided the accusation that hair policy explicitly made exceptions for one group and not another.

At Williston, the hair policy is not gender specific. One morning I count four boys (three Indian and one Black) sitting outdoors for punishment because they had violated the school's hair code. A set of Indian twin boys had gel in their hair, the other Indian boy and the Black boy had their hair shorn shorter on the side than the top—"fancy"—and all four were made to stand out in the school plaza until their punishment was complete. Mrs. Samantha Vaughn, the head of the English department, walked by and commented on the boys' "fancy" hairdos and mentioned how they made excuses that they did not have enough time or forgot to have their hair "properly" cut over the past weekend. "The hair policy is so difficult, you know," Mrs. Vaughn tells me. "The military has the same problem, I think. Now that we have the White and Black kids together, it's hard to say what's 'natural.' You have the Black and White or Negroid and Caucasian hair, and it's hard. Then you have the Indian girls and their hair grows here (she points to the center of her lower back) and it's so beautiful and thick. White people don't get their hair like that," Mrs. Vaughn continued without skipping a beat. "We tell them that they have to be neat and tidy. We're trying to teach them conformity. We took them over to the Kellogg factory, and they couldn't believe that workers had to wear nets over their hair. They [students] said that they wouldn't do it, and I told them, 'Well you won't get a job then.' Normal is so difficult to define today, but no extensions and frizzy afros are allowed."

Full disclosure is in order here. I was annoyed by the continual reference to "normal," so I mentioned that some black hair is quite curly and frizzy. "We're careful to say that hair must be in its natural state," Mrs. Vaughn responded. She continued, "A friend of Caryn's (Mrs. Billups) from Canada, who was visiting, said to her, 'Are you sure you want to die trying to push this issue up a mountain?' It's a lot more relaxed than it used to be. When it was just a white school, it was a lot more strict. We're really struggling with this issue," she said.

The school's policy implied that ethnic hairstyles such as braids, twists, and locks were not "normal," and some of the school's leaders explicitly stated this, although descriptions were tempered by the euphemism "fancy." Remarkably, Principal Billups and Mrs. Vaughn uttered these words with straight faces as they looked directly at me, an African American woman who wears her hair natural in short, corkscrew twists. Given my own hair style and stature as a professor and researcher from an elite American university, I reasoned that this was why a group of girls had approached me initially in 2001 to take up this matter with Principal Billups and the SGB, who still resisted a change of policy three years later when I began this research and four years after that when I went back for a follow-up visit.

Aware of cultural differences, Mrs. Billups reasoned that her African learners could practice their (time-intensive) hairstyles "over the weekend after and before school." In producing a hierarchy of cultural meanings, Williston's approach mandated that all learners acculturate to a dominant "white" hair aesthetic and that no special efforts be made to consider the cultural preferences, differences, tastes, or styles of Black learners.

In principle, these educators believe that they constructed a policy such that no group is given "special privilege," although in practice, a special privilege was given to White youth. Their hair aesthetic had become the standard, albeit with some exceptions.[16] Nonetheless, Principal Billups and the SGB were willing to make an exception as in a case that they perceived to be about civil rights. That is, Mrs. Billups and the SGB made an exception for a Sikh Indian boy and allowed him to ignore the school's hair policy by wearing a turban and growing a beard, which was also forbidden by the school's hair code. Billups justified this allowance as religious tolerance and a respect for religious diversity. In contrast, Williston's educators and governance structure relegated nonreligious, ethnic hair forms to mere changeable styles—not upheld by any specific creed or protected by law—that could be worn on the weekend. Thus, Black learners found themselves bearing the disproportionate burden of adapting to the White educators' aesthetic about hair.

As some legal scholars have written, visual representations of ethnic and gender identity are often perceived as threatening.[17] And not unlike the cultural gatekeepers of other states in the global community, including several European nations such as Germany and France, which require that their residents demonstrate national belonging and loyalty to the state through linguistic competence and modes of bodily performance (e.g., the removal of Muslim women's head scarves in schools),[18] some South African educators in former white-only schools now confront African students with forms of cultural exclusion for the sake of educational inclusion.

The ways schools address ethnocultural issues reflect how their organizational-racial habitus varies, and the differences in organization-racial habitus among schools do not necessarily correspond to the racial and ethnic makeup of the students, per se, but rather to varying normative and political values. A school's "organizational habitus" encompasses a combination of expectations and aspirations of students based on norms about appropriate academic and social behaviors, which—as numerous scholars and researchers have documented—are predicated on a tacit acceptance of middle-class ways of being.[19] The school's organizational-class habitus is not the only force influencing students' well-being within the school, however. Its organizational-*racial* habitus matters, too, and as intangible as habitus may be, its influence within schools is indicated by the differential treatments and experiences of students by race and ethnicity across socioeconomic classes.

Other issues ensued at Williston that struck this observer as particularly indicative of its organizational-racial habitus. My research assistant and I ran across a group of five Black students who had been locked outdoors behind gates on the school's plaza for misbehaving in class. Shivering in their brown and gold uniforms, they sat on benches and spoke to us through the gate's rails. My assistant, Fagan, and I were particularly troubled by this sight, of students being punished for misbehaving in class (namely, talking) by being made to wait in a "prison" outside in cold weather. What is most striking about this form of student punishment is the historical symbolism of the politics of race and resistance that it signified. Standing there, I was reminded of the tiny jail cell that I had visited several times on Robben Island where former President Nelson Mandela had spent eighteen of his twenty-seven years in confinement. Equally troubling is the fact that students and staff at Williston actually referred to this space where punished students were sent as "the prison." The correspondence between the imprisonment of Black freedom and resistance fighters under apartheid just decades prior and Black students who challenge educational authorities and are punished by being sent to the school's "prison" cannot be lost here. Black students were being criminalized for talking too much in their White teachers' classrooms.[20] They transgressed by defying teacher authority.

What are noticeable are the symbolic messages emitted to the school's community about not only racial status and punishment but also the severity of punishment for African youth who overstep their bounds with their White teachers. Black students were disproportionately represented among the punished, those labeled the "bad" students. In all of my time at Williston, I never saw a White youth punished in this extreme manner. When I later questioned Mrs. Billups about the "prison," she proudly boasted about this type of punishment. Not only did Mrs. Billups and her staff fail to show any awareness about the inhumanity of punishing students by making them sit out in the cold, but also they showed no signs of introspection about the racial undertones that characterized the school's social and cultural climate.

## Cultural Difference May Become Radically Egalitarian

The ideological orientation of the school leadership often shapes a school's sociocultural and socio-political climate. Kelvin Welner and his colleagues have introduced the concept of "zones of mediation," the idea that individuals' or groups' tolerance of and behaviors toward equity in school—specifically, racially minded policies—depend on the different constituents' social positions and the salience and strength of their identities by race, class, or other social categories.[21] The zones of mediation also differ by political ideology, which can pose a considerable challenge to the implementation of specific equity-minded educational policies, especially when the implementers do not wholly accept the change in policy.

We may expect that schools are situated within *varying* zones of normative and political values in terms of their breadth of outreach to different social groups. Writing about how White South African educators have adapted to school desegregation, educational policy expert Linda Chisholm, for example, has discussed one of three cultural-political approaches taken after Black students were admitted: 1) *cultural difference*, in which educators acquiesce to the inclusion of different racial groups in a school; yet they stop there and do not practice a deeper inclusion of those groups in terms of participation, treatment, exchanges, or consideration of cross-cultural differences; 2) *equal treatment* or *opportunity*, in which educators ignore the vastly different material or historical realities of students despite disparate outcomes because of these varied conditions, expect assimilation by the previously disadvantaged group(s) and therefore attempt to treat all students in the same manner; and 3) *radical egalitarianism*, in which educators aim intentionally to hold fellow educators, students, and SGBs accountable for mechanisms that perpetuate the racial divide in schools.[22]

Taken together, Welner's and Chisolm's perspectives on how schools may handle particularly sensitive organizational matters that pertain to culture and equity should shed some light on why Palmer High School handled the matter of hairstyles quite differently than Williston.[23] John Dalton, Palmer's principal (who had been participating in a leadership course at the Coast City University) also wrestled with the contentious cultural issue of hair. Like Principal Billups, Mr. Dalton's dealing with the hair matter signaled his and other school officials' qualms about the diffusion of tastes from "black" cultural repertoires to White learners. On the one hand, he and his predominately white staff sought to recognize cultural differences, but they also sought to preempt any transmission of cultural styles across racial identity boundaries by maintaining a dual policy for Black and White learners:

**DALTON**: It's always a contentious issue, the question of hair...and what's quite interesting, particularly with "open" schools...so for White people it's not too difficult to design a hairstyle. Black people have curly hair. Now in the Xhosa tradition, your traditional Xhosa boy should have his hair cut as short as possible; that's a sign of respect. If a White boy cuts his hair short, it's a sign of being a punk. So he's now making a statement, whereas the Xhosa boy is not. So it's almost as though you've got different rules for Blacks and Whites, which creates a few problems. Then there's the question [of] braiding. Now, it used to be that only females braided their hair, but now the boys think it's quite cool to braid their hair. And this school is one of the few schools that allow the boys to braid their hair…It looks neat, as long as it's neat and tidy, not sort of a Bob Marley sort of style, it's got to be neat and tidy.

**PRUDENCE**: White kids can't wear the braids?

**DALTON**: White kids, no, which is very strange. Our rule says that if your hair supports the braid on its own, then you can have braids. So the *Black* kids don't need to have little ribbons and beads and things like that to hold it because their hair naturally holds it. But if I tried to braid my hair, I'd have to have little elastics and things all over the place to keep it in, to keep the actual plait or the braid in. So we don't allow that, because then you've got this sort of Christmas tree effect.

Self-admittedly, Principal Dalton struggled with the notion of inclusion, but he "opened" the school's hair code to allow Black learners more options for hair styling as he took phenotype into account—implicitly acknowledging both biological and cultural conceptualizations of race, while simultaneously bounding or constraining the options of White learners so that the practices of the Black learners would not become too culturally diffuse and influence White kids' behaviors. At the time, Principal Dalton and his school were not alone in this racialized approach. A headline in the Johannesburg *Sunday Times* reads, "Posh School Says Girl's Braids Are 'Unacceptable,'" and describes why an upper middle-class White female ninth grader at an exclusive private school was sent home for sporting long, blond "African-style beaded braids."[24] While Lauren-Lee Wilson was told that wearing braids was "unacceptable for her because she has long, blonde hair and further, "looked out of place in a school uniform" [for a White girl], it was acceptable for Black girls to have braids. Dalton and Lauren-Lee's principal took the "cultural difference" approach, where the school aims to teach its learners the variations in cultural tastes and forms but to impede any process of cultural diffusion or sharing in the other direction—that is, White students' emulation of Black students' cultural practices.

With time, thought, and exposure, ideological transformation occurs, nonetheless. Four years after my first visits to Palmer High School, I revisited the school, right before the class of 2008 (eighth graders when I first met them) was due to take its National Senior Certificate exams for graduation and university eligibility. To my surprise, Principal Dalton had changed his school's hair policy after further consideration and after a Scandinavian masters degree student had visited his school and continued to push him about the culturally unequal hair policy:

**PRUDENCE**: What about the hair policy? I remember your talking about that [in 2004].

**DALTON**: It's changed!!! It's changed!

**PRUDENCE**: How?

**DALTON**: We had a fascinating discussion. Let's see. There was a girl here called Maddy Madison. She came here from Denmark and she came and did her master's based on diversity in South Africa, and she came here a year or two after you came here, and she spent an entire year with us and at the end. She said, "You know, this hair thing, I still don't get it." And some of the kids were starting to make noises about this hair thing and so we said, "Okay. Let's have a look at it again." And we've changed, and there's a whole new policy now. Anybody can cut their hair, short, you know, it used to be only the Black kids could cut theirs short. Now White kids can cut their hair short and they can braid their hair as long as it's, you're not using ribbons and things to keep it in place. Now if your hair is naturally curly enough to braid it, then it's cool, you can braid it, you know? We're still a little conservative when it comes to length and things like that.

John Dalton and his staff proved themselves to be open to social and cultural change. With the prompting of foreign visitor (a graduate student from a Scandinavian country)[25] and the persistence of its majority- Coloured and Black student clientele, Palmer had shifted its position on how students could style their hair, especially when it came to so-called ethnic hairstyles. Dalton was fully aware that his and his staff's attitudes were "conservative" and that "cross-cultural understanding" evolves. While Dalton and his staff had arrived at this position and had implemented a fairer hair policy, Caryn Billups and her staff at Williston, hundreds of kilometers north, had not retreated.

Palmer now leaned more toward cultural egalitarianism. On the one hand, Principal Dalton and his students struggled with equity policies implemented to open the doors to Blacks and Coloureds who had been historically denied access to good schools and better academic resource contexts. At the same time, Principal Dalton and his staff were vigilant about specific in-school policies or codes that unfairly targeted their non-White students. As mentioned earlier, Palmer was also committed to its Diversity Trippers program, which provided overnight retreats for scores of its ninth- and tenth-grade students to challenge themselves and each other and to discuss social differences and contentious issues that could impede their abilities to relate as peers in school. When I met with group of Diversity Trippers who had returned from their trip just a couple weeks prior, the potential intrapersonal and interpersonal effects were noticeable:

**ASHTON**: I learned, well, when I went into a camp it was like, you know, the whole camp was about racis[m]…you know, the whole Diversity Tripper camp…judging and stuff and when I went away from the camp it was a real eye-opener because I didn't realize that I judge people for so little things, and it just becomes a part of you that you can't really get away from, you know, the judging and stuff.

**DANIELLE** (talking together)…me and Claire are having a conversation and before, we would have made a comment about Penny because she's Black. And then…camp…happens. And then I get back to school and Claire makes a comment and I'm supposed to laugh with her, but instead I say, "No, don't say that." She was very confused. They [non-Diversity Trippers] don't know how to deal with it.

**PRUDENCE**: Can you say anything, or do you just keep quiet?

**DANIELLE**: Well, instead of saying you're wrong, because then you're actually degrading them, you say, well, I think that, or I don't see it like that.

**ALICE**: And hopefully it will rub off on them, instead of telling them what to do and say how you're familiar…and they'll go, oh, my word, maybe she's right.

Palmer's Diversity Tripper Program, guidance counselor Jennifer Benson's brainchild, more than tripled in size over the course of four years, having now reached hundreds of students. And as Alice and Danielle shared, a transformation in individual racial attitudes, and by extension the school's ethos, was quite possible.

## The Township Schools and their Organizational-Racial Habitus

Neither Groveland nor Montjane, the township schools, in comparison, reinforced symbolic ethno-racial boundaries by having explicit hair policies. Braids, locks, twists, and closely shorn hairstyles were a common sight at both schools. Thus, the hair matter highlighted the limited cultural and organizational flexibility of some of South Africa's desegregated schools. Another arena of the racial and ethnic habitus of schools pertained to language policy. Compared to Williston and Palmer, Groveland and Montjane appeared to be more organizationally flexible in this vein, too.

The South African Ministry of Education mandates that all schools ensure the proficiency of their learners in at least two languages. Primarily, the desegregated schools choose English and Afrikaans and not the mother tongue of the majority of the nation's populace.[26] Thus, individual school language policies are not immune to political and cultural meanings of the in-group versus the out-group. Williston did not offer IsiZulu, IsiXhosa, or SeSotho (the first languages of many of the students present), while Palmer offered IsiXhosa as an elective; the majority of its Black students were Xhosa.

Black learners and their parents are not without agency, however. Each SGB is allowed to set its own language policy, and it is the duty of the provincial department of education and the SGBs to provide classes in certain languages if a sufficient number of learners request them. The perceived better resource context of the desegregated schools masks the hegemonic nature of the schools' cultural and educational practices. Many Black families consent to not being formally taught in the African languages and are willing to forego the preservation of their home languages in exchange for fluency in English. And perhaps, this desire is attributable to the forces of globalization, labor-market demand, and English as the lingua franca of the international community.

The two township schools, Groveland and Montjane, nonetheless, offered several of the national languages, catering specifically to the tongues of their student populations. Montjane offered five of the national languages, the first languages of four of the main Black ethnic groups enrolled in the school plus English. In addition to English and Afrikaans, the first language of most of South Africa's Coloured population, Groveland offered Xhosa. These three languages comprised the home languages of all of Groveland's learners. Educators in the township schools consciously acknowledged the symbolic nature of language while seeking to preserve African languages. Montjane's principal, Jonah Nkomo, a forty-something and friendly Black man who had been the head principal since the school's opening less than a decade prior, as well as a long-term active member of the African National Congress and the national teacher's union, said the following:

Our school policy states that we are using English as our medium of instruction, okay. But there is also this period that would always be dedicated to our mother tongue, and that therefore, we shall take English as a second language, and our mother tongue as a first language. And that's how we do differ as a policy [from] Williston High. At Williston High they will say our medium of instruction is English, and our first language is English, and our second language is Afrikaans.

**PRUDENCE:** So is this one way to privilege your first language?

**NKOMO:** Yes. Yes… To preserve our own language.

Principal Nkomo contrasted Montjane's approach to Williston's, incidentally the school that his fourteen-year-old daughter attended. Days after I spoke with Principal Nkomo, Andrew, a White male twelfth grader at Williston and Nkomo's daughter's schoolmate, shared his concern regarding the fact that his school did not teach any of the African languages.

What I think is we shouldn't be learning Afrikaans in school. We should be learning a black language, because… as a White person, I'd love to learn a language to communicate with Black people, because Afrikaans—the Afrikaans', like, way of living is like kind of dying out.

On the one hand, Principal Nkomo acknowledged the necessity for cultural preservation through language, while Andrew, who is learning Afrikaans at Williston, foresaw that he most likely needs to know one of the languages that will be spoken by those in the majority—that is, a black ethnic language. Andrew's comment also points out the necessity for a more strategic multilingualism that includes an African language. As the South African economy develops and the African consumer base grows, Andrew's generation would benefit from knowledge of either IsiZulu or IsiXhosa, the two most widely spoken African languages in the nation, among others. What both of these excerpts expose is the dominance of both English and Afrikaner cultures in South African society, despite the transition—at least, discursively—to a nonracial democracy in post-1994 South Africa. Furthermore, Andrew's comments indicate the dominance of the native languages of the white minority[27] and exposes how his school ignores the linguistic background of more than 40 percent of its learner population.

As others have argued elsewhere,[28] what the exclusive language programs signify is not only the organizational-racial habitus of the schools but also the zones of their normative and political values. At Williston, especially, the absence of any African languages as mandatory pointed to a contradiction in practicing equity for a school steeped in a larger political context espousing radical inclusion. Meanwhile, Palmer, like the township schools whose academic resource contexts were extremely limited, proactively maintained some semblance of egalitarian cultural space that would represent the diversity of their students.

## Are American Schools More or Less Organizationally Flexible?

The American principals at South County Prep and North Village Prep, the two majority-white schools, held varying ideological approaches about how to incorporate their racial and ethnic students and address social boundaries, though neither could be described as proactively egalitarian, according to Chisholm's framework. Consider the following activities. Religious sentiments run deep at South County Prep. On the wall of nearly every classroom there, a plaque reads, "In God We Trust." On Friday mornings at 7:30, before the school bell rings at 8:15, South County Prep holds meetings for one of its largest student groups, the Christian Sportsman Union (CSU). Upon walking through the door of the gym, students find tables with donuts and orange juice and several kids greeting others. One particular morning, four White male faculty members sat off to the left side. At first glance, it appeared as if the males were supposed to sit on one side and females on the other, but after a while the students began to mingle and sit across genders.

The CSU was attended by about twenty Black students, mostly males, that day; only one Black female was present. The remainder of the more than one hundred students in attendance consisted of White males and females. All the students intermingled with each other; there was no distinct separation of racial groups. Priscilla, an African American female tenth grader, brought in a boom box, playing contemporary Christian rock music. A Black male wearing a red beanie, gray sweatshirt, and black athletic pants announced the speaker for the morning, and the man who spoke was a forty-something White male wearing jeans and a suede jacket. He walked up carrying a Bible and gave a brief message about his life, using scriptures from the Book of Revelation, the last book of the New Testament, to underscore his points. "You know that this [state] is the Bible Belt? Well, you are in the buckle of the belt," one of South County Prep's French teachers, Ms. Jamie Harrison, informed me.

South County High made no attempts to hide its incompliance with the "separation of church and state" principle. And, being in the "buckle of the

Bible Belt" may explain why it was not uncommon for my research assistants and me to walk into a classroom on a given day and observe a teacher playing Christian music quietly in the background as students worked silently during a core class or have a Christian scripture from Romans 2:1 (King James version) written on the board, while Joshua, a boy wearing a Jewish yarmulke, sat nearby. Joshua was one of about five Jewish students who attended South County High and was a member of the small Fellowship of Jewish Students (FJS), which for several years had prepared a schoolwide PowerPoint presentation on the Holocaust for tenth-grade world history students. South County Prep was aware of cultural difference to an extent, although its practices of equity and social differences did not have much depth.

Consider other examples. An observant visitor would notice that representation of students by race in classes at South County Prep did not come close to reflecting the overall student population. While sitting in the lounge area of Ms. Marion Benjamin's classroom—a home economics room with a full-fledged kitchen and lounge—Jessica, an eleventh-grade White female, shared her newly released school yearbook with me. Thumbing through the pages, I saw pictures of Jasmine Thomas, a National Achievement semifinalist, and Farah Roman, the two most visible African American students involved in the elite academic and extracurricular activities at South County Prep that were not sports. Jasmine and Farah were usually the only students of color receiving academic awards on Awards Day.[29] I had observed soft-spoken and warm Jasmine, whose bright eyes shone in a mocha-brown face marked with adolescent pimples, in a calculus course. She was also enrolled in physics, advanced placement (AP) English, AP biology, and a computer science class. On occasion, I would watch her tutor the son of one of the school's security guards after school.

Jasmine's fellow achiever, Farah, tall and slender with shoulder-length, straight brown hair and light skin, was one of the two African Americans out of seven maidens on the homecoming court. Further page turning in the yearbook revealed that Farah was also active in the thespians and teenage Republicans groups, the only Black student participating in the latter. Her schoolmate Brad, who, like Jessica, was enrolled in Ms. Benjamin's class for students with individualized learning plans, had already told me that most of the Black students did not even talk about politics at the school, so Farah was truly an exception. Farah's academic and extracurricular efforts paid off, too, as she was the only student of color to be inducted into South County Prep's Hall of Fame at the end of her graduating senior year—an especially high honor for any student at the school.

At South County Prep, sports and other extracurricular activities also reflected the social boundaries among students by race at the school. In terms of student participation, basketball and steppers are to "Black" and "Black female" as baseball and cheerleading are to "White" and "White female," respectively. Consequently, students formed close relationships with those participating in the same activities. Cheerleading, baseball, the Fellowship of Christian Athletes, and the Young Republicans largely exclude minorities, who are well-represented participants in basketball and football, however. Students were learning their places, their boundaries, their "lines" from the real and symbolic distinctions they see mirrored in their social organization within schools.

## North Village Prep

After an assembly introducing the student body to a program ("Challenge Day"), which was making its way across the country to motivate educators and students to deal with social differences, including at North Village Prep, I walked into a sociology classroom. Prior to the assembly, as students walked into the auditorium, they were given randomly assigned, color-coded pieces of paper and told to sit in the area designated by its color. Being rebellious adolescents, students ignored the directions and chose not to, especially since color-coded random assignments would have taken them out of their comfort zone of sitting with their friends. Students watched video excerpts of the program's feature on the Oprah Winfrey Show, and then they were encouraged by two senior co-facilitators, an African American female and a White male, to participate in North Village's own upcoming "Challenge Day."[30]

Since the sociology teacher, Tim Nolan, was absent that day, his substitute invited me to facilitate some discussion about what we had just witnessed in the assembly; I agreed to moderate a conversation among this class of seniors. At the u-shaped table directly in front of me sat six African American students, five of whom were students from the VDP. The back horseshoe-shaped table was comprised of a group of White students, including an exchange student, a petite, fair-skinned girl with brownish blonde hair from Austria. The first to begin the discussion was Shari, a medium-height, round African American girl from the North Capital City area, who said that she stood up when the facilitators asked the question of whether anyone had been called a bully. Shari said that she was not a bully; rather, she just tells people what she thinks! Her tone was saturated by bravado. "I just speak my mind, and if I don't like you, I don't like you," she claimed. Immediately, I could tell that

Shari could be intimidating, and I asked her if it's possible that she could tell people that she does not like their behaviors versus stating that she does not like them. I also made it a point to affirm her own understanding of herself as someone who is not a bully. A slim, fair-skinned, White male dressed casually in jeans and a button-down shirt sitting away from her then said that he does not see Shari as a bully. "I just think that she's opinionated, and she expresses her opinions." A dark-haired White female sitting behind Shari stated that what the video evoked for her was the problem of girls calling other females "sluts" when they had trouble with boys doing it. "I mean, if we don't want the guys calling us that, she says, then why do we do it?" she queried.

One of the African American students likened the "ho" example to how kids use the "n-word" (nigger) and said that some (Black) kids use it to talk about their family and friends who are close to them—as an endearment. A White male sitting closer to the window chimed in and said that he has Black friends and that the "n-word" has been demystified and that everyone uses it now. I asked them if there was any danger in that. An African American girl with a scarf tied around her hair said that she would not appreciate hearing that word from a White person. There were several mumblings going on around this. Then BJ, a White male sitting at the back table, stated that he believed that the film did more harm than good. He says, "Our school is doing very well compared to other schools. I mean, like we don't have those kinds of problems." He said that his friends at other schools talk about fights and interracial tension but that he did not experience that at North Village Prep. A White girl sitting across from him on the other side of the room agreed. One of the African American girls disagreed and mentioned that she is from the town of North Village and that people assume that she is a VDP student because she is Black. "Although my family is not poor, they always make that assumption," she said, often rendering VDP participants synonymous with poor families. Later on, someone in the group also pointed out that they all sit together divided along racial lines and noticed how that never changes. The girl who made the "ho" comment said that sometimes she wanted to engage with the Black girls, and then she stopped talking: "Oh, I'm going to cry," she said, becoming emotional, but then continued, "but then I am afraid that I'm going to be rejected." I tried to validate this girl's feelings and took her sharing as a moment to relate her experience of feeling like a member of the "out-group" to how the VDP students explained feeling daily, coming into affluent and majority-white North Village Prep. I saw several Black heads nodding as I mentioned this. The end-of-class bell rang before we could delve further. Yet, the intensity of the moment signified to me that the boundary making that students conduct at North Village Prep is painful and divisive, even if it is not as violent or overtly conflict ridden as BJ claimed it was at other schools.

North Village Prep began to acknowledge some of its cultural differences and even attempted to do something about it by bringing along the Challenge Day program, which would reach at least one hundred students. Still, other issues threatened to undermine this work. The social organization of students within classes and racially demarcated extracurricular activities reinforced the establishment of de facto ethnically and racially segregated spaces.[31] From completing paper assignments to getting tutorial assistance to playing chess and talking politics to merely hanging out with one another, most VDP students spent at least some time in the "VDP room," away and separate from their White peers. Beyond their class time with White peers in their general comprehensive and college preparatory classes, nearly all of the students of color at North Village Prep—namely, the VDP participants—had limited social contact with White students outside of class time.

Additionally, the school's efforts were challenged by the impact of residential segregation on VDP student participation on nonacademic aspects of school life, as well as their social cohesion with school mates. Almost all of North Village Prep's VDP students are bused into the district from the urban center and surrounding areas of North Capital City. VDP students disliked the lack of neighborhood proximity because they could not be full participants in every aspect of school life, and school officials had found no easy way around the matter. While they did have a "late" bus, which left at 5:30 p.m. daily, this prevented VDP students from participating in any evening programs or early morning meetings that occurred before the bus arrived. Substantive academic incorporation would entail educators, and students, in the in-group valuing a full engagement of the VDP students in the school's programs and acknowledging their particular needs, values, and perspectives—processes, I would argue, that are central to the practices of equity.

## Chapter Summary

In this chapter, I have offered an organizational-level analysis of the reproduction of social boundaries, showing how schools *act* and *behave*, too, via policies and practices. When I decided to return to high school over the last several years, while I was able to recoup some of my limited knowledge about various classical and contemporary poets and writers or remember how to take the derivative of a function in calculus, what I learned most was how our schools reproduce the lines between those viewed as "us" (the in-group) and "them" (the out-group). School leaders, the cultural and organizational gatekeepers, commonly reproduce (even unintentionally) ethnic, racial, and other social boundaries through the reinforcement of implicit and explicit patterns, rules, codes, and policies. But the nature of boundaries in schools varies depending on the social and political environment in which the students are situated. This was the case both in South Africa and the United States.

From an observational standpoint, my research assistants and I witnessed more overt reproduction of symbolic boundaries through specific school policies in South Africa. School diversity was a relatively new phenomenon for these educators. Still, these schools vary in their organizational-racial habitus and their normative and political values about equity and inclusion, nonetheless. Comparatively, the dispositions of the organizational-racial habitus of the study schools in the United States were less obvious through specific school-based, culturally-focused policies than the South African ones, although American and other developed societies have also wrestled with the political and cultural meanings of hair, dress, and language practices, too.[32]

Other observed representations of inequality in both academic and non-academic practices marked the U.S. schools' organizational-racial habitus. Sociologists John Meyer and Brian Rowan have argued that the norms, values, and cultural aims of the educational institution can often be "decoupled" from what occurs on the ground in schools every day.[33] These findings suggest that while more resource-rich schools enable students to traverse particular physical boundaries, racial and cultural differentiation in these schools continue to cultivate strong social and symbolic boundaries that undermine the schools' equity goals. Students will succumb to social divisions in academic and extracurricular activities, unless otherwise compelled to interact in a class activity or even a group interview for a researcher's project. Yet, as Meyer and Rowan articulated years prior, it is the "street-level bureaucrats," the principals and teachers in a school, who shape the local cultural and social climate. They set the example for the sociocultural goals students should emulate.

Though much attention has been given to the *value* and functions of multiracial schooling for the attainment of educational opportunity, a paradox emerges in school-communities where demographic changes and access to equal material conditions are the primary focus, but where attention to symbolic and ideological structures is either absent, minimal, or superficial. Although some students of various ethnic and racial backgrounds across the class spectrum are enrolled in "good" schools in both South Africa and the

United States, can we dare say that the organizational-racial habitus of some of these schools really promotes equity? Findings presented in this chapter suggest that the answer is "Not really." Students of different races can come to have different understandings, sensibilities, and expectations of "other" students depending on the school context.[34] The implication here is that the school's organizational-racial habitus shapes the level of its own cultural flexibility. And now we must consider the relationship between the schools' and their students' self-reported cultural flexibility.

*Why is there not much equity?*

*what is preventing it?*

# 4

## Cultural Flexibility

### THE (UN)MAKING OF MULTICULTURAL
### NAVIGATORS

IN THE DIMLY lit, modestly stocked, and thinly insulated library of Montjane Secondary School, some of its "cream of the crop"—students who had survived the curricular transition from grade nine to grade ten (a point at which many township schools face their highest attrition rates and at which the compulsory age for schooling is met at age 15)—discussed their futures in what South Africans then referred to as the "new dispensation" of democracy. I sat with this small group of tenth, eleventh, and twelfth graders, aspiring accountants whose accounting class was held in the library because classroom space was limited. We talked about their reasons for wanting to be accountants, a rapidly growing and lucrative profession in South Africa and a reasonable means out of poverty, provided that they could attain a university degree and pass the certified public accountant exams. As the conversation evolved, language differences were mentioned. I asked how they felt about English being the dominant language in the corporate sectors to which they aspired; their first languages were Sesotho and IsiZulu. They spoke these languages even in their classrooms, at a school where English is the language in which subjects are supposed to be taught.

*why?*

"How do you negotiate your desires to be upwardly mobile in this society with the expectations that you make cultural adjustments to thrive in it?" I asked. "I do it and learn from them [Whites]," declared high school junior Lerato, a medium-height African girl sporting a short Afro. "But they must also learn from my culture, too," she continued. "It's a two-way process. They must also learn from my culture, too!" she said emphatically.

Lerato was willing to be culturally flexible, but she believed that her White peers and teachers needed to be flexible as well. They needed to learn African languages (affirming Andrew's claim earlier) and understand the traditions of some ethnic African cultures—those of the majority of the South African people—as much as it had been demanded that they learn about white South African ways of life descending from British and Afrikaner cultures. Lerato's educational trajectory was a particularly striking one; she had been enrolled briefly at Williston High School, which was less than five miles away. She had been expelled, though, because she defied what she called the "cultural police." Lerato reasoned that her behaviors were a response to what she perceived as a one-way cultural diffusion process. "Ma'am, there were too many rules about what you could not do or be," she said to me. (Williston's Principal Billups later told me that Lerato had violated the school's disciplinary codes extensively by defying authority and accumulating a horde of demerits.)

"Cultural diffusion" refers to how practices spread beyond the margin of a particular social group, organization, or other society entity. Increased social interaction among different groups of students should, in theory, compel them to expose one another to either new or different cultural practices or tastes. When African English language learners living in black-dominant neighborhoods choose to privilege English at home; or to purchase fast foods like pizza and hot dogs, as opposed to local African pies (bulky rolls filled with an assortment of meats); or to acquire new tastes in clothing styles (such as those associated with a specific youth subculture like "skater culture"), the cultural diffusion process is at work—at least in one direction. It becomes even more widespread as those dubbed as Model C'ers, namely African youth attending ex-Model C's, share their new food and dress tastes with peers who attend segregated township schools. Through them, cultural tastes and practices now spread beyond the desegregated school walls and into the neighborhoods, communities, and townships where learners of color live. They meet with some resistance, however, from less economically advantaged peers and others who consider themselves the guardians of Black South African (youth) cultures. And the symbolic boundaries remain as these youth continue to label some of these cultural tastes as "white" and others as "African."

The cultural diffusion process (from the school's vantage point) primarily operates in one direction, from white to black and coloured. Some school officials, as we read in chapter 4, minimized or staunched the spread of purported "black" cultural practices—for example, the acquisition of African languages and hairstyles—among White learners. Such controlled diffusion indicates how resources and power shape the contours and limits of symbolic boundaries in multi-racial schools that are now inclusive of non-White students. In reaction, some African students like Milton, another Montjane student and a ninth-grade boy with closely shorn hair (forbidden at Williston), asserted the following: "We can come here [to the township] school and get the same education [as at the ex-Model C schools] and still have our culture!" An informed reader, no doubt, would challenge Milton's claim that he could "get the same education" at Montjane; it is unlikely that township schools fare better academically than former Model C schools, which are significantly greater resourced. Milton was aware, nonetheless, that Montjane had performed relatively well on the previous years' National Senior Certificate exam, with pass rates greater than 90 percent. Still, although a significantly high percentage of matrics at successful township schools like Montjane might pass the National Senior Certificate exam, very few performed well enough to attain endorsement level qualification for admission to the national universities, which required scoring at least 40 percent on at least five subjects, among other criteria. What strikes me about Milton's declaration is that he, like Lerato and even school leaders at both Montjane and Williston, felt a threat of losing his cultural identity; consequently, they reinforced symbolic boundaries to stave off one-way cultural diffusion.

In contrast, students who are willing to cross the borders and accept the requisite rules of participation in new sociocultural environments like schools may take the newly acquired cultural knowledge that they obtain and share it with peers who do not have access to the same cultural practices. I began to discuss some of these issues from an organizational standpoint in chapter 4. Major sociological studies of schools contend with the tensions between *structure* and *agency*, aiming to avoid overdeterminism in one direction or the other.[1] With this understanding, I wanted to ascertain more fully the interplay between a school's and students' perceived cultural flexibility. After I left South Africa and returned to the United States, I added another component to the student survey. It examined how students' *cultural flexibility* varied by school context, since now I had a grasp on how some schools' organizational-racial habitus and flexibility differed. In the forthcoming pages, I share survey results of analyses of the American case studies and then return to the observational and interview data to provide some clues to why certain patterns occurred.

For several reasons, I analyzed these survey data on the U. S. sample only. First, here is where major contextual differences would complicate any hypotheses or statistical models. That is, the statistical models incorporate conceptual variables whose influence on cultural flexibility would not necessarily be equivalent in the two national contexts. For example, tracking, as curricular differentiation is known in the United States, is not widespread in South Africa. Yet, I hypothesize that it could have some influence on cultural flexibility in the case of U.S. students. After all, prior U.S. studies have indicated that students are also known to attach meanings and to associate specific groups with different classes in tracked systems, depending on the representation of identities in those classrooms.[2] Students can be flexible in the meanings that they attach to school practices and to each other, however, depending on the academic context.[3] Second, curricula are standardized in South African schools so that students of varied social backgrounds are, in theory, exposed to the same academic material, although the resource contexts of their schools may be quite disparate. Given these factors, the determinants of students' cultural flexibility may vary in the South African context. Still, the observational and interview data (which I discussed earlier and in other chapters) suggest just how school practices there, as in the case of the United States, may influence students' inclination to move across social and cultural lines.

## Student Cultural Flexibility in the United States

In various subfields of educational research, scholars inquire about the associations between students' cultural identities and their school participation.[4] Thus, we know that students negotiate their own social identities in ways that compel them to make decisions about whether or not to engage across the social categories ascribed to them. Some researchers have investigated the dynamic nature of cultural identity and discussed multiple forms of identity transitions, from the subtractive, where students lose touch with their native/home culture identity;[5] to the additive or feeling closer to the host/dominant cultural identity, although with some maintenance of one's cultural heritage;[6] to the affirmative (or sometimes perceived as oppositional), where students reject the mainstream cultural identity and maintain their own cultural centrality.[7] Studies of biculturalism show consistent results of positive academic, psychological, and social attainment, compared to their relatively monocultural peers.[8] They suggest that ultimately, bicultural students possess the ability to interact, participate in, and traverse different social and cultural settings, to embrace other forms of cultural knowledge and expand their own understandings of self, and to hold inclusive perspectives about others who differ in diverse social aspects or identities.

Cultural flexibility, in contrast to bicultural identity, comprises both a social psychological and a behavioral process. It encompasses the student's ability to cross different social and symbolic boundaries and to utilize variable cultural tools to negotiate multiple sociocultural environments. To be culturally flexible, students most likely will have to maintain an "intercultural" identity,[9] one in which they define themselves as world citizens and are able to interact appropriately and effectively in multiple cultural settings.[10] The difference in the intercultural strategy from the identity strategies mentioned earlier is that not only do individuals possess multiple cultural competences, but also they do not denigrate one culture in favor of another and instead conceive of themselves as multifaceted cultural beings.[11] Now, we must ask how students come to acquire these flexible skills in schools. How does the school's social organization correspond to its students' propensities to be culturally flexible?

## The Survey Findings

I first examined the idea of cultural flexibility with a nine-item scale that I created and first tested in 2007 on 652 American students.[12] Students who completed the surveys comprised a random stratified sample of a range of 25 percent to 35 percent of each of the four schools' populations and yielded a total survey sample size of 471 Black and White students across the four schools. For the purposes of these analyses, Asian and Latino/Latina students were excluded due to low numbers and nonrepresentation at half the schools. As a measure, cultural flexibility was not just a student's inclination for racial bridging. Instead, students were asked about their propensity to engage with persons of various social and cultural traits. Specifically, students were asked nine questions: "On a scale of 1 to 5 in which 1 means 'makes a very large difference' and 5 means 'does not make a difference at all,' would the following characteristics make a difference in whether or not you would become friends with another student?"[13] These characteristics covered differences in gender, race, and ethnicity, as well as some popular adolescent styles, including language (e.g., slang vs. Standard English), musical tastes (e.g., classical, hip-hop, pop, and rock), clothing styles (i.e., not wearing "cool clothing"), social traits ("nerdiness"), and media habits (like for television).[14,15] Higher scores represent more cultural flexibility. The Cronbach's alpha for the cultural flexibility scale equals .86 for the American students.

I also used mother/female guardian's and father/male guardian's highest level of education to control for certain family background effects, and I included a categorical variable for gender (Male = 1). Students were asked to self-report their grade point average (GPA) using categorical variables ranging from 0 (less than 1.0) to 4 (4.0 or higher). To ascertain individual and group-level differences, I used categorical or dummy variables for school compositional type ("majority-minority" and "majority-white"). Following research studies, which reveal that the social organization of students in schools have an impact on their behaviors, I also used a dummy variable to indicate whether the student was enrolled in either an AP or honors course in English, math, history, science, or foreign language and a continuous variable for the number of extracurricular activities in which the student participated —which, in many multiracial schools, increases the opportunity to meet across race, ethnicity, and other categories of social difference.

Students also have their own personal preferences and prejudices, which they may acquire from their home communities and wider society.[16] Therefore, I chose to include predictors of students' personal preferences for living in neighborhoods and attending school with only members of their own racial, ethnic, and socioeconomic backgrounds; and their academic, gender and class identities. Students were asked to respond whether the following statements were either "true" or "false": "I prefer to attend a school where most of the students come from the same racial or ethnic background as mine;" "I prefer to attend a school where most of the students come from the same economic background as mine;" "I prefer to live in a neighborhood where most of the people come from the same racial or ethnic background as mine;" and "I prefer to live in a neighborhood where most of the people come from the same economic background as mine."

Culturally flexible students may possibly maintain strong levels of individualism and confidence in participating in and moving across diverse social and cultural environments. Therefore, self-esteem could be a major determinant of culturally flexibility. A strong sense of one's self might imbue an individual to move comfortably across different identity contexts. In other words, the culturally flexible individual enabled by strong self-concept and self-esteem—which social psychologists show to be positively related to individualism[17]—may not necessarily feel great pressures to conform to narrowly defined group-based identity markers; group separatism; or thick and salient in-group/out-group boundaries. Rather, he or she could expand his or her choices about social interactions and participation in different cultural activities. First, I examined whether there might be differences in self-esteem among students and then explored how self-esteem might influence students' levels of cultural flexibility. I added a continuous variable measuring self-esteem to the models, using Rosenberg's reliable, widely used scale.[18] The alpha for the nine items of the Rosenberg scale is .80.[19]

Since U.S. history and prior research inform us that regional differences in terms of race relations might influence intergroup dynamics,[20] I also included a dummy variable for region (North = 1). To ascertain significant differences among students by race and ethnicity, I included dummy variables for Black (with Whites as the reference group). Table 4.1 reports the descriptions, means, and standard deviations for the student-level variables tested in the regression models, and Table 4.2 presents the means of the dependent variable, cultural flexibility, by school, race, and ethnicity.

I found varying results in the determinants of cultural flexibility among the American students. First, those with preferences for same-race schoolmates and neighbors revealed lower levels of cultural flexibility.[21] That is, those who preferred to attend school and live in neighborhoods only with others of a similar racial background reported lower levels of cultural flexibility (refer to Table 4.3). In the full model including selected controls, self-esteem, participation in AP or honors courses, and the number of extracurricular activities, all were positively associated with cultural flexibility. Also, Black students reported lower levels of cultural flexibility, on average, than White students, although the significance of this result was only marginally significant ($p < .10$).

These patterns changed somewhat when I disaggregated and examined the effects of the predictor variables in an *intra*racial comparison of Black and White students across the four schools. For example, cultural flexibility differences between Black students in the multiracial, majority-minority and multiracial, majority-white school contexts appear to be accounted for by significant differences in self-esteem ($b = .23; p < .05$) and participation in AP or honors courses ($b = .20; p < = .10$). That is, Black students at South City Honor and North City Tech had higher self-esteem, on average. Furthermore, those Black students enrolled in either AP or honors courses showed a modest though greater level of cultural flexibility than those enrolled in non-AP and honors classes, and these particular students were more likely to attend the two majority-minority schools. Black students' preferential attitudes about the racial and ethnic composition of their schools and neighborhoods had no influence on their cultural flexibility (see Table 4.4).

Table 4.5 tells yet another story. For White students, the school type did not matter. Rather, those White students in both majority-minority and majority-white schools had similar degrees of cultural flexibility, all other factors held constant. Their preferential attitudes about their schools' and neighborhoods' racial, ethnic, and class composition did not matter, either. White students enrolled in AP or honors courses (b = .30; $p < .05$) and those

Table 4.1  Descriptions, means, and standard deviations for selected variables, by school

| | | | Mean (standard deviation) | | | |
|---|---|---|---|---|---|---|
| Variable | Description | Metric | North City Tech | North Village Prep | South City Honors | South County Prep |
| Cultural flexibility | Would the following characteristics of a person make a large or small difference in whether or not you will become friends with another student? The person is... 1) of a gender different from yours; 2) of a race or ethnicity different from yours; 3) speaks proper Standard English all the time; 4) does not wear cool clothes; 5) prefers to listen to classical music; 6) does not like rap or hip-hop music; 7) prefers to listen to rock music; 8) does not watch TV; 9) is nerdy | 1 = Makes a very large difference 2 = Makes a large difference 3 = Makes neither a large nor small difference 4 = Makes a small difference 5 = Does not make a difference | 4.10 (.89) | 4.07 (.78) | 4.05 (.83) | 3.74 (.93) |
| Preference for same-race schoolmates | Is the following statement true or false? "I prefer to attend a school where most of the students come from the same racial or ethnic background as mine." | 0 = False 1 = True | .28 (.45) | .32 (.47) | .25 (.44) | .38 (.49) |

(Continued)

Table 4.1 (Continued)

| Variable | Description | Metric | Mean (standard deviation) | | | |
|---|---|---|---|---|---|---|
| | | | North City Tech | North Village Prep | South City Honors | South County Prep |
| Preference for same-race neighbors | Is the following statement true or false? "I prefer to live in a neighborhood where most of the people come from the same racial or ethnic background as mine." | 0 = False<br>1 = True | .33<br>(.47) | .31<br>(.46) | .26<br>(.44) | .40<br>(.49) |
| Preference for same-socioeconomic-status schoolmates | Is the following statement true or false? "I prefer to attend a school where most of the students come from the same economic background as mine." | 0 = False<br>1 = True | .26<br>(.44) | .28<br>(.45) | .23<br>(.43) | .33<br>(.47) |
| Preference for same-socioeconomic-status neighbors | Is the following statement true or false? "I prefer to live in a neighborhood where most of the people come from the same economic background as mine." | 0 = False<br>1 = True | .36 (.48) | .43<br>(.50) | .36<br>(.48) | .45<br>(.50) |
| Student's grade point average | Student report of grade point averages | 0 = < 1.0<br>1 = 1.9–1.9<br>2 = 2.0–2.9<br>3 = 3.0–3.9<br>4 = 4.0 or higher | 2.51<br>(.71) | 2.74<br>(.66) | 2.78<br>(.66) | 2.70<br>(.76) |
| In advanced placement or honors courses | Students' report of whether they are enrolled in any advanced placement and/or honors courses | 0 = No<br>1 = Yes | .44<br>(.50) | .60<br>(.49) | .75<br>(.43) | .49<br>(.50) |

| Number of extracurricular activities | Count of the number of extracurricular activities mentioned by the student | 0 = Minimum<br>6 = Maximum | 1.05<br>(1.36) | 1.54<br>(1.81) | 1.33<br>(1.30) | 1.50<br>(1.42) |
|---|---|---|---|---|---|---|
| Family background/ parents' education | Composite of single or two parents'/ guardians' educational background | 1 = < high school<br>2 = High school diploma/GED<br>3 = Post high school vocational/trade school<br>4 = Some college<br>5 = College degree<br>6 = Graduate degree | 2.72<br>(1.34) | 4.58<br>(1.27) | 4.28<br>(1.21) | 3.93<br>(1.24) |
| Self-Esteem (scale) | i) Good luck is more important than hard work for success; ii) Every time I try to get ahead, something stops me; iii) When I make plans I can usually carry them out; iv) On the whole I am satisfied with myself; v) I am able to do things as well as most other people; vi) I certainly feel useless at times; vii) I take a positive attitude toward myself; viii) I wish I could have more respect for myself; ix) At times, I think I am no good at all; x) Planning only makes a person unhappy because plans hardly ever work out anyway. | 1) Disagree strongly<br>2) Disagree<br>3) Agree<br>4) Agree strongly | 2.97<br>(.53) | 2.98<br>(.43) | 3.04<br>(.47) | 2.94<br>(.50) |

Table 4.2 Mean parent education and students' cultural flexibility (CF) scores, by U.S. schools and race (number of responses)

| | North Capital City | | South Capital City | |
|---|---|---|---|---|
| | North City Tech (majority-minority) | North Village Prep (majority-white) | South City Honors (majority-minority) | South County Prep (majority-white) |
| **Mean parent education** | | | | |
| Asian | 2.14*** (48) | 5.31 (26) | — | — |
| Black | 3.12 (60) | 3.70*** (32) | 4.10** (68) | 3.70*** (103) |
| Latino | 2.49** (65) | 3.88*** (25) | — | — |
| White | 3.14 (38) | 5.11 (58) | 4.65 (30) | 4.20 (80) |
| **Mean CF scores** | | | | |
| Asian | 4.01 (48) | 4.25 (26) | — | — |
| Black | 4.10** (60) | 3.84 (32) | 4.10** (68) | 3.67 (103) |
| Latino | 4.05 (65) | 4.21 (25) | — | — |
| White | 4.25** (38) | 4.15 (58) | 4.05 (30) | 3.88 (80) |

Parent education ranges from 1 "did not finish high school"; 2 "completed high school or got GED only"; 3 "attended vocational or trade school after graduating from high school"; 4 "attended 2-year college"; 5 "graduated from college with BA or BS; 6 "graduate degree"

*Significance* levels (within schools): *** $p < .01$; ** $p < .05$

Table 4.3 Regression coefficients of cultural flexibility on school type, region, self-esteem, and other selected variables: Black and White students[a]

|  | Model | | |
|---|---|---|---|
|  | 1 | 2 | 3 |
| School type (majority-minority = 1) | .27 (.08)*** | .22 ** (.08) | .17 (.09)* |
| Student attitudes |  |  |  |
|   Preference for same-race schoolmates |  | −.14 (.10) | −.14(.10) |
|   Preference for same-race neighbors |  | −.21* (.10) | −.18 (.10)# |
|   Preference for same-socioeconomic-status schoolmates |  | −.20# (.10) | −.17 (10)# |
|   Preference for same-socioeconomic-status neighbors |  | −.00 (.09) | −.05 (.10) |
| Self-Esteem |  |  | .16 (.08)* |
| In advanced placement or honors courses |  |  | .23 (.09)** |
| Number of extracurricular activities |  |  | .05 (.03)* |
| Controls |  |  |  |
|   Parent educational background |  |  | −.01 (.03) |
|   Student grade point average |  |  | −.03 (.07) |
|   Black |  |  | −.16 (.09)* |
|   Gender (male = 1) |  |  | −.03 (.08) |
| Region (Northeast = 1) |  |  | .21 (.08) ** |
| Intercept | 3.84 | 4.04 | 3.54 |
| Adjusted $R^2$ | .02 | .06 | .10 |
| N = | 469 | 466 | 458 |

[a]*Metric* coefficients (standard errors); *$p < .10$, **$p < .05$, ***$p < .01$ (two-tailed tests)

living in North Capital City (b = .25; $p < .05$) were more likely to have higher cultural flexibility.

In sum, there were several patterns found overall with the survey data. Controlling for parent educational background—a proxy for students' socioeconomic background—and their self-reported grades, neither of which was statistically significant, and a host of other factors, I learned that students attending the majority-minority schools in the United States reported higher levels of cultural flexibility than those attending the majority-white schools. The number of case studies is too limited to declare a particular school effect. However, what I discuss forthcoming with the ethnographic and interview data is that students in these schools

Table 4.4  Regression coefficients of **cultural flexibility** on school type, region, self-esteem, and other selected variables: Black students only[a]

|  | Model | | |
| --- | --- | --- | --- |
|  | 1 | 2 | 3 |
| School type (of color = 1) | .39 (.11)*** | .33 (.11)** | .20 (.12) |
| Student attitudes |  |  |  |
| Preference for same-race schoolmates |  | −.12 (.13) | −.14 (.13) |
| Preference for same-race neighbors |  | −.22 (.14) | −.16 (.14) |
| Preference for same-socioeconomic-status schoolmates |  | −.17 (.14) | −.16 (.14) |
| Preference for same-socioeconomic-status neighbors |  | −.11 (.14) | −.14 (.14) |
| Self-Esteem |  |  | .23 (.11)** |
| In advanced placement or honors courses |  |  | .20 (.13)* |
| Number of extracurricular activities |  |  | .05 (.04) |
| Controls |  |  |  |
| Parent educational background |  |  | .00 (.04) |
| Student grade point average |  |  | .02 (.09) |
| Gender (male = 1) |  |  | -.12 (.12) |
| Region (Northeast = 1) |  |  | .20 (.13) |
| Intercept | 3.70 | 3.93 | 3.02 |
| Adjusted $R^2$ | .04 | .08 | .10 |
| N = | 263 | 261 | 256 |

[a]Metric coefficients (standard errors); *$p < .10$, **$p < .05$, ***$p < .01$ (two-tailed tests)

had significantly different educational experiences, especially the African American ones. This is a particularly striking finding given that, in theory, one would predict that cultural flexibility would correlate more positively with socially diverse, integrated schools. Yet, the finding is not entirely counterintuitive since notable scholars have argued repeatedly that a multiracial school in which its teachers, principals, and staff do not fully engage with the meanings of integration in all of its facets would struggle in its incorporation of previously disadvantaged social groups.[22]

In addition, these results highlight some of the processes within schools that appear to be associated with school composition and social organization via classes and extracurricular activities. Among all students, placement in

Table 4.5  Regression coefficients of cultural flexibility on
school type, region, self-esteem, and other selected
variables: White students only[a]

|  | Model | | |
|---|---|---|---|
|  | 1 | 2 | 3 |
| School type (of color = 1) | .17 (.12) | .12 (.12) | .06 (.13) |
| Student attitudes | | | |
| Preference for same-race schoolmates | | −.17 (.14) | −.19 (.14) |
| Preference for same-race neighbors | | −.21 (.14) | −.18 (.15) |
| Preference for same-socioeconomic-status schoolmates | | −.15 (.13) | −.19 (.16) |
| Preference for same-socioeconomic-status neighbours | | .04 (.13) | .09 (.13) |
| Self-Esteem | | | .04 (13) |
| In advanced placement or honors courses | | | .30 (.05)** |
| Number of extracurricular activities | | | .05 (.05) |
| Controls | | | |
| Parent educational background | | | −.03 (.05) |
| Student grade point average | | | −.11 (.10) |
| Gender (male = 1) | | | .08 (.12) |
| Region (Northeast = 1) | | | .25 (.11)** |
| Intercept | 3.99 | 4.16 | 4.15 |
| Adjusted R² | .00 | .04 | .06 |
| N = | 206 | 205 | 202 |

[a]Metric coefficients (standard errors); *$p$ < .10, **$p$ < .05, ***$p$ < .01 (two-tailed tests)

either AP or honors courses appeared to be positively related to cultural flexibility. This result signals something about the academic experiences in such classes. Prior research has already informed us about the different degrees of curricular content and exposure, creativity, analytical rigor, pedagogical techniques, and support of student curiosity in academically rigorous courses versus "regular" or standard classes.[23] Studies show that AP and international baccalaureate programs in some high-poverty, urban minority high schools provide the opportunity for students to learn and utilize various cultural codes.[24] Such classroom-level factors collectively may augment cultural flexibility. Paradoxically, while exposure to AP and honors classes—both proxies for a certain type of classroom experience—are positively associated with cultural flexibility, they constitute an organizational structure highly correlated with race and inequity in many schools.[25] In this study, there was greater representation of African American students in AP and honors classes at the two majority-minority schools—South City Honors and North City Tech. In contrast, they were significantly underrepresented in these classes at South County Prep and North Village Prep.

I had no way of knowing whether prior academic disparities existed among these students across the four schools before enrolling in high school or whether their prior elementary and middle school experiences account for some of their high school cultural orientations. What is known is that many of the African American students at North Village Prep and South County Prep began their schooling in their respective, high-performing school districts in both elementary and middle school. Although neither self-reported GPAs nor test scores (analyses not provided here) proved to be significant predictors of cultural flexibility in the regression models, one may not be able to fully dismiss some association between academic experiences and the differences in sociocultural experiences between Black students at majority-minority and majority-white schools. The black-white test score differences at North City Tech and South City Honors (two majority-minority high schools) were significantly lower than those in the two majority-white schools (Refer to Table 4.6). No significant differences were found between Black and White students in the study on their state's English test at South City Honors, while Black students performed slightly better than White students on English at North City Tech. In math, White students performed better at South City Honors but no differently than Black students at North City Tech. In contrast, at both South County Prep and North Village Prep, African American students (of similar socioeconomic status as their peers in the other two schools) scored significantly lower than their White peers on both tests.

Finally, a social psychological factor such as self-esteem proved to be significant, especially for African American students. Prior studies have found that Black students in desegregated schools have higher self-esteem and confidence and do better in school than those in segregated contexts.[26] That was not the pattern in these data. Rather, the results from this study revealed that Black students attending high-performing majority-minority schools in the two urban areas of both North and South Capital City possess significantly higher self-esteem than their counterparts in majority-white schools nearby within these same regions. These findings are congruent with the work of

Table 4.6. Mean student test T-scores: By U.S. schools and race (number of responses)

| Mean T-scores on tests | North Capital City | | | | South Capital City | | | |
| --- | --- | --- | --- | --- | --- | --- | --- | --- |
| | North City Tech (majority-minority) | | North Village Prep (majority-white) | | South City Honors (majority-minority) | | South County Prep (majority-white) | |
| | English | Math | English | Math | English | Math | English | Math |
| Asian | 45 (48) | 53 (48) | 58 (21) | 54 (21) | — | — | — | — |
| Black | 50** (58) | 52 (58) | 49*** (26) | 38*** (27) | 52 (46) | 51** (31) | 48* (41) | 46*** (62) |
| Latino | 48 (63) | 53 (63) | 52** (24) | 42*** (24) | — | — | — | — |
| White | 46 (37) | 52 (37) | 57 (56) | 51 (56) | 55 (19) | 58 (11) | 52 (37) | 52 (61) |

Significance level (between-race): *$p$ < .10; **$p$<.05; ***$p$<.01

Note: Since the available student test scores varied by state and by grade, all scores were standardized into Z-scores and then converted into T-scores for comparison purposes. T-score (subject test) = (Z-score * 10) + 50.

psychologist Morris Rosenberg, who has argued that unlike in majority-minority schools, Black children in majority-white schools perceive and experience more distance in their social comparisons to White classmates.[27]

Why are some students more culturally flexible or inclined to move beyond their own social, cultural, and even academic comfort zones than others? What is it about a social and academic context that encourages students to be culturally flexible? How can we come to understand why the students at the majority-minority schools in the study demonstrated more cultural flexibility than those in majority-white schools? And finally, what were some of the differences between the schools that could be associated with the difference? The remainder of this chapter examines these questions by going more deeply into the ethnographic and interview data, inquiring about the following: 1) individual and social factors associated with the cultural flexibility of Black and White students in both majority-minority schools and majority-white schools and 2) different facets of school and society that students discussed as associated with their tendencies (or not) to move across social and cultural boundaries. Both observations and interviews divulged that cultural flexibility is a function of both individual student choices and traits, as well as school organizational factors.

## Unpacking Survey Data through Ethnography and Interviews

### The Interplay between Organizational and Individual Determinants of Cultural Flexibility

The student who navigates various social and cultural boundaries has to possess certain traits and, even more critically, must have access to multiple social, cultural, and material contexts. Certain boundaries in schools, the economy, and neighborhoods are more easily permeable today because of legalities that enable boundary spanning. Yet, whether individuals situated in various contexts are empowered to be culturally flexible beings may depend on a host of factors, from the social psychological (personality, self-concept, self-efficacy, or self-esteem) to mesostructural (family, peer group, neighborhood, school, organization) to the macrostructural (e.g., normative climate, policies, laws, economic conditions). In our interviews, my research team explored what would make it easy or difficult for students to cross social lines in order to ascertain some understanding of the social dynamics behind cultural flexibility. Analyses of observations and interviews, both individual and group-level ones, suggest associations with various factors, specifically 1) the context of feeling personally and collectively secure, 2) social relationships influenced by academic course placement and extracurricular activities around which symbolic boundaries are drawn, and 3) societal norms and enduring practices regarding intergroup contact, specifically racial and ethnic interactions. These various sociological and social psychological factors were illuminated most clearly during comparative analyses *between* schools *within* each of the two urban contexts. Such analyses really allowed me to comprehend the survey findings that signaled something about the differential experiences of students within the multiracial, majority-minority and multiracial, majority-white schools and between the two regions.

## Individuals and Groups Feeling Safe and Secure

South City Honors (majority-minority) and South County Prep (majority-white) are two schools that are twelve miles apart. By state accountability standards, these two schools fluctuate between "exemplary" and "very good" ratings, indicating that for the most part, they meet the testing performance requirements and expectations for nearly every racial, ethnic, class, and ability-level group mandated by the federal NCLB legislation. South County Prep, whose student population is three-quarters White, is a wealthier school in a predominantly white neighborhood where the median household income is nearly 50 percent higher than the median household income for students at South City Honors, a Title 1 school where 93 percent of the students are African American.[28] Just a year prior to our arrival, South City Honors had been commended nationally as an outstanding high school, while South County is often lauded for its exemplary results at the state level.

While many of South City Honors' African American students are from low-income families, many also come from middle-class ones. Of those who participated in this study, 60 percent had parents with at least some college experience, and 54 percent of the African American students at South County Prep had parents with at least some college experience. Yet, despite the similarities among the African American students in terms of their socioeconomic backgrounds, the performance contexts of their respective schools, and the schools' proximity to one another (a few times we met students at either South City Honors or South County Prep who mentioned that they had a sibling who attended the other school), the level of cultural flexibility between these two groups of students was significantly different. One observation we found was that African American students at South

County Prep did not possess the sense of ease and confidence that many of their peers at South City Honors did. Three African American females, all graduating seniors, pointed out a pattern we heard and observed on many occasions: Black students at South County Prep were uncomfortable moving across racial and other social boundaries, so they stuck together:

INTERVIEWER: Would you say that it's easy or difficult to become friends with someone from another background?

ANGELA: It depends on the type of person.

TASHA: Like if you, like, easy going and can really decide to really get into anything, stuff like that, it's not gonna be hard, but if you like [are] totally different, you come from like totally different background, then it's going to probably be a little different...little hard to get into.

INTERVIEWER: So what group are you all...?

SHERRY: The Black people. Yeah.

TASHA: So we all just hang out together. That's how it is. We just all hang out together.

These young women collectively refer to the student who is a boundary crosser as someone who is flexible, "easy-going," and "can really get into anything." Tasha, Angela, and Sherry suggest that a strong sense of self and ease is necessary for moving across distinct social and cultural lines. However, they admitted that they prefer to hangout together and find it difficult to interact across racial lines. And they were not alone, which the survey data confirmed. On average, the African American students at South County Prep scored lowest in both self-reported cultural flexibility and self-esteem. Later on in the conversation, this same group of girls contrasted themselves to "Josh," an African American male who had effectively moved across social lines and accomplished a rare feat in this southern majority-white school. Josh had been elected "Mr. South County Prep," and the girls in the group made sense of Josh's success because he was able to participate and excel in an extracurricular activity that was symbolically associated with White students.

TASHA: ...I mean, he was athletic but he really went like, ...

ANGELA: Soccer?

TASHA: Yeah.

SHERRY: He played soccer?

TASHA: Yes.

INTERVIEWER: Soccer gave him a lot of...

**ANGELA**: Yes, well, especially with the White people.

**TASHA**: Yeah. That's what I'm saying.

**SHERRY**: Oh, wow.

**TASHA**: With the White people, you know, they hang out and, you know, he got to know people so they [Josh's supporters] got the majority vote over what we did.

The girls believed that Josh, who was one of the school's strongest athletes (see more below), had been elected Mr. South County Prep because he had expanded his extracurricular and social activities beyond the repertoire of activities that Tasha, Sherry, and Angela said many of his Black peers at South County Prep labeled as "black." These girls attributed Josh's ability to participate and excel in soccer—which was explicitly considered a "white" sport in their high school—as the reason for his popularity among his mostly White schoolmates. Thus, certain Black students who exhibited a certain type of fortitude spanned the boundaries at South County Prep, but many could not.

Compare and contrast Angela, Tasha, and Sherry's assessment with those of students from South City Honors nearby. Three males, Ugo, a Nigerian immigrant boy whose accent is noticeably different from the other students in the group; Nathan, an African American male; and Zach, a White male, in responding to a question about how students become a part of or fit into the school culture at South City Honors, responded as follows:

**UGO**: If you're a new student coming, if you have the same quality as somebody else, you become friends with them. Share your view and your styles and, you know, people [also] like somebody if they are different. (laughs) And I come here. I speak a different language, different accent or whatever.

**INTERVIEWER**: Where you from?

**UGO**: Nigeria. I came here and I do some funny stuff nobody does, you know?

**NATHAN**: Yeah. He does. (laughs)

**ZACH**: He does do some goofy stuff. (laughter)

**RESPONDENT**: Yeah.

**UGO**: That's what makes me, me, and as long as I find somebody else, I appreciate what I do, you know, that's a good way to start. We have a lot [of that] at this school. A lot of independent people...

**NATHAN**: Like he was saying, he does what, you know, he does...he's not going to change who he is with regard to where he comes from or where he come to. He ain't going to try fit in and be like, be like [other students],

and they don't care. You know, be whoever he is and like whatever he
wants to like. Just like Zach. Zach don't try to fit in with certain people. If
he's like wearing Girbaud, he wears Girbaud. If you want to play football,
you can play football.[29]

These three males mention two things in their conversation: first, the
ability of students to be independent, which Ugo, an immigrant student who
was apparently a zany character, experienced firsthand; and second, the claim
that their school's culture did not inhibit students from crossing specific
culturally symbolic and racial boundaries. For example, Zach, a White male,
could even wear popular "black" styles of wear (Girbaud) or play football,
if he so desired, as Nathan, an African American, said—alluding to the fact
that the team is predominantly Black; and no symbolic boundaries set the
contours of who was in or out of particular activities at South City Honors.

That was not the case at South County Prep, however. On another occasion
and at a later date, a small group of White male seniors at South County Prep
picked up the topic that Tasha, Sherry, and Angela had introduced earlier
about Josh, the boundary spanning African American soccer player who also
played baseball. Mark, William, and Grant offered some insight into symbolic
boundaries reinforced by school leaders and how they made sense of the few
African American males' participation on South County's baseball team:

INTERVIEWER: Are there expectations about who should participate in dif-
    ferent sports, student government, or other extracurricular activities?
MARK: I think everyone has an equal chance on those, especially sports.
INTERVIEWER: What about baseball?
MARK: Baseball is a little different, I guess.
WILLIAM: I don't know what's going on with them but, I mean, it's just like I
    hear people be like they don't get equal...they don't get a chance to show
    what they can do because like [the coach] knows who can do what, and
    [the coach] just puts them out there. [Some players] never get a chance to
    show what they can do. I never been to a baseball game because I know the
    same people that you hear about...you hear about, that's all the people
    who kind of play.
INTERVIEWER: So does Josh get good playing time? He's an African
    American?
GRANT: Josh is like (pause) good in every sports he's been in.
MARK: Yeah. He's good at basketball, baseball, football. So that's just a natural
    talent for him and like for other people who like...just for example, Todd

Dedham, everybody knew he could play baseball, but he didn't really start shining until like going into his twelfth grade.

**GRANT:** You're right.

**WILLIAM:** Because every... all the White boys was in it... in his spot because McCourt wouldn't let him play, but when they got hurt, then he had to put [Todd] in, and then he was a star shot, so it led all the way up to his twelfth grade year. And people found out how good he really was—almost breaking into like the record here at school for home runs.

**GRANT:** He broke the record here for the school.

**WILLIAM:** Yeah.

**INTERVIEWER:** So he's been in baseball, but he hasn't been able to play.

**WILLIAM:** Until his 11th... he wouldn't probably but until his 11th grade year when that boy got hurt or something like that, he was like the only person left in that position to play and then that's when his light started to shine from then to all the way up to this year but... if Coach McCourt would have gave him that chance before, I think that he would have been... he would have had way more scholarships; he would have been way more popular; and then he would probably got a lot of scholarships like Josh and them did so... that's how I think.

At first, Mark declared that no expectations existed about which groups would participate in select sports. The researcher asked explicitly about baseball, after having heard previously from the girls that symbolic boundaries were drawn around certain sports. In this case, these three students believed that Todd, another African American student, missed a critical college scholarship opportunity because he only got to show off his athletic skills for one year. Before that, he was sitting on the bench waiting on the opportunity to play. Whether Todd deserved to be second string and had to earn a starting position is not the point here. Rather, it is that these students *perceived* that baseball, as an extracurricular activity with the potential to make higher education affordable through scholarship, had been deemed the domain of "White boys" and not "Black boys." Baseball participation, in this case, emerged a signifier of social boundaries between Black and White males that could translate into a higher education benefit for the latter group.

Up north in North Capital City, the between-school differences in educational experiences for African American students appeared differently, too. Like South City Honors, North City Tech is a Title 1 school, although it is significantly more multiracial and multiethnic than the former, and many of its language course offerings, for example, reflect the diversity of its immigrant student population. In addition, many of the Black students who took a bus daily to affluent North Village Prep, the wealthiest school in the study, would have been eligible to attend North City Tech.

Forty-seven and 32 percent of the Black students in the study at North Village Prep and North City Tech, respectively, had parents with at least some college experience. Black and White survey respondents at North City Tech resembled each other in terms of family background, with 32 percent of White students having parents with some college experience. In comparison, nearly triple that number, 88 percent of White students at North Village Prep, had parents with some college experience. Students at North City Tech came from neighborhoods all across the city, so that it was difficult to ascertain the median household income of their neighborhoods. In comparison, the median household income for the community where North Village Prep resides was over $120,000 in 2007. In addition, North Village Prep's school budget in 2007 was more than triple that of North City Tech, which has a slightly larger student population, at over $19 million.

Despite the disparate resource contexts between these schools, both Black and White students at North City Tech reported significantly higher levels of cultural flexibility than those at North Village Prep. Beyond simply mentioning their willingness to cross racial and ethnic boundaries, North City Prep students proudly described the bases of their cultural flexibility. For instance, Cherise, an African American ninth grader at North City Tech, spoke frankly about why she had decided to enroll in a Chinese language class at school; most of her friends, since seventh grade, were Asian American— Chinese, to be more specific—and she wanted to converse with them in their language. Cherise's was not an exceptional case. Two of her schoolmates, both White high school seniors at North City Tech—one an Italian-Irish American girl and the other an Irish Catholic—who perceived themselves as "minorities" in this predominantly Black, Asian, and Latino school, discussed their own cultural flexibility:

NATALIA:...I was the only Italian-Irish girl, and everybody thought I was some type of Latina so they were like, "Oh, what are you?" and they thought I was Cuban and White. Like, "No. I'm Italian." So then everyone thought that I was in the Mafia because they saw my father. (laughter)...I hang out with a lot more Latino people just because, I don't know, so I like learn how to speak Spanish and stuff....

Later in this same group conversation with White seniors, Anthony provided a further example that adaptation to being a "minority" at North City Tech entailed some cultural flexibility:

**ANTHONY**: It was kind of hard being the only White kid around for a little while, but you got used to it so…

**INTERVIEWER**: Can you say more about that? Like was it…was it socially that it was hard? Was it like trying to kinda feel like you belong here? Like what parts about it do you feel like made it difficult in the beginning?

**ANTHONY**: Well, personally, I came from a really, really small all Italian Catholic school. Hard core, northern…think everything about Italian people and it's there, and that was all and then I went to Cuomo [pseudonym] for a year, and it was all Italian or Latino people, and then I came here, and it was totally different. Like everything was just different and you have to get used to different characteristics in cultures, and I didn't know what a Guyanese person was. I didn't know…I had no…I went to a Catholic school and they still use the word "Oriental." Like, I didn't know of anything else. So you just have to get used to things like that.

**INTERVIEWER**: Do you feel like, though…like having to get used to that affects how people do in school?

**ANTHONY**: I think it makes them better because it broadens their horizons.

Anthony discussed the values he felt that North City Tech offered him in terms of its racial and ethnic diversity—even if it meant his being in the minority as a White student attending the school. For him, experiences at North City Tech were making him a "better" person because he broadened his "horizons," because his interactions with diverse peers made him more culturally flexible.

Proactively broadening students' cultural horizons is common at North City Tech. Some of the first things I noticed when I arrived on the main floor of the school was the centrality of its library and the wall displays throughout the hallway, including the paintings, pictures of historic and artistic figures of various races, ethnicities, and genders, and a trophy display case of North City Tech's successful sports teams (track in particular). A middle-aged African American woman with shoulder-length salt-and-pepper colored corkscrew twists and a sharp tongue named Cheryl Terry was in charge of the displays. Clearly, Ms. Terry was proud of the library that she had created, filled with shelves and displays of books that spotlight various African, Asian, Latino, and European American writers, which is not only an academic space for students but also a place where students would gather socially after school. An Afrocentric woman who wears dresses made of kente cloth, Ms. Terry was intentional about the visual, knowledge signals that she transmitted to students, insuring that multiple perspectives were represented on the bulletin boards and doors that she decorated outside of the library. The displays commemorated the histories and contributions of various previously marginalized groups, including African Americans, Asian Americans, Latinos, and women—all groups represented in the school.

Cheryl Terry was not the only educator doing this; our field notes are filled with descriptions of numerous teachers' classrooms that marked the histories and affirmed the realities of various immigrant groups, disabled people, various peoples of color, and women. One popular retiring history teacher, an African American man named Peter Thomas, proudly shared with us on several occasions how his African American history class, enrolled by students of diverse backgrounds, had days prior raised $4,000 schoolwide in support of the establishment of the Martin Luther King memorial in Washington, DC, which opened in 2011.

Overall, it was little surprise that Anthony's, Natalia's, and Cherise's admissions about their intercultural pursuits converge with what the survey results tell us: North City Tech High students, on average, scored highest on the cultural flexibility scale. And White students at North City Tech were the highest scoring racial subgroup. All in all, these three youth explicitly mentioned something about their school's social climate that encouraged students to not only embrace its racial and ethnic diversity but also to actively participate in other cultural practices—some of the basic attributes of cultural flexibility.

## Structuring Relationships through Classroom Organization and Other School Activities

We have like kind of blurry lines a lot of the times . . . but like, you know, you have that group and you can't really like relate to that group. You can individually, but like not as a whole group, but a lot of the other groups just like they've learned their lines a lot. Like we have a lot of people that are in the AP classes, and they hang out together a lot and there's like theater groups and stuff like that and they hang out and just like random small groups from like different . . . just from being in high school together for so long and stuff like that. (Ashley, White female, eleventh grade, South County Prep)

Students learn their "lines," their places, and the value of cultural flexibility from interactions with the organizational habitus, and that habitus encapsulates social, academic, and cultural dynamics that influence the contours of particular social groupings within the school. Ashley, a White female participating in a coed, all-White, eleventh-grade group interview at South County Prep, shared openly that how students are organized in academic and extracurricular activities structures their friendships. Her views and that of others with whom we spoke confirmed what we already know from the research on multiracial schools and sociability.[30]

Differential participation rates by groups can concretize the "lines," boundaries, and perceived differences to the point that they can endure throughout high school. At South County Prep, not only were highly visible and high-status extracurricular activities, including cheerleading, the Young Republicans Club, baseball, and football, characterized as racial "turfs," but also specific academic classes drew symbolic boundaries, too. In an informal poll I took, teachers designated only about five (out of 302) African American students bright enough to be enrolled in advanced classes, and generally there was only one, or at the most two, student in these classes when we visited them. Both the number of extracurricular activities and participation in advanced or honors classes were positively correlated to cultural flexibility in the survey analyses.

These meaning-making processes are not unique to South County. Students at North Village Prep made similar comments about how their schools might influence their ability to move across social boundaries more easily and frequently. Will, a graduating White senior, lamented what he found one of the most negative aspects of his high school, which had participated in a voluntary desegregated school for decades:

**INTERVIEWER:** If you were able to change one thing about your school, what would that be?

**WILL:** I think one thing I would change is I would try to make this school more welcoming for…all people. I kind of, I mean, as with any high school, probably, you tend to form…tend to break down into groups I mean, I hang out with people who do a lot of the same activities as me and, you know, get the same grades and are in the same classes, and I think that's one disadvantage of having kind of tracked classes. I'm glad that we don't have them in English or History. I think that helps a little bit but, yeah, I'm certainly glad that we have the "Be the Change" program this year, I think…I really think that will make a difference in the school.

Will told us that tracking, as well as the lack of diversity in extracurricular activities, prevented much student interaction across racial lines in school. And survey data confirmed his personal observation, showing that at North Village Prep, 71 percent of White students and 88 percent of Asian students were enrolled in at least either *one* honors or AP course, compared to 30 percent and 48 percent of their Black and Latino peers, respectively. Similarly, at South County Prep, White students were more than one and a half times as likely to be enrolled in either AP or honors courses as their Black schoolmates—62 percent and 38 percent, respectively. In Will's case, the opportunity for social contact across racial lines was limited because of his course placement (and, no doubt, the small percentage of students of color at North Village Prep). Nonetheless, Will and some of his fellow students (of various races) and some school administrators demonstrated their willingness to build relations across social lines through other means that, as Will says, could potentially "make a really big difference," a program that urged students to be proactive about crossing boundaries (see discussion in chapter 5).

Notably, White students at North Village Prep High reported significantly higher cultural flexibility than their Black peers there. In addition to the significantly wider socioeconomic gap that existed among African American, Latino, and White students at North Village Prep, the cultural and educational opportunities' gap loomed large, as well. With a few exceptions, Black and Latino students at North Village Prep did not reap the advantages of attending a well-resourced school with strong parent support and fundraising. For instance, in the spring of 2007, the air was abuzz with the eager anticipation of students and a few fortunate teachers, who were preparing to head to Japan on a band and orchestra trip for a two-week exchange to Japan. Although one of the only two Black teachers, Mr. Clifton Moman, was going on the trip as a chaperone, none of the African American and Latino students who participated in the VDP at North Village Prep were headed to Japan. Every year students took trips abroad through Europe, Asia, Latin and Central America—after numerous car washes, bake sales, and parental financial support—but North Village Prep's Black and Latino students—the majority of whom are lower income and voluntarily bused to the school via the VDP—either could not afford or were not financially subsidized by the school to participate in these trips. Conceivably, these are experiences that can also broaden cultural horizons and facilitate more cultural flexibility.

Moreover, at various break times and free periods during the day, the VDP student participants at North Village Prep socialized and took study breaks in two rooms where only they gathered. While some of the space was also allotted to students who were facing academic and behavioral challenges in the classroom, these rooms had been assigned to the VDP program for student support, housing the desk of the program's in-house tutor, Beverly Kite, an African American woman who was an alumna of the VDP program at another high school in the area. Beverly was one of the first to bring my attention to how classroom life corresponded to boundaries and even flexibility. She was in charge of closely monitoring classes that VDP students took and making recommendations. On any given day, I chose to sit in on a different sampling of courses, and one morning I mentioned to Beverly that I was headed to a class on ancient Roman society. When I asked Beverly if she knew the teacher, she responded, "Who?" I said, "Ken Mack. He teaches a class on ancient Rome." Beverly retorted, "Oh, that's why I don't know him. He ain't on none of my lists. These [VDP] kids don't take classes like that." I quickly discovered that some classes were not even on the radar for the VDP kids—another reminder that desegregation is not a sufficient condition for integration and full academic incorporation.

North Village Prep's principal, Stuart Beckman, who was due to retire at the end of the year, acknowledged Will's and other students' concerns, which were heightened by the conspicuous racial achievement disparities at his school, which sent more than 90 percent of its graduating (White and Asian) seniors to college. Some of his staff held regular weekly discussions about this matter; and my research assistant and I attended several of their meetings. Teachers and VDP staff looked for ways to understand the VDP students' material or historical realities better. Still, academically their participation rates in college preparatory courses, which are known to expand students' knowledge bases in significantly different ways than regular comprehensive high school in courses, and in cultural activities such as band, orchestra, theater, and model UN (United Nations), were much lower than the participation rates of their counterparts at the majority-black schools in the larger study.

Principal Beckman and his staff took a different approach toward equity, not necessarily a cultural difference one and not nearly egalitarian. Rather, North Village Prep staff observed the disparate backgrounds of their students, encouraged some discussions—generally among smaller groups—and ignored the academic and extracurricular patterns that corresponded with racial (and class) backgrounds. Similarly, South County Prep's principal, Mary Jennings, did not appear to have any concern that only 5 out of over 302 African American students at her school were enrolled in the most advanced college preparatory classes. She and her staff, however, took the cultural difference approach in which they accepted the inclusion of African American students at South County Prep and signaled that they did not believe these students were as academically capable as the majority of White students in their schools. Furthermore, Jennings and staff did nothing even symbolically (at least during the time that we were there) to advocate for integration or a deeper inclusion in terms of intimate mixing and cross-cultural communication in the classroom and beyond.

In comparison, we found that the structuring of student relationships at both North City Tech and South City Honors (both majority-minority) was different; Black students' academic placement in the schools had a broader range from the most accelerated and advanced courses to the most remedial courses. In addition, Black and White students were enrolled in at least one AP or honors courses at the same rate: 75 percent and 76 percent, respectively, at South City Honors, and 50 percent and 42 percent, respectively, at North City Tech—two schools known for their strong promotion of academic rigor. For Asian and Latino students at North City Tech, the participation rates were 40 percent and 48 percent, respectively. At both of these schools, we observed that not only did many students of color share equal academic status with White students, but also they participated in diverse extracurricular activities. At South City Honors, Black students also participated in Model UN, a program for high school students in which they learn about the organization and international policy building of the United Nations, and the National Forensics League. Both of these programs allow students to meet other students from dissimilar places and to compete with them locally and nationally.

In short, while both North Village Prep and South County Prep had stronger material resource contexts—they were significantly wealthier— Black students enrolled in these schools were significantly less likely to either have access, be encouraged to participate, or to avail of such opportunities as their peers at the two majority-minority schools: North City Tech and South City Honors. The latter schools, in comparison, had programs that signified a breadth of cultural and academic possibilities and interests for the different racial groups of students.

## Summing Up

Overall, the main implication is that cultural flexibility is a social and psychological process, which may determine the extent to which individuals of diverse backgrounds are really willing to realize the visions of social integration. From students' perspectives, their sense of self and their social organization within school have a great deal to do with their tastes for cross-cultural participation. The power to create and maintain rigid social and symbolic boundaries particularly within schools is within the hands of both students and educators. Yet, often the former learn their lessons and behaviors from the latter. Educators, as well as other key adults in youths' lives, set the examples; and they signal whether they would allow the values, sensibilities, practices, or participation of other social groups to cross the "lines" or even eradicate social and symbolic boundaries.

Today students in the United States, like South Africa, attend both poor, segregated schools and well-resourced, multiracial schools. What we also know is that even in numerous cities around the United States—areas where the per capita income and educational levels are high—students of color attending middle-class, white-dominant schools are performing less well in some cases than their counterparts in poorer schools.[31] For the most part, though, reports on some of the nation's most affluent schools and districts reveal that while Black students lag behind their White peers within the same schools, generally they perform better on achievement tests than Black students in segregated schools.[32]

Although previous studies show that mixed-race, predominantly white schools generally benefit racial and ethnic minority students, offering better academic resource contexts,[33] the question remains whether they necessarily engender the cultural and social environments to enable all students—whether African American, Asian American, Latino/Latina, or White—to avail fully of critical academic skills and to develop civically by crossing social boundaries, diminishing symbolic ones, and forming relationships that would extend well into adulthood and influence their residential, social network, and friendship choices.[34] While racial proximity is a necessary condition for long-term engagement across racial and ethnic boundaries,[35] social forces such as discrimination, racism, ethnocentrism, classism, and other forms of inequality continue to permeate many schools' walls and to counteract students' ability to attain cultural flexibility.[36] And while new research shows that African Americans and Latinos feel more attached to school when they attend it with greater proportions of their own race or ethnicity, racial proximity with other groups in schools remains a necessary, albeit insufficient, condition to realize the visions of social integration for all students.[37]

One of the implications of the findings here is that many students attending minority-dominant schools perceive that they can do as well as or achieve highly because affirming messages are deeply inculcated into them.[38] For example, Massey, Charles, Lundy, and Fischer found that Black first-year college students, who graduated from urban, minority-dominant high schools and later attended some of the nation's most elite universities, maintained very strong senses of self and aspirations.[39] Paradoxically, these students maintained very high confidence levels, despite having significantly lower grades than their Asian and White peers in their first year of college. While Massey et al. may have labeled this self-concept and achievement paradox as "overconfidence," such findings still indicate how different school contexts influence students' identities, self-concept, and the boundaries they create within them.

Self-esteem is a significant and positive predictor of cultural flexibility for Black students, and those Black students enrolled in the two majority-minority schools, North City Tech and South County Honors, revealed higher self-esteem than their racial counterparts in the two majority-white schools, North Village High and South County Prep. Studies find that for Black students, critical identity issues may emerge for those educated in school contexts where their social and cultural realities are either muted or invisible.[40] In a developmental period when identity means much to them, many youth of color find meanings in how classrooms and school activities are organized and the degrees to which they are encouraged to interact with one another both socially and academically. Therefore, the relationship between minority students' high self-esteem and cultural flexibility in majority-minority schools may not have much to do with whether these students sit in the classrooms with White students[41] but whether positive familial, economic, and social supports are in place, in addition to effective teachers and adequate educational resources.[42] When these students witness daily that their coethnic peers cross the spectrum of ability levels and smartness, athleticism, and leadership potential, their reference group for achievement expands and includes some representation of others who share similar social backgrounds.

In short, the promotion of cultural flexibility by educators is critical to the academic incorporation of many students. As social agents, students can either consciously or unconsciously choose to be culturally flexible in their identities.[43] The opportunities that schools permit for them to mix across various social boundaries both inside and outside of the classroom matter, too, however. If schools reinforce social and symbolic boundaries whereby some groups are less fully incorporated into the fabric of school life than others, then they are actively reproducing structures of inequality.[44] Some school practices, therefore, threaten educational equity by signaling disparately among social groups who is either "in" or "out" of the opportunity system of education.

# 5

## *The More Things Change, the More Threatening They Feel*

WHITE YOUTHS' ATTITUDES ON EQUITY

AS FIDGETY STUDENTS sat listening in rows of chairs, sitting shoulder to shoulder, in the assembly hall at South Africa's Williston High on a bright, cool afternoon, Principal Caryn Billups strongly proclaimed to them, "We are all South Africans." Urging these youth to return to their country even if they took a few "gap years" abroad, she continued, "Go away and earn some money, if you'd like, but come back, buy a home, and settle in your country. We are all South Africans," she declared again. Clearly, Mrs. Billups was speaking directly to the White students in her school. By and large, they were leaving the country, headed for the United Kingdom, Australia, the United States, and elsewhere, where chances of being in a white majority were greater and where they invested their hopes of strong economic returns for their human capital.

Four years after meeting them for the first time, I gathered a group of about twenty school matrics at Williston for a discussion about how things had changed in their high school over their five academic years there. Adolescents can be frank, very frank, if they trust that you are listening and allow them the safety of knowing that what they say matters. I must admit that I was unable to mask my incredulity when more than half of this group—all of the white, a few Coloured, and two Black students—expressed with a level of certitude that they intended to leave their country and live elsewhere as adults. For the White learners, several frustrations surfaced: fear of their national leaders' capability to run the nation, disgruntlement over how much the country was doing to redress the apartheid-stained past, and the belief that no jobs were available for Whites because of "reverse racism." The group had fewer

White students than I recalled some years prior because the White student population had declined by about 10 percent. Fear of the "other" translated easily into these families' flight to other (mostly white) private schools that are more expensive but whose educational results did not differ vastly from Williston's, according to Principal Billups.

When I asked why so many of them wanted to leave South Africa, Bernard, a Coloured male sitting directly in front of me, responded immediately in a sardonic tone, "the Blacks." Some students gasped; that was not the politically correct thing to say after all. Unaccustomed to limited political and top-down decision-making power, many non-African, especially White, students were feeling it. "Ours is a country where nothing but criminals have been president," cried Jason, a White male. I wondered if this group of "criminals" included "Madiba," the Xhosa clan name that South African people use to refer to former president Nelson Mandela, a national hero, nonagenarian, a conciliator who has kept civil war away from a black nation boiling with anger and resentment for its decades of disenfranchisement. "What do you mean that you have had nothing but criminals for your president?" I asked. "Are you including all, including Mandela?" I inquired. "Well, yes," proclaimed Megan, a White female. "He was in prison, too," she explained.

I could understand some reservations about the extant president, Jacob Zuma, who was elected in 2009. After all, he had been indicted for rape charges of which he was absolved, and at the time of our conversation, he had been indicted for serious corruption charges surrounding bribes for which his associate in the matter had already pleaded guilty. But Megan and Jason did not merely include Mr. Zuma in their estimation of black criminality; they included former President Mandela because he had spent nearly three decades in prison for resistance against the apartheid state (and ostensibly Thabo Mbeki—the former president of South Africa who was in exile under apartheid). Historical record informs us, on the other hand, that these notable men fought against the nefarious effects of a racist and rigidly separate nation-state that denied citizenship rights to all of its inhabitants. Biographies and history books describe them as heroes, resistance fighters, and advocates of social justice and democracy.[1]

Learners at Williston were not alone in their stereotypes about black competency. Similarly, both White and Coloured learners at Palmer High School (Coast City) made similar comments, deriding affirmative action policies in the country because allegedly "incompetent" Blacks were being hired over perceived more qualified Whites and Indians and Coloureds. To the outsider, learners used their perceived state of their economy as evidence of South Africa's imminent downfall. "Our economy has been going down the tubes for the last fifteen years," Vijay, an Indian male, remarked derisively during my final wrap-up visit to Palmer in 2008, specifying the period in which the black-dominant African National Congress (ANC) came to power and brought democracy.

In the last chapter, we saw that some preferences for same- race and same-class group members are related to students' cultural flexibility. In addition, wider social forces such as residential segregation and homogeneous social networks continue to provide the fodder for the endurance of attitudes and beliefs that groups hold about their position, their status, and their interactions with others.[2] The goal of this chapter is to discuss other individual- and group-centered dynamics that may influence the processes of cultural flexibility and ultimately inclusion. To do this, I focus now on the meaning making that non-Black, namely White, youth and educators have produced to make sense of the changing world around them and within their schools. Attitudes and beliefs are often the ones that reinforce the social boundaries that groups draw between themselves and the "other," and how they shape social reality has critical implications for cultivating not only cultural flexibility but also equity, a social condition that holds the key for the full realization of any inclusive, just democracy.

## An Enduring Past: Racial Attitudes and Schooling in South Africa

In educational research, students' attitudes, aspirations, and beliefs about matters relevant to their economic mobility have been used as indicators of their individual class habitus.[3] Similarly, we can learn something about their individual racial habitus via their attitudes and beliefs about interracial relations, cross-racial boundary crossing, and racial differences and disparities in their respective communities and societies. Such attitudes and beliefs can serve as a barometer of the intensity and closed nature of the social boundaries that students (re)produce.

Overall, the South African students in the study were significantly more likely to believe that Whites experienced "some" to "a lot" of discrimination in education in comparison to the U.S. students. Conversely, South African students were less likely to believe that Blacks experienced "some" to "a lot" of educational discrimination compared to American students. Figures 5.1a through 5.1f show that differences in perceptions of educational discrimination varied by nation and race. In both national cases, White students were significantly more likely than Black and Asian students to believe that Whites

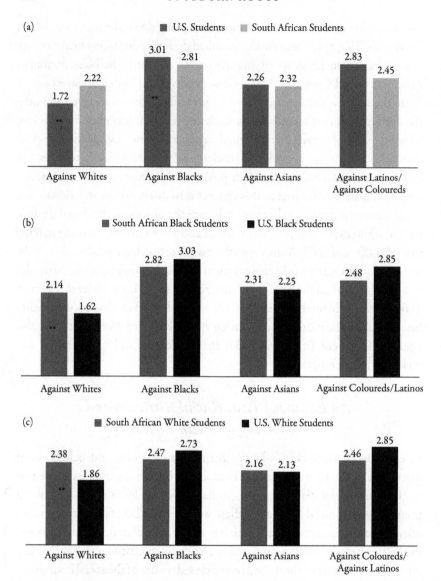

Figure 5.1 (a) Students' Views about Educational Discrimination against Different Racial/Ethnic Groups, by Nation

(b) Black Students' Views about Educational Discrimination against Different Racial and Ethnic Groups, by Nation

(c) White Students' Views about Educational Discrimination against Different Racial and Ethnic Groups, by Nation

Note: Response categories were 1 (none), 2 (a little), 3 (some), and 4 (a lot); **$p <= .00$.

Figure 5.1 (Continued)

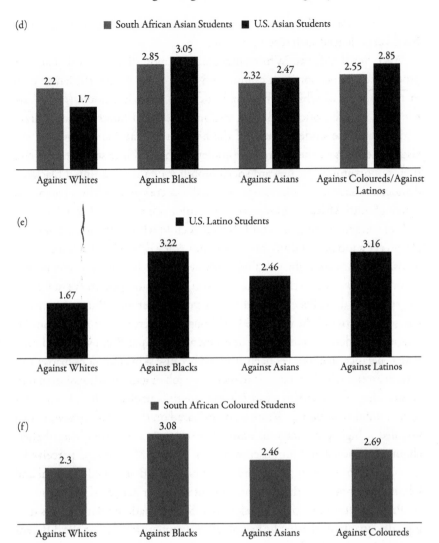

(d)

■ South African Asian Students ■ U.S. Asian Students

Against Whites: 2.2, 1.7
Against Blacks: 2.85, 3.05
Against Asians: 2.32, 2.47
Against Coloureds/Against Latinos: 2.55, 2.85

(e)

■ U.S. Latino Students

Against Whites: 1.67
Against Blacks: 3.22
Against Asians: 2.46
Against Latinos: 3.16

(f)

■ South African Coloured Students

Against Whites: 2.3
Against Blacks: 3.08
Against Asians: 2.46
Against Coloureds: 2.69

(d) Asian Students' Views about Educational Discrimination against Different Racial and Ethnic Groups, by Nation

Note: The cell sizes are likely too small for conclusive, statistically significant results among Asian students.

(e) U.S. Latino Students' Views about Educational Discrimination against Different Racial and Ethnic Groups

(f) South African Coloured Students' Views about Educational Discrimination against Different Racial and Ethnic Groups

Note: Response categories were 1 (none), 2 (a little), 3 (some), and 4 (a lot)

experienced some educational discrimination and less likely to believe that Blacks experienced such discrimination.

Also, South African White students were more likely to feel that they experienced educational discrimination than U.S. White students, even in the context of white-dominant leadership in their schools ($t$ = -6.46, $p$ = .00). While Principal Billups attributed some of South Africa's "brain drain" to White students' fears of the high "crime rate" and "poverty," she also acknowledged that there is a problem in how White students perceive their opportunities for upward social mobility in a newly minted black-led democratic nation. "Look, I hope eventually, there's going to be a balance, if you're a South African, regardless of what color you are. I think it will take us a bit of time to get to that. And I think any child whose attitude is right will always get a job here. I don't care what your color is," declared Billups. "Kids whose attitudes are right will find work here, regardless if they're male and White. I think it's a myth, you know, if you're male and pale you're not going to get a job. I don't believe that; I believe you can get jobs. But your attitude has got to be right," she continued. Although she perceived that "attitude" is a significant determinant of job attainment, Principal Billups also believed that a "balance" had not yet been attained because skin color does matter to a certain extent, whether it comes to securing a job or gaining admission to university. She referred to this white fear as a "myth," but clearly there is a perception of unfairness among White students based on the school surveys, which revealed a high percentage of affirmative responses regarding their beliefs about educational and job discrimination. Even if Mrs. Billups perceived a disconnection between the White students' fear and actual educational and job mobility practices, the students did not share her conveyed optimism.

Principal John Dalton at Palmer High School made similar remarks during a discussion of whether he had observed competition among the different races within the school:

> Some of the White kids are a little bit tense about it and they say, "You know, why must we get punished effectively or get shut up?" And the message I keep saying to them is that I have never known a White kid in all of the years that I've been teaching when the whole question of affirmative action came in and you got extra points if you were Black or Coloured or female…I said, you know, I've never known a White male not to be able to get in if they were absolutely determined to do so. It's just a question of motivation, will, desire—all those things and to say, "I am going to become a doctor."

Like Mrs. Billups, Mr. Dalton pointed to the importance of a student's attitude or "motivation" in gaining access to university, but he also openly acknowledged that White students perceive themselves as being at a considerable disadvantage. As our conversation evolved, Mr. Dalton also stated that he considered preferences given to Black students at his school, who were middle class, as "unfair." Moreover, his response suggested that he tries to allay the fears of these students by discounting the effects of affirmative action. He took the position that regardless of the benefit provided by affirmative action policies, he had never known of a White student who did not get into a South African university, if so desired.

White students at both Williston and Palmer hail from middle-class communities with unequivocally the best performing public schools in the nation and comprise a segment of the population that faced practically 0 percent unemployment under apartheid and 8.9 percent for those with only a high school (matric) degree in as recently as 2002, compared to 56 percent and 24 percent for the Black and Coloured South Africans with matric degrees only, respectively.[4] The 2009–2010 Annual Employment Equity Report shows that White males and females constitute 7 percent and 5.5 percent of the economically active population in South Africa, respectively. Combining the genders, Whites are doubly represented in the skilled labor workforce: 28 percent. White males and females hold the largest percentages of professional jobs, occupying 27 percent and 16 percent of all professional jobs; and 54 percent and 9 percent of top management positions across public and private sectors, and 46 percent and 16 percent of all senior management jobs across public and private sectors, respectively. Whites dominate, especially in the private sector, holding more than 50 percent of all skilled and professional jobs collectively at any given level. All other race-gender groups appear to be proportionately represented in only government-sector jobs.[5] Nevertheless, we know from numerous research studies and statistics that the legacy of white dominance endures within economic and educational spheres, even as White South Africans continue to constitute a numerical minority.[6] Still, there are obvious signs of fear among these White youth about any equity-minded educational and economic policies in the country.

## A More Perfect Union? Racial Attitudes and Schooling of American Students

It is very likely that in the first decade of the twenty-first century, U.S. high school students are accustomed to issues of racial diversity and tolerance significantly more than their South African counterparts, since the United States has been at it for more decades. More than two-thirds ,of American students declared that they prefer to attend mixed-race and mixed-class schooling, 68 percent and 72 percent, respectively. Being accustomed to the dialogues of diversity is certainly not the same as the practice of it for all students, however. For instance, twice as many White students (39 percent; $N = 139$) in majority-white schools preferred to attend schools where Whites are in the majority than White students attending majority-minority schools (18 percent; $N = 68, p = .00$).

Like their White peers, nearly four in ten Black students (38 percent; $N = 128$) attending majority-white schools expressed preferences for attending a school where Blacks were in the majority. However, no significant differences were found among Black students by school composition type; 33 percent of Black students attending majority-minority schools ($N = 135$) preferred to attend black-dominant schools. For Latinos, it was 30 percent ($N = 70$) and 27 percent ($N = 33$), and 7 percent ($N = 27$) and 21 percent ($N = 48$), respectively, for Asian American students in terms of preferences for schools where their ethnic or racial groups were in the majority (refer to Figure 5.2).[7]

Patterns of students' same-class group preferences in school were similar to their same-race preferences. About a third of White students in majority-white schools preferred that the majority of their schoolmates share their socioeconomic background, compared to sixteen percent of White students attending majority-minority schools. For other racial and ethnic groups, class preferences mirror their racial preferences, although no significant differences

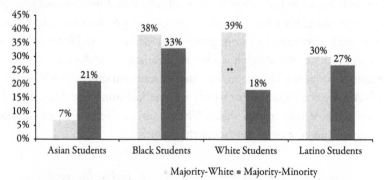

**p < = .00

Note: Asian cell sizes are small.

Figure 5.2 Percentage of Students Preferring to Attend Schools Where Majority of Students Are of Their Race, by School Composition Type were found by school composition type. That is, among Black students, 33 percent of students attending majority-white schools preferred to be in schools with peers of a similar class background, compared to 26 percent of those attending majority-minority schools. For Asian students, it was 22 percent and 29 percent, and for Latinos it was 24 percent and 27 percent, respectively (see Figure 5.3).

Students' neighborhood preferences reflect their desires for schoolmates. White students in both school types were equally as likely to want to live in same-race neighborhoods (39 percent of those in majority-white schools and 31 percent of those in majority-minority schools). In this case, significant differences were found among Black and Asian students and not Latino students. Among Black students, 37 percent of those attending majority-white schools and 24 percent of those in majority-minority schools preferred to live among their own racial group ($p < .05$); and for Asian students, it was 15 percent and 40 percent, respectively ($p < .05$). As Figures 5.4 and 5.5 show, similar patterns hold for these students' preferences in terms of their neighbors' socioeconomic status. Neither Asian, Black, Latino, nor White students could escape the historical, separate, and sometimes divisive, racial, ethnic, and class lines that characterize their families, schools, and communities. Ethnic and racial boundaries in schools and communities abound.

Sociologists Lawrence Bobo, James Kluegel, and Ryan Smith have provided a sophisticated sociohistorical analysis of racial attitudes to show how Whites in the United States have shifted in their viewpoints, moving from

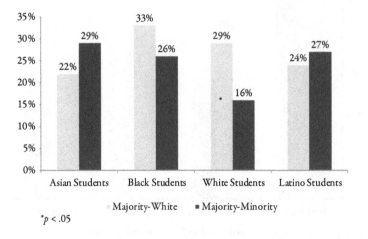

Figure 5.3 Percentage of Students Preferring to Attend Schools Where Majority of Students Share Their Socioeconomic Background, by School Composition Type

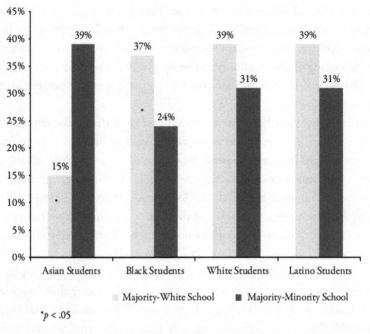

Figure 5.4  Percentage of Students Preferring to Live in *Neighborhoods* Where Majority of Students Are of Their Race, by School Composition Type

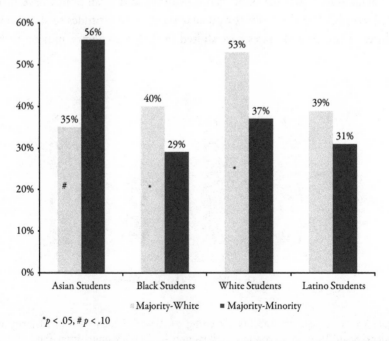

*p < .05, # p < .10

Figure 5.5  Percentage of Students Who Prefer to Live in *Neighborhoods* Where Majority of Students Share Their Socioeconomic Background, by School Composition Type
*p < .05; # p <.10

closed to tolerant from the mid- to late twentieth century.[8] Nonetheless, Bobo and colleagues found another interesting paradox: While White Americans did not profess to believe in overt forms of racial discrimination and inequality as cohorts of Whites did in earlier periods, they still engaged in behaviors that belied their avowed acceptance of Blacks, Asians, and Latinos. Bobo et al. argued that Jim Crow racism mutated into a new form of racial intolerance— what they refer to as "laissez-faire" racism—in which American Whites demonstrate their real feelings of the "other" (i.e., non-Whites) through their housing choices, segregated neighborhoods, social networks, and framing of current inequality as a by-product of culture and misplaced values of specific racial and ethnic minority groups, as opposed to attributing their fortunes to institutionalized forms of inequality. The racial and class habitus existent in segregated communities and schools undoubtedly shape many American students' attitudes and positions toward the racial and class "other," students who do not share either their skin color or socioeconomic background. And in this study, same-race and -class preferences appeared to be especially stronger among those attending majority-white schools.

## *The Variable Nature of White Students' Racial, Ethnic, and Symbolic Boundaries*

As students and educators sustain the boundaries that they use to demarcate "us" from "them," the very nature of the social and cultural tools and ideas that they use to differentiate themselves could vary substantively. One of the first ways to ascertain the extent to which students invoke boundaries is to think about how they identify themselves with a group. I asked all of the students in the study to self-identify both ethnically and racially. In the United States, students tend to rely on racial terms such as "Black" or "White" or a pan-ethnic one such as "Latino," which encompasses Spanish-speaking groups of various ethnicities and national origins. Generally, when asked to identify in terms of ethnicity, the majority of American White students tend to label themselves as White or Caucasian, which Doane describes as a "dominant group ethnic identity."[9] More than three-quarters of students of European ancestry identified ethnically and racially as "White" at South County Prep, South City Honors, and North Village Prep High Schools: 89 percent, 86 percent, and 74 percent, respectively. These statistics are not terribly surprising, especially since scholars of race, specifically of "whiteness," have found a decline in ethnic identity among Whites throughout the late twentieth and early twenty-first centuries.[10]

Though social boundaries manifest in many forms in a stratified society, the symbolic nature of these boundaries signifies the levels in which members within ethnic groups are likely to either span or transcend those lines of difference in terms of interactions, behaviors, and exchanges. Sociologist Andreas Wimmer's multidimensional framework outlines several characteristics of boundaries that signal the degree to which members of a group may align with members of other groups; these boundary traits include "*social closure*" (or the extent to which an ethnic group is either exclusive or closed-off to outsiders), "*political salience*" (or the intensity levels in which coethnics form groups to compete over resources), and "*cultural differentiation*" (or the demarcation of group boundaries based on symbols, customs, practices, traditions, and other cultural artifacts).[11]

An examination of the aggregate survey data on ethnic identity reveals that ethnoracial boundaries exist in different forms in schools, too, and vary in the degrees in which the boundary traits specified by Wimmer are prominent. Which trait becomes more apparent is associated with the social and political contexts of the surrounding communities of the schools. For instance, White students at two of the U.S. high schools—North City Tech (North Capital City) and South County Prep (South Capital City)—stood out in terms of the strength of their symbolic boundaries, but the nature of these boundaries varied significantly. First, those at North City Tech pertained primarily to *ethnic and cultural differentiation* among students, many of whom were first- and second-generation immigrant students. In contrast, *social closure* mostly characterized the nature of social boundaries at South County Prep, a school where students reported the lowest levels of cultural flexibility and high levels of same-race preferences.

As Table 5.1 shows, White students at South County and North City Tech were more than five to eight times as likely to believe that members of their group should show their loyalty by hanging out with other members of their own group than White students at either North Village Prep or South City Honors were: 15 percent, 16 percent, 2 percent, and 3 percent, respectively. In addition, twice as many White students at South County (57 percent) and North City Tech (65 percent) expressed a strong attachment to their ethnic group than White students at North Village (29 percent) and South City Honors (33 percent). Also, more than a third more White students at South County (80 percent) and North City Tech (86 percent) expressed feeling "good about their ethnic or cultural background" than students at either North Village (62 percent) or South City Honors (60 percent). In sum, White students at South County and North City Tech reported great pride and attachment to either their white or

Table 5.1 Feelings about ethnic identity and group attachment, by school, region, and race/ethnicity, percentage who agree (N = )

| | North Capital City | | | | | | | | South Capital City | | | | | | | |
| | North City Tech | | | | North Village Prep | | | | South City Honors | | | | South County Prep | | | |
| Item | Asian (48) | Black (59) | Latino (65) | White (37) | Asian (26) | Black (33) | Latino (25) | White (58) | Asian | Black (67) | Latino | White (30) | Asian | Black (103) | Latino | White (81) |
|---|---|---|---|---|---|---|---|---|---|---|---|---|---|---|---|---|
| I feel good about my ethnic or cultural background. | 81 | 86 | 87 | 86 | 76** | 70** | 84*** | 62 | | 82** | | 60 | | 74 | | 80 |
| I feel a strong attachment toward my own ethnic group. | 65 | 76 | 74 | 65 | 56** | 58** | 72*** | 29 | | 72** | | 33 | | 73* | | 57 |
| I have a lot of pride in my ethnic group. | 77 | 82 | 82 | 84 | 65*** | 73*** | 88*** | 40 | | 88*** | | 35 | | 86*** | | 56 |
| I understand pretty well what my ethnic group membership means to me. | 69 | 84 | 77 | 71 | 62 | 75** | 92*** | 48 | | 85*** | | 50 | | 77** | | 64 |
| I have a strong sense of belonging to my own ethnic group. | 73 | 82 | 80 | 70 | 58** | 63** | 88*** | 35 | | 81** | | 50 | | 67 | | 73 |
| I am happy that I am a member of the group I belong to. | 75 | 87 | 91 | 87 | 85 | 76 | 96*** | 71 | | 93** | | 67 | | 80 | | 86 |

Continued

## Table 5.1 (Continued)

| Item | North Capital City | | | | | | | | South Capital City | | | |
| --- | --- | --- | --- | --- | --- | --- | --- | --- | --- | --- | --- | --- |
| | North City Tech | | | | North Village Prep | | | | South City Honors | | South County Prep | |
| | Asian (48) | Black (59) | Latino (65) | White (37) | Asian (26) | Black (33) | Latino (25) | White (58) | Black (67) | White (30) | Black (103) | White (81) |
| I have a clear sense of my ethnic background and what it means to me. | 83 | 88 | 85 | 84 | 58 | 76** | 92** | 59 | 80** | 67 | 76 | 69 |
| Members of my ethnic group should show their loyalty by hanging out with other members of our group. | 21 | 18 | 9* | 16 | 15 | 6 | 4 | 2 | 6 | 3 | 18 | 15 |
| Members of my ethnic group should only date members within our group. | 8 | 7 | 11 | 16 | 0 | 0 | 4 | 2 | 1 | 3 | 11*** | 33 |
| Students in my ethnic group should attend schools where the majority of students are like them. | 4 | 8 | 9 | 8 | 0 | 6 | 0 | 3 | 6 | 3 | 29 | 16 |
| Schools where my ethnic group is in the majority should have teachers and administrators from my group. | 10 | 32 | 17 | 5 | 8 | 12 | 16 | 3 | 19 | 3 | 27** | 12 |

White and non-White comparisons: ***$p <= .00$, **$p < .05$, *$p < .10$

ethnic identities, and the differences between White students at these two schools were statistically greater and significant than those White students at the two other schools.

What sets these two schools apart from one another, however, is how the White students in each responded differently to questions that indicated something about the symbolic boundaries that they maintained. Students at South County High, a large, conservative, comprehensive high school, which is proud of its southern history steeped in the Confederacy, showed the strongest and most palpable evidence of racial boundaries behind its school walls. A main indicator of the links between the school's organizational-racial habitus and the (re)production of social and symbolic boundaries is the difference between survey results at South County Prep and those of White and Black students at its sister school in the study, South City Honors, a majority-black school not very far away.

One-third of the White students surveyed at South County believed that White students should only date only White students, signifying a symbolic boundary they constructed around intimate relationships and romance. Nearly another third of White students reported that they neither agreed nor disagreed, while the remainder disagreed. The percentage of agreement among White students at South County Prep was ten times that of White students attending both South City Honors (their local majority-minority school counterpart) and North Village Prep (their northern white-dominant school counterpart), and more than double than that of those White students attending North City Tech. Even within South County Prep, White students were three times as likely to disagree with interracial dating as their Black schoolmates (11 percent) were.

Similar patterns hold for beliefs about which students should attend their schools. When asked to respond to the statement, "Students in my ethnic group should attend schools where the majority of students are like them," nearly two in ten students at South County (16 percent) agreed, compared to only 8 percent, 3 percent, and 3 percent at North City Tech, North Village Prep, and South City Honors, respectively.[12] A similar pattern was found among White students' responses at each school regarding their agreement to the statement that the majority of teachers and administrators at their schools should share their ethnoracial identity. White students at South County Prep were four times more likely to agree than White students at South City Honors and North Village Prep and more than twice as likely as those at North City Tech.

The racial habitus of South County Prep is implicated in the survey results. Both White and Black students there showed the most striking notes of the political salience of boundaries through the construction of "whiteness" and "blackness." A significant number of Black students attending majority-white South County Prep, where only three Black teachers worked, made a statement; more than a quarter of them believed that more students and educators from their respective ethnic groups should be in their school.

In contrast, the symbolic boundaries for White students at North City Tech, an urban, exam school attended by a critical mass of immigrant and working-class students, appeared very differently than those at South County Prep. Students there relied on cultural differentiation and tended to identify in ethnic European-American terms, demonstrating the degree of connection they had to their ethnic cultures—whether they were either what sociologist Herbert Gans has referred to as "symbolic" or real ethnicity.[13] Unlike White students at the other schools, nearly half of the students at North City Tech reported an ethnic identity such as "Albanian," "Bosnian," "Greek," or "Italian," among others. Their self-reported identities suggested that their ethnic cultures, signified through languages, traditions, and other conventional cultural practices, had not become as diluted for these students as their peers, whose ancestors had been in the United States for many generations. At the same time, North City Tech White students' attitudes did not appear to engender exclusion or taste for a shared identity steeped in historical privilege and subordination of others, as their survey responses attest. As the group of students who reported the highest levels of cultural flexibility, than other White students, in the study, their strong ethnic affinity did not appear to inhibit their exchanges across different social and cultural lines with their fellow North City Tech students.

## Let the Past Be the Past: We Didn't Have Anything to Do with It

That's the only, like, I would have to say real problem, is just that they [Blacks], I think that like we owe them something, and it's like, okay, almost like your great, great father. Oh my gosh, it was like your great, great, great, great, great grandfather. Honestly. We're past that, but they [Blacks] still bring up. It's kind of ridiculous. I was like we were slaves first in Egypt, and we did it, so... (Susan, eleventh-grade White female, South County High)

Sixteen-year-old Susan made these comments in a group of peers, all White, expressing what she believed was one of the thickest symbolic boundaries between the black minority and white majority of students at South County High School. African Americans, Susan believed, still felt that they were owed reparations from Whites because of the legacy of slavery. And further, her peers were not the ones to create this injustice; their grandparents several times removed, in Susan's opinion, were. She could not understand why African Americans had simply not shaken off the mental shackles of slavery and moved forward. After all, her ancestors had, and she reached far back into the vestiges of human history to the Hebrews' toiling in labor in Egypt (a biblical reference, no doubt) to show how "her" people had overcome their difficulties. Susan's commentary reflects an early onset of "racial fatigue,"[14] a frustration and impatience with the residual distrust and collective storytelling of events in an era in which she was not even born. Susan was not alone. The staff of South County High implicitly supported Susan's position. As a whole, the school did little to observe the Martin Luther King holiday in January, for example; instead, they observed Heritage Day, celebrating General Robert E. Lee's birthday.

An ocean and a continent away, Jason, a White male who has gained a green jacket, a sign of many academic and extracurricular honors earned at Williston High school, struck a similar tone to Susan's. His historical timeline was not as long, yet the onset of racial fatigue was evident. It had been fourteen years in South Africa since rigid state-mandated racial separatism was the law. Still, Jason said the following when I asked him and a group of matrics what they would do if they were policy makers given the task to redress the economic legacy of apartheid:

> What I'd do is…not necessarily forget about [it], but stop teaching it in schools. I know that from grade one, we get apartheid this and that—every single year, every single year. Just enforcing it, just enforcing it…And the thing is that I feel that's, you know, there isn't racism as such between the people now, the youth today, like our generation because we haven't had that sort of thing. The only reason that it's there is because they keep on teaching it in schools, and this is what happens…this is what the White people…this is the Black people. I really think that's it's…If you think that, you should stop teaching that and teach a new thing of harmony and equality and not reliving the past the entire time. With BEE [the Black Economic Empowerment policy],[15] the thing is that the majority of the people that have benefited are the people that were already the rich Black people before; and they've become richer and what are they doing to the

other Black people that are still in townships and things like that? It's
not the White people that are doing it anymore. It's the people that are
greedy and things like that... Because you know they put Black people in there who don't know what they're doing and the thing is, it's
not... not... uh... a racist thing.

Jason did not believe that maintaining a collective memory and teaching
about South Africa's apartheid past was necessary. Furthermore, he felt that
the South African government's attempt to redress economic inequality
with a redistributive affirmative action policy that encouraged corporations
and businesses to either subcontract to or hire nonwhite companies and
individuals was only benefitting the African middle class; similar arguments
have been made in the United States in opposition to affirmative action—
the idea that it has failed to reach the economically lowest segments of
black society. In the estimation of Jason, a South African, and Susan, an
American—both White youth who have not lived the with de jure forms of
racial discrimination, the proverbial social playing field has been leveled.

Students in both the United States and South Africa exhibit paradoxical, attitudinal value-behavior "stretches."[16] On the one hand, many agree
that inequality and segregation are not healthy social phenomena. On the
other hand, many care to do little to ameliorate these problems or to consider
"hitching the framing of these issues to the past." "Why am I supposed to feel
some guilt, or be responsible for what happened in the past" some asked—
something that I have occasionally heard in my university classrooms, too,
from students in response to articles by scholars about historical accumulated
disadvantage and the "education debt"[17] or historic and state-mandated forms
of "affirmative action" that benefited Whites in the post–World War II era.[18]

Whereas many White youths articulate a common humanity with
their non-White peers, there exists quite a bit of psychic dissonance when
it comes to thinking about and acting concretely in terms of policies and
practices that would enable their peers to have access to either the same
or similar resources to which they feel they are rightfully entitled. There
is a disjuncture between attitudes and behaviors—a paradox—that we
observed repeatedly throughout discussions in both the United States and
South Africa, as the data have shown. This disjuncture between attitudes
and behavior is consistent with a similar paradox described by sociologist
Roslyn Mickelson who observed that students hold positive "abstract" attitudes toward education even if their behavior contradicts their attitudinal
embrace of education.[19]

## White Youth Emulate White Adults

I began to wonder if the transmission of ideas like the ones uttered by students earlier were being transmitted both explicitly and implicitly through the commentary of the school's leadership. On my last day of visits at Williston, I asked Caryn Billups what her future plans were, and she said that she would retire within two years; by that time she would be sixty. Knowing that she had worked with the same deputy principals for at least the seven years during which I had been visiting, I asked if one of them would move into her place. "Well, most likely they will put in a Black," she remarked. "I mean after all the school is becoming more Black, and even if we recommend our first, second, or third choice, they can override that decision. The funny thing is that the Black learners come here because we have a White principal. They know that we work hard and that we have discipline. With a Black, they won't get that."

And perhaps, one of the last vestiges of apartheid schooling in contemporary South Africa is the lack of diversification of the teaching staff in the former white-only schools, the ex-Model C's. Curious about why I rarely saw Black, Coloured, or Indian educators teaching in the former white schools, I asked Principal Billups the question. "Black teachers are lazy," she responded. "Plus, why would they come to our schools and be expected to work harder when they can get the same salary teaching in the townships for doing less work?" she continued.

Several things struck me about Principal Billups's comments that day as we sat over lunch: first, I wondered how Black teachers and principals would be any less dedicated than their White counterparts to the (mainly middle-class) Black and Coloured students, who in many instances constitute the majority in the ex-Model C's. Second, I was struck by how similar the stereotypical discourse about native South African Blacks was to African Americans. Third, it did not escape me how comfortable Principal Billups felt again making impertinent remarks about Blacks to me, an easily identifiable Black woman. Insulted but trained to maintain a neutral researcher's face, I remarked, "You know, that's the same thing that they say about African Americans in the U.S." Principal Billups retorted, "But oh, African Americans are so *clever*, not like South African Blacks. Look at what they have accomplished over time." It is both ironic and enlightening sociologically, though disheartening too, how one nation's deeply stigmatized group (African Americans) is accorded a significantly higher social status in another society, where the economically or socially dominant group (Whites) considers others of the same racial category in their national context (Black South Africans) subordinate.[20] In that moment, my higher social status as an African American in South Africa had even accorded me the "backstage" experience of being told without reservation that Black teachers and principals in South Africa were lazy.

Principal Billups is partially correct that South African teachers are generally paid on the same pay scale; salary scales for teachers have (in theory) been nationally standardized based on qualifications since the 1990s. Yet, Black teachers, on average, still earned less at that time than white teachers, given significant differences in credentials because of apartheid-based inequalities during their training years. Plus, as Mrs. Billups divulged to me, the governing bodies of ex-Model C schools like Williston tend to subsidize their teacher salaries with revenue that they generate from their substantially higher fees, as compared to those of township schools. Still, she believed that there was little incentive for Black teachers to move from the comforts of their own communities, as well as the convenience of their schools' geographical location, to teach in schools where they would likely be in the minority and experience social distance.

Mrs. Billups confirmed what Mr. Ephram Mguni, a Zimbabwean, one of the three Black teachers at Coast City's Palmer High, had already told me: Black teachers were believed to be averse to the fraught interracial dynamics that they perceived would breed between Black and White teachers at the former white-only schools. In the mean time, White teachers might stumble along in their limited cultural knowledge of many of their students of color. Running to attend a class of one of the students whom I was shadowing at Williston, I encountered an incident between Mrs. Frances Hall, who was standing in the door of her classroom, and Thabo, a Black male learner. Mrs. Hall was reprimanding Thabo for a misdoing, and Thabo kept his eyes averted and head down. His body language further incensed Mrs. Hall, but unbeknownst to her, children in Thabo's Zulu culture were taught to be deferent to their elders by not looking them in the eye when spoken to with authority. Thabo received a demerit for his transgressions, and the severity of his punishment was further compounded by his teacher's lack of cultural awareness. I heard about what little the teachers knew about their students' cultural differences later in the school quarter, while sitting in a Zulu language workshop with a few of the teachers and Principal Billups. They had decided that they were unfamiliar enough with their student clientele, that it would be worth it to learn a few Zulu phrases. Yet, I could only wonder if, had some of the teachers from Thabo's background—the heritage of the majority of Williston's students—worked at the school and engaged in pedagogic and cultural exchanges with their White colleagues, would the outcomes be substantially different.

South Africa's challenge with trying to change many White youths' and adults' thinking about the out-group in schools may depend on how the country manages its fears of experiencing economic competition and job unemployment for the first time, as well as Blacks being in charge of high-status job positions. In a black-majority country, it might be obvious why many Blacks would suddenly acquire economic and political power, but if White learners in schools view it as a form of discrimination and reverse racism, then the framing of these social policies, by educators, parents, and the media, may impede critical discussions about the alleviation of racial inequality in the country. Today, many non-Black youth and adults in South Africa do not perceive themselves as having to compete equally; they are the underdogs now, and there is much discussion about race and incompetence in the schools.

In *Knowledge of the Blood*, South African scholar and current vice-chancellor at the University of the Free State, Jonathan Jansen has documented how White South African youth arrive at university, in this case the prestigious University of Pretoria, under the influence of direct and indirect "knowledge" that they have gathered from the critical adults in their lives. In riveting detail, Jansen recounts story after story about his exchanges with White university students who believe and think very much like the student Megan and Principal Billups—maintaining strongly negative stereotypes and beliefs about their Black compatriots, perceiving them as criminals, intellectually inferior, and sometimes unworthy of acknowledgment in public even when they know the person.[21]

Fear of the other and fear of loss of status position[22] undergird and characterize a significant amount of contemporary race relations in South Africa. Sociologist Graziella da Silva has found that Black South African professionals are likely to attribute contemporary racism in South Africa to just that—to the realm of the nonrational—to ignorance and fear emerging from a separatist history through which apartheid's beneficiaries were indoctrinated and taught to believe in the superiority of their own kind.[23] Like Jansen, I learned early on that many of the ideas about the "other," particularly about Black South Africans, persist among the first generation of "postapartheid babies." As two White male students taking part in a mixed-race group interview of boys at Palmer High School told me, racism had been "imprinted" in them:

**ROBERT**: Racism, you just can't get rid of it. It's still here. We're only ten years out of democracy. You can't just expect, hey, apartheid's finished, let's all forget what's just happened for the last sixty, seventy years. So many people have died to bring this country to freedom; let's just forget about it. You can't say that.

**NICHOLAS**: That's where racism still plays a big issue in this country… [Say] this guy, say he's Black, or say he's White; a White person will choose a White person. Say there are twenty-five Black people and five White people, he'll choose a White person. It's just—he might not be racist. Look, everyone's prejudiced; everyone's got their own form of prejudice. Everyone. It's just part of us; we've just grown up with it and it's become imprinted in us. Some people are more prejudiced than others, but that's just the case. You know, this guy who's choosing the suitable person for the job might not be a racist, but it's just that blood is thicker than water. He might think, oh, this is my race; I'll just take some of it. That's where racism unfortunately still plays a big issue.

Candidly, Robert and Nicholas spoke about their perceptions of the racial reality of their society, and consequently, their daily behaviors, at that time a decade after democracy had developed in South Africa. While the degrees of racial prejudice varied, according to them, the historical legacy for this first-generation in school after the end of apartheid is the racial socialization inculcated that compels them to prefer to hire others who share their racial identity and to acknowledge and deal with the institutionalized practices inherited from their parents. Falling back on a biological notion of race, Nicholas declared that "blood is thicker than water," meaning that preferences for in-group racial members would necessarily be stronger than those for out-group racial members.

Nicholas and Robert are not unlike the hundreds of White South African youth whom Jonathan Jansen describes in his book, students whose racial frames have been passed down from their parents, the progeny of apartheid. When he was the dean of education at the University of Pretoria, Jansen faced a continual barrage of racial stereotyping and interracial conflict between White and Black university students, often living among each other for the very first time in their lives. In pondering the enduring theme of the belief that "blood" is thicker than water , Jansen offers a remedy of what he calls "postconflict pedagogy." Postconflict pedagogy incorporates an approach of respectful disagreement and transformational thinking through an empathetic understanding of how racial actors like Megan, Principal Billups, and the Indian student Vijay have come to learn their places in society. Postconflict theory, Jansen maintains, does not take sides, but rather, this seemingly postmodern approach acknowledges that "all knowledge is partial" and that the bearers of received knowledge do not come with one story about the past, a common understanding of the present, and a shared vision of the future.[24]

Whether postconflict pedagogy is effective remains an empirical question. First, we must educate teachers about it and then utilize well-designed intervention studies to test whether it works. What we do know, nonetheless, is that in spite of the massive rewriting of history textbooks and curricula for postapartheid South African schools, in addition to the multitude of laws and educational policy changes that have occurred since the mid-1990s to allow access to better school resource contexts for historically disadvantaged students, changes in the white minority's racial attitudes are slow to follow. In other words, material changes have been necessary albeit insufficient for changes in the meanings of race and shared South African identity. These findings, like Jansen's, beg for more focus on the sociocultural realm of schooling, the substance and context of social relations in schools to which policy makers and educators have paid little attention.

Another striking aspect of the sentiment of letting the past be the past is the underlying threat of allowing history to repeat itself if both educators and students are not encouraged to remember and comprehend what has transpired. A critical aspect of Jason's (South Africa) and Susan's (United States) views is that they reflect a wide and palpable social and cultural divide among racial groups in these schools. On the surface, learners and even educators claim that students get along—although they sit separately in cafeterias and outside in the school plazas. In comparison, their parents yelled at one another across picket lines and barricades as schools desegregated in the United States or protested loudly at rallies and marched the streets to protest the inequalities of township schooling in South Africa. Jason and Susan share school spaces with non-White schoolmates, passing each other in the hallways, sitting in close proximity in a science or history class, and even holding up the mantle of school pride as they compete and represent their respective schools in athletic events. Yet, some of the discontent that we heard and interactions and that we witnessed from the "other side," from African and Coloured and Black and Latino students in these two nations, contradict the claim that students get along cross-racially.

## White is a Minority, Too

The experiences of White students in schools vary just as much as it does for other groups of students.[25] Pamela Perry, for example, found that the contours of whiteness may appear differently in a majority-white school than it does in a school where Whites are in the minority. In the former, white identity in the United States becomes coterminous and is tacitly understood to be the same as "American" and "middle class." In the latter, students are more likely to view themselves as racial and cultural beings, drawing contours around indicators such as dress, speech styles, and musical tastes to distinguish themselves from other racial groups in the school and even to maintain a stronger awareness of inequality, discrimination, and racial privilege.[26]

When White youth are the numerical minority in American public high schools, they can face social and cultural challenges just as American minority students do. Athena, an eleventh-grade White student who attended multiracial and multiethnic North City Tech in North Capital City, exemplified the anxiety caused by this experience. She did not like her school because of her "minority" experience. When an interviewer asked Athena and another student their likes and dislikes about their school, Athena, frowning and wearing a look of disgust, immediately responded that she did not like North City Tech. Carla, the graduate student interviewer, asked why, and Athena said that she wished it were "more diverse." For Athena, North City Tech felt more like a "jail cell" than a high school. Ironically, it is one of the most racially and ethnically diverse schools in the entire metro area of North Capital City. We learned as the conversation continued, however, that Athena really wished her high school were whiter. She explained that she wished the racial makeup was "more spread out"—that she would prefer not to be one of only "a few White people".

Athena said that as a White person, she was constantly made to feel "inferior," and she used this word repeatedly throughout the conversation and throughout the day that Carla shadowed her from class to class. Sometimes kids made her feel "inferior," and at other times teachers did. On the point of the students, she described how once in the girls' bathroom, an African American girl said to her, "Wow, a White girl who can actually dress!" Athena was offended by the couched compliment and implicit stereotype made by this Black schoolmate that White girls cannot dress stylishly (according to whatever adolescent-style barometer the student had in mind).

Athena's complaints moved then from the clothing comment to her government class, as she described Mr. Alexander Fine's class and the ways in which his AP government class made her feel inferior, like a "racist White person . . . like I'm in the KKK or something!" Athena felt that Mr. Fine was teaching an African American history course rather than a U.S. government course, that he "forced" the topic of race into any and every subject they covered, and that he overdid it. As one of two White students in the class, Athena felt like the spotlight was on her—a representative of her race—and that the consistent focus on the history and sociology of people of color made her feel like she doesn't matter—"inferior." Halla, an Egyptian girl sitting with Carla and Athena, interjected that she did not find anything wrong with Mr. Fine's teaching, but that if it were making Athena uncomfortable, she should say something. Athena went on for a good while during that conversation about Mr. Fine's class and how she feared that she was completely underprepared for the AP exam, which is not an exam on African American history.

Strikingly, Athena was experiencing the angst that multitudes of students of color face daily in their schools—invisible, perceived as representatives of their race, and unsure about what the content of the curricula in their classes have to do with their own social, historical, and material realities. She believed that Mr. Fine's racial habitus influenced greatly his approach to epistemology, about what is knowledge. Her AP history teacher defied Athena's conventional notions of what is "real" history. Mainstream American history, as multiculturalists have noted often,[27] thoroughly decenters the historical realities of peoples of color to the extent that when these perspectives are folded into the curriculum, they are often qualified by modifiers such as "African American" or "Chicano/Chicana" history and not simply U.S. history. Meanwhile, by bringing in those histories away from the margins and centering them during his teaching, Mr. Fine challenged Athena's sense of what "American" history is. Consequently, she feared that she would not be prepared for her AP history exam.

Athena could very well be an outlier case at North City Tech; only a mere 8 percent of White students at the school believed that students of their ethnic/racial group should attend schools where they were in the majority. Although Athena experienced some angst as the minority in school, other White students like Anthony, who also attended North City Tech, can have very rich experiences that the average U.S. White public school student does not have—experiences that can broaden their thinking and expand their social and cultural horizons. Anthony, introduced earlier, was glad to be at North City Tech because his cultural tastes had broadened, and he also learned why referring to his Asian peers as "Oriental" was problematic.

## In Their Footsteps: When Extraschool Forces
## Undermine What Schools Do

South City Honors, North City Tech's southern majority-minority high school counterpart, was an all-white high school until the late 1970s. It had not been immune to "white flight" into private and surrounding county district schools after school desegregation occurred. Still, a steady mass of Whites continued to attend it—noteworthy for decades for its strong academic programs, even in its incarnation as a predominantly African American high school. Administrators, teachers, and students understood that the school's historic reputation and consistent production of strong test results kept some White families (even those of some faculty at a nearby prestigious liberal arts college) invested in the school. Nevertheless, students believed that sanctions could ensue for too much racial mixing in South Capital City. Adam, a White senior at South City Honors, discussed at length his interpretation of a situation in which he believed that he was penalized for socializing intimately across racial lines:

> I was talking to [the coach at the local college] and everything was going good...we were emailing back and forth. He's just like, "I'm going to have you come by Monday, Tuesday or Wednesday to sign for your scholarship." And that Monday I was out with my girlfriend who happens to be Black, and it just so happened we was at the mall, and he happened to be there. We were at this little booth or whatever and he was like, "Hey, you!" You know, he called me over, and I came over, and I talked to him and he introduced me to his...I don't know if it was his wife or girlfriend at the time. I was like, "Hold on just a second. I want to introduce you to my girlfriend," and she walked over...he just...there was this look on his face like "I can't believe what you're"...you know, that I was dating a Black girl, you know? And he never called me...for that Tuesday or Wednesday, he never called me back. He hasn't said word to me since then, and he ended up signing my friend; and not that I'm not glad my friend got a scholar-ship and that. It's just that I know that I was better than my friend in that aspect and I really do believe that that is the reason that he didn't [call]...

Adam believed that he was a better soccer player than his friend:

> [My friend is] another White guy from [a nearby suburb] and...and we were playing soccer pretty much the same amount of years, but

I just naturally was a little…you know, a little better than him…I was just a little faster. I had a little bit better touch. You know, I just read the game a little bit more.

Adam could only reason that the coach's failure to follow up on a promise to recruit him was because he introduced the coach to a girlfriend "who happens to be Black." Along with schoolmates Fred (White male) and Jeremy (Black male), Adam described how racial dynamics of the region, families, and communities countervailed what flexibility in social boundary crossing the school environment enabled:

**FRED:** At South City Honors for…(pause) you know, people tend to disperse to who they're more related to; and I guess being White and the minority (laughs)…is, I don't know…I guess you can relate maybe a little…easier to White people and it's kind of easier to get along with them but…uh…and it's kind of how it is but…uh…I mean, everyone is cool. Everyone is generous, you know, they're good people and it's…it's kind of like a school friendship, but away from school you don't really keep the same friendships…

**JEREMY:** It's harder for some people to accept you outside of school. I can say, "What's up?" and hang out with you in the lunch room but, you know, I can't go out on the weekends with you or something like that.

**ADAM:** Yeah. Their parents might not be comfortable with you coming over their house or whatever. It's just…it's just there. I mean, and that's still the way it is here because there's still a little bit of racism.

**FRED:** Really. I don't know. South City Honors doesn't have too much…

**ADAM (INTERJECTS):** Yeah. South City Honors doesn't but, you know, outside is what I'm saying.

According to a report by Gary Orfield and Chungmei Lei of the Civil Rights Project, most White students, except in the South and Southwest, have little contact with minority students.[28] Thus, White students at South City Honors and North City Tech are the exceptions. And they informed us how they negotiated their relationships with their Asian, Black, and Latino peers. At least for them, intergroup relations at school appeared to achieve some of the social goals of the Brown decision. However, those like Adam and Fred also understood how macrosocial relations may negate what advancement in interracial relations they made in school once they left for home at the end of the day. They mentioned explicitly how the attitudes and practices of some critical adults in their lives—parents, coaches, and others—could countervail any diminishing or blurring of boundaries that occurred at school.

Some of their South African peers at Palmer High School agreed that parents, especially, could be a problem. In my conversation with the same group of Diversity Trippers introduced earlier, several students shared some of the familial challenges they experienced:

**ASHTON**: I don't know about the rest of you but...your parents...
**DANIELLE**: Because they grew up with that. They grew up with apartheid.
**PRUDENCE**: So you had a difficult time with your parents?
**ASHTON**: It was a very difficult time—I mean, I don't want to exaggerate but, I mean, your parents are of that generation where they have been...by these things and they make comments like, I don't necessarily agree with that, and they sort of brush you aside because that child/adult relationship is difficult.
**ALICE**: And they've got more reason to say that because...because if she's Black or whatever, "It's oh, because she's Black." I mean, my father, even my father will always sit there and make some comment about any politician, anyone in government, anyone. "No, it's because they're Black." And I just sit there and I say, "Dad, it's got nothing to do with that. They wouldn't be there if they weren't meant to be there."

Alice, Danielle, and Ashton made it clear that while the changes in their attitudes were influenced by certain school practices that promoted the weakening of social boundaries, they could not escape the historical, divisive racial attitudes that permeate their family lives and communities. Even as a decade of a racial democracy had made some inroads on the mindset and worldviews of some of Palmer High School's youth, the apartheid generations—their parents and grandparents—still struggled with evolution of the society.

## Concluding Thoughts

In both the United States and South Africa, White students and educators like their counterparts in other racial groups are generally the products of their social environments. These environments encompass deeply ingrained ideological, moral, and racial views that shape their behaviors about how to include out-group members not only into the elite academic, economic, and political realms but also into their personal lives. As a researcher, I have sometimes found it distressful to have to choose where to sit among racially (and ethnically) segregated lunch tables in school cafeterias that I have visited. With Whites here, Asian students next to Whites, and Latinos not far from the Black students who are over there, I have learned the lunchroom's physical geography by its social layout in these mixed-race schools. These observations necessarily beg the question: Are we teaching our youth to accept racial segregation as a natural part of the human condition? Further, are some of our schools worse off than others in transmitting these messages?

Some schools and their leadership are in a position to uproot the weeds of inequality and exclusivity by being vigilant about where they sprout. Others have taken a "laissez faire" or a hands-off approach. At the same time, the work that schools may do to cultivate equitable relations among students and between groups can be undermined by what happens in families and communities. Any wall that separates a school from its community is an illusion, after all.

Issues of equity are invariably linked to issues of fairness and the distribution of resources. And one of the greatest challenges to modern democracies like the United States and South Africa is the limited ability to redress the past without offending the sensibilities and inciting senses of fear, threat, and anxiety in either their economically dominant or higher status populations. Thomas Labelle argued years ago that the implicit goals of desegregation in the United States and South Africa, first, were to persuade or to compel subordinate group members to adapt to the cultural and structural interests of one or more of a society's dominant groups; and second, to limit the dominant group's own need for protecting the status quo.[29] Labelle reasoned that dominant groups are likely to permit school programs to reflect greater social rather than structural diversity as long as the existing social structure and balance of power among groups are not threatened.

Herbert Blumer's seminal argument about race prejudice as a function of *group* (as opposed to individual) position is also a key one to draw on here. Blumer argued that there are four basic types of feelings that are present in group prejudice: 1) a feeling of superiority, 2) a feeling that the subordinate group is intrinsically different and alien, 3) a feeling of proprietary claim to certain areas of privilege and advantage, and 4) a fear or suspicion that the subordinate group harbors designs on what are perceived as the prerogatives of the dominant group. Blumer acknowledged that members of the dominant group could vary in their individual orientations toward subordinate groups, from being exclusionary, hard, and callous to open, benign, and polite. The sense of *group* position and perceptions of "what ought to be" that dominant group members subscribe to is what is critical to Blumer's framework. Perceived threats to that sense of position can activate collective racial prejudice or even what others refer to as "racial antipathy"—indifference to racial and ethnic inequality or issues of equity.[30]

Sociologists Nina Eliasoph and Paul Lichterman have written that people do not believe things should change unless they view them as a problem. Namely, the situation must affect them personally before it is really viewed as something potentially harmful.[31] Although it is commonly found that White students are not hurt academically by desegregation or the adjustments in the racial composition of schools, researchers have yet to point to significant academic gains for Whites attending multiracial schools.[32] Social gains are different. How do students come to embrace and respect their fellow schoolmates if fear and apprehension about the other's social group is firmly planted in their consciousness?

Feelings of group threat are a particular mechanism that can undermine both access and the expansion of opportunity structures and the spanning of boundaries.[33] Feelings of group threat are sustained by symbolic boundaries. Those who harbor either fears of the racial "other" or racial antipathy are likely to show the least amount of flexibility when it comes to issues of equity in schooling and in social relations. And if cultural flexibility is a moderating factor in diminishing social and symbolic boundaries and school inequities, then these findings have critical implications for the reproduction of power, privilege, and inequality.

# 6

## Equity and Empathy

GROWING EQUALITY OF OPPORTUNITY

*What does equality of educational opportunity mean?*
*Does it mean the same opportunity to get an education?*
*Or does it mean an opportunity to get the same education?*
*Or opportunity to be educated up to the level of one's capa-*
*bilities and future occupational prospects? Or opportunity*
*to learn whatever one needs to develop one's own pecu-*
*liar potentialities?... Is only racially integrated education*
*equal, irrespective of whether lack of integration is inten-*
*tional or accidental? Is equality of educational opportunity*
*a moral as well as a mathematical concept?*[1]

JUDAH HENDERSON OF North Village Prep, introduced in the opening of this book, declared one afternoon, "If [our society] wants to rid itself of the achievement gap, it must first reduce the empathy gap." I am rarely shocked these days by the incisive comments and thoughts that our youth have to offer, but I must say that this is one that really stirred me up. Indeed, Judah may have hit the proverbial nail on its head. He understood that improvement in student learning and achievement goes beyond a dependence on whether the adequate teacher and facility inputs will improve test scores. He got that schooling is more than a testing factory where kids have to disavow their social experiences and the connections among history, family, neighborhoods, government social policies, resources, culture, politics, student engagement, and achievement. Even resource-rich schools like his need to attend to the reduction of the social and cultural distances among its various student clienteles if they want to diminish the academic achievement gap. Diverse, resource-rich schools are vital not only for bolstering achievement outcomes of historically disadvantaged or excluded students—that is, increased test scores, graduation and college-going rates—but also for promoting social cohesion in a democratic society.[2]

But then I heard later from an esteemed colleague, "People don't care anymore about school integration. They want choice." I admit that I winced at this comment, partly concerned that the sociologist was correct. Was school integration merely a fleeting policy ideal that used a civil rights frame to promise equal educational opportunities, and has it had its heyday as a possibility of transforming schooling in a democracy as other educational policy fads such as school choice have come along to "fix" the system? After all, many educational policy trends come and go with the changes of the political winds.

In the United States, the venerable goals of school integration advocates were to diminish the impact of accumulated disadvantages of the past. As one of the most critical educational practices of the twentieth-century, it was meant to offer better educational opportunities and to prepare historically disadvantaged groups with the human capital they needed for economic advancement in a modern capitalist economy. In the mid- and late twentieth century, White Americans began to favor integration, both residentially and educationally, in their attitudes.[3] However, as researchers have pursued the study of changes in racial attitudes over time, they have found that the levels of tolerance for increased racial interactions and proximity are so low that it would take much push and pressure to achieve both residential and school integration.[4] Historic battles brought by White American parent plaintiffs from Hartford, Connecticut, to Charlotte, North Carolina, to the heartlands of Detroit, Michigan, and Milwaukee, Wisconsin, to the Pacific Northwest city of Seattle, Washington, expose the limited tolerance for the amelioration of the educational conditions of the racial "other."

David Labaree has written provocatively that there exists a paradoxical relationship between the framing of education as a public good to promote democratic equality and citizenship and the framing of education as a private good or a vehicle for individual social mobility. In principle, both of these frames aim to expand access to education to all social groups, Labaree writes. The frame of education for democratic equality characterizes schooling as egalitarian. In contrast, classical neoliberal values for personal liberty, choice, and free markets and a meritocratic ideology—or the idea that opportunity should mainly be awarded to those who work the hardest and/or score the highest (which tends to ignore whether equal access to resources has even leveled the playing field across groups)—undergird the frame of education for social mobility. Labaree argues that these two frames overlap—educational opportunity and individual achievement, and they define core liberal educational politics. Yet, the individual-centered social mobility frame foments competition, credentialism, and an inability to view how the blind pursuit of educational degrees and status as means to an end (for example, jobs, careers, and wealth) breeds practices in schools and communities that reinforce social stratification and thus inequity.[5] That is, educational equity is an especially difficult state to attain in societies where liberal national values espouse individualism, competition, and a denial of how historic, discriminatory practices placed specific social groups in the economic and academic predicaments in which they currently find themselves.

At present in American society, the children of the middle and upper-middle class are so concentrated in resource-rich schools and compete against one another for selective college and university admissions that they dampen each other's probabilities of admission, becoming effectively small frogs in big ponds.[6] Meanwhile, their parents utilize "concerted cultivation"[7] and enroll them in numerous extracurricular activities to increase the odds that their child will excel significantly to maintain one-up on one another and to insure their admissibility to the finer schools. Parents want the best schools for their children. For the middle class, across the racial spectrum, that means little to no contact in the classroom with many low-income children of color are associated with low test scores and limited academic achievement. The establishment of "good" schools, as we know them conventionally, in stratified societies such as the United States and South Africa, is rarely a race- or class-neutral project.

Essentially, how school-communities either support or ignore issues of equity and inclusion of other social groups indicates something about their commitment to the advancement of the public good, to the progress of an enlightened democratic society, or to the idea of equality, in general.[8] Studies even show that when schools implement programs that do not compel either balkanization or assimilation among students, then social boundaries diminish.[9] A school's social and cultural environment can either facilitate students' (and educators') propensity to move across social lines, affiliate, and share common cultural frames of reference , or instead it can establish rules, codes, and other tools that reproduce certain levels of social distance and privilege for the dominant and disadvantages for the subordinate social groups. Many schools in the United States and South Africa are committed to equity for all of its students. They vary, however, in how they perceive themselves as practicing it. Their organizational-racial and -class habitus expose the extent to which what happens daily in them really engenders equity.

Understanding the difference between "desegregation" and "integration" offers additional insight into Judah's comment about the links between the achievement and empathy gaps. Although a number of desegregated school districts exist, which intentionally work to diversify their student populations, there exist significant groups of students who feel that the schools they attend do not even value them, let alone fully include them. "True integration in our schools…is transformative rather than assimilative. That is, while desegregation assimilates minorities into the mainstream, true integration transforms the mainstream," writes legal scholar john powell.[10] In other words, social relations are very different under desegregation—mixed-race schooling for the sake of proximity and exposure to certain educational resources—versus integration— the intercultural exchange among students of different social groups for both academic and nonacademic functions. Integration entails not only the reduction of resource disparities but also the cultivation of social cohesion through equitable practices, which would till the soils of a blossoming democracy.

To attain that type of school integration, I argue in this chapter that educators should consider ecological differences even *within* schools and be mindful of the degrees to which the *type*, *practice*, and *moral* tone of the policies and discourses in their schools indicate something about either their openness or closed-ness—something about their own organizational and cultural flexibility or lack thereof. By "openness" and "closed-ness," I mean the degree to which either the academic or social environment is accessible in material, political, social, or cultural terms to all participants or community members.

This chapter flows out of the analyses included in the previous chapters, and it posits a new typology based on the sociological lessons learned from this cross-national study of schools. Just as I discussed earlier, that schools comprise dual structures, the processes of school integration can be broken into two contexts, as well: the *resource* and the *sociocultural*. Overall, evidence from the eight school cases highlight at least three broad domains within each of these contexts: 1) the *form* or *type* of social organization that schools can develop for school integration, or deeper inclusion and academic incorporation of all groups of students, 2) the actual *practices* that ensue from educators' approaches to inclusion, and 3) the *moral* values underpinning the conversations and practices that officials engage to accomplish it.

Table 6.1 summarizes my arguments about the multiple dimensional aspects of the dual structures that would constitute school integration.

Table 6.1 Domains of inclusion in diverse schools

| Type | Material or resource Context | | Sociocultural context | |
|---|---|---|---|---|
| | Practice | Moral condition | Practice | Moral condition |
| Open | Full desegregation (spatial proximity) | Justice<br>Fairness<br>Equality/Equity | Integration<br>Radical inclusion<br>Radical egalitarianism | Sharing/Caring society<br>Egalitarian pluralism<br>Communitarian |
| Semiopen/ Semiclosed | Semidesegregation (tracking by race/class/ gender or other social status) | Mildly tolerant<br>Laissez-faire | Acculturation/Anglo-conformity<br>Cultural difference model<br>Symbolic multiculturalism | Tolerant<br>Liberalism<br>Free market competition<br>Rugged individualism |
| Closed | Segregation | Intolerant<br>Inegalitarian | Ethnic Separatism | Intolerant<br>Inequality<br>Inequitable distribution of resources |

It depicts a 2 × 2 × 3 table that outlines two events (practices and moral condition) for the two specific domains of integration (the "resource context" and the "sociocultural context"), which can fall along the three-point spectrum of boundary types ("open," "semiopen/closed," or "closed"). Let me state from the outset that the characteristics of the different dimensions of integrated schooling are "ideal types," which represent theoretical notions of what should occur in practice. The actual manifestation of the theoretical concept is never totally pure or exactly mirrors the intent of the object.[11] How would I apply this typology to the five desegregated schools in the study? And how do they compare across the two national contexts?

## Type

The "type" of integration in a school pertains to its degree of accessibility and its express purpose to create educational conditions where students of diverse social backgrounds learn with one another. Schools can be either "open," "closed," "semiopen" or "semiclosed" in their daily practices within both their material and sociocultural contexts. I do not have to say much about a "closed" school. While avowed segregationists, ethnocentrists, and separatists are still around, few national, state or provincial, or local educational officials, if any, would actively advocate for closed schooling, for complete separation of the races. That is unconstitutional in both the United States and South Africa. Although "open" can more broadly encompass specific conditions of *both* the material and sociocultural contexts of schools, over time, its application has primarily referred to the accessibility of the material context. This is where most researchers, policymakers, and proponents of school integration have focused mainly in trying to reduce educational inequality. From a resource standpoint, an "open" integrated school is one where students across all of these groups have roughly the same chances of access and opportunity to attend a school. The permeability of residential or school organizational boundaries, for instance, enables openness.

Conventionally in South Africa, the concept of "open" has denoted issues of access to more resourceful, formerly segregated white schools. " 'Open' simply means 'Ok, we won't resist and allow you here, but we won't mix with you,' " Jennifer Benson, Palmer's guidance counselor, explained. " 'Integrated,' on the other hand, signifies a willingness to be truly multicultural and diverse," she continued. Like powell, Jennifer refers to a tension that exists if we do not consider the conceptual and policy/practice distinctions between the spatial proximity of students of different social backgrounds (because the law mandates it) and the sociocultural context ("integrated," willingness to be *truly* multicultural and diverse). Indeed, a more holistic meaning of "open" would encompass the school's sociocultural climate. Thus, I appropriate the term and broaden its applicability to both the school's resource and sociocultural contexts. That is, an open, integrated school provides a strong probability that students of disparate backgrounds can attend a school—even if access is determined by lottery. In an open integrated school system, residential segregation does not dictate the socioeconomic profile of the school. Also, an open, integrated school supports academic, social, and cultural exchanges that neither scorn differences nor impose acculturation to the extent that it annihilates the identities and symbols of people-hood for nondominant groups. From a social and cultural standpoint, boundary crossing vis-à-vis efforts toward school desegregation have frequently signified assimilation in which historically disadvantaged students move from one school to another and embrace the school's cultural codes and mores without any real change to an existent racial and cultural hierarchy within it.[12] Open integrated schools, in contrast, would produce flexibility among students and educators to deal with academic and social conflicts in values, cultures, and perspectives.

## Practices

The everyday routines, manners, and ways of schooling needed to fully include many groups of students academically, socially, culturally, and politically constitute the "practices" of integration. Of the eight school case studies included in this study that would fall into the "open" category in terms of access to the resource context, North City Tech, a multiracial and multiethnic exam school in North Capital City, comprised mainly of working-class students, is the one that comes closest to this ideal type. The white and black student population at North City Tech nearly mirrors their proportions in the overall public school populations, while the percentages of Asian and Latino students are overrepresented and underrepresented, respectively. Nevertheless, each of these groups is respectably represented.

The school, nonetheless, is challenged ecologically by the low percentage of White families who refuse to send their children to the public schools in North Capital City's district. While more than half of the residents in the metropolitan area identify as "White," less than one-fifth (about 14 percent) of the students in the public schools are White. Other than will and choice, there are no structural reasons that would preclude these families from being more heavily represented at the school. Still, North City Tech is a very diverse school, composed of a student population where scores of different home languages are spoken, including Arabic, English, Spanish, French, Italian, and Russian, to name a few.

In terms of access and attendance, most of the other schools in the study would be characterized as either semiopen or semiclosed—the flip side of the same coin. The four white-dominant, multiracial schools in the study would fall into this category since access is primarily determined by either who and which groups live in the surrounding areas (South County High and North Village Prep in the United States), or which students' families can afford to pay the relatively expensive school fees in South Africa (Palmer and Williston High Schools). In the case of the U.S. schools, the doors are open to relatively small percentages of Black and Latino students via the forty-year-old VDP program at North Village Prep, while only one in five students are Black at South County Prep, whereas the Black population in the metropolitan area is over 40 percent. These schools are located within middle- and upper middle-class neighborhoods with low representations of racial minority families.

The mere existence of school desegregation as an educational practice is threatened at the moment in both the United States and South Africa. According to a report produced by Gary Orfield, codirector of the Civil Rights Project/Proyecto Derechos Civiles at the University of California, Los Angeles, African American and Latino students were more segregated in public schools by 2006 than they had been over the previous forty years. Moreover, nearly three out of five Black and Latino students attend schools where the average student is poor (using the proxy of eligibility for either free or reduced lunch), which, according to Orfield, creates a "double jeopardy" of the effects of race and class.[13] In comparison, a large percentage of South African youth attend intensely segregated schools, like Montjane, which are located in extremely racially homogeneous communities and poor townships and rural villages around the nation.[14]

In both countries, White families have fled from urban to either suburban and private communities or schools couched in terms of seeking "good schools" and out of a desire to maintain higher status and capital.[15] The problem in U.S. society, particularly, is that the feeble and uneven implementations of diverse schooling over the last fifty-five years appear to correspond more to social closure or exclusive racial and class boundaries than they do to these other values. While attitudes shifted greatly over the course of the twentieth century, so that the favor of racial integration became a normative value in the United States among White Americans, they are still least likely to attend racially mixed schools and to reside in integrated neighborhoods.[16] Likewise, the patterns of "white flight" from South African desegregated schools— already primarily a social and educational experience among lower-middle and middle-class South Africans—render racial distrust and racism as the primary culprits for the increasing failure of both of these societies to realize the goal of equality of opportunity through diverse schools. Consequently, a significant number of public school students in both nations attend conspicuously segregated schools, and according to my typology, these educational contexts would be labeled as "closed."

There is the popular saying, "Don't judge a book by its color," which is an appropriate metaphor to distinguish between how a school looks in terms of social composition and what is going on behind its walls to educate youth. Inside a school, the degree of its openness extends beyond which groups constitute its student population. Still, many wonder, reasonably so, why, when students of color and poor students move into well-resourced, white-dominant schools, those students still do not fare as well as their more affluent White (and sometimes affluent Asian) peers. Very likely, one answer pertains to how we believe that these various groups of students are nestled within similar *ecological* structures within education. The ecology of education encompasses multiple dimensions, and various levels of sociological forces exert influence on youths' over educational well-being.

Taking into account the multiple contexts that influence students' ability to learn, adapt, and fully engage in school means to take into account their lives inside and outside of school. Because of macrostructural factors such as racial segregation, past legalized and extant forms of unconstitutional discrimination, economic transformations such as the decline of U.S. central cities, joblessness, and class-linked out-migration from urban communities, the array of social contexts and resources available to students varies significantly across social groups. Consequently, they have ecologically dissimilar educational experiences. "Ecological dissimilarity," according to sociologists Robert Sampson and William Julius Wilson, indicates the degree to which the structural contexts of a social environment are vastly disparate by race and class.[17]

Sampson and Wilson's "ecological dissimilarity" concept is also useful when thinking about schools at an organizational level, when examining the forces and dynamics *within* the new resource context. For example, in the United States, ability grouping continues today as a dominant form of organizing students as families jockey for advantage in the college-access market.[18] Generally, racial and ethnic minority students are not found within the upper echelon courses at multiracial, white-majority schools. The converse pattern is rarely, if ever, found at multiracial, majority-minority schools. If anything, White students who are a minority will be overrepresented in such schools. Tracking, therefore, has begun to be referred to as a form of resegregation in the former schools because it has evolved into a type of semiclosed educational practice, frequently excluding on the basis of perceived ability by race or ethnicity.[19]

At North Village Prep, for example, none of the Black and Latino students in the school were enrolled in the advanced math and science classes (English and history were not tracked). Aware of this academic divide and comparing himself to the more privileged students at his school, Judah continued to expound on the boundaries between VDP and non-VDP students, commenting as follows: "[W]hen I got here, looking at kids my age who are taking trigonometry, and I'm here in geometry...I'm here in Algebra 2; I'm looking at kids who are in calculus; and I'm still here in Algebra 2, being where I'm supposed to be. And I feel like I have to catch up to them because if I don't, then thirty years down the line, who is going to be the clerk and who is going to be the one who is leading the company?"

A similar pattern held at South County Prep. Although our research team observed five African American students (out of 302 overall) in several advanced placement and honors courses there, generally, these were the same students across these classes. Mrs. Denise Spann, one of the three Black teachers at South County Prep, gave me her take on the issue of low black representation in the most advanced and demanding classes. I met Mrs. Spann in her first year at South County Prep, and she taught students communications skills. She had no plans to remain at South County Prep long because she was on the administrative track to become a principal. I attended one of her classes at the last period of the day and remained after school to talk to her. When I mentioned the low statistic of very few high achievers among the African American students, Mrs. Spann remarked, "There are many more smart students, but you should notice the color of the skin of those who get classified as 'smart.' You'll notice that some of the students because of the way they look will never get deemed as smart, even though they are quite competent and intelligent," she continued.

Mrs. Spann suggested that actual skin color plays a role. "Yes, Tonya is light. I haven't met Renee (the other African American girl deemed a high achiever) and perhaps, Benson is included because his father is so famous. Some of the kids don't fit the image that the staff prefers," Mrs. Spann claimed. Although Tonya, Renee, and Benson, the son of a local newscaster, would all be classified as light-skinned, the number of cases is too few to prove Mrs.

Spann's allegations. She confirmed, nonetheless, that very few Black students were mentioned as the prominent star pupils among an entire racial subgroup of students at South County Prep. In comparison, African American students at South City Honors, down the road from South County Prep, as well as at North City Tech, did not encounter so few black student models of high achievement.

Both South County Prep and North Village Prep maintained semiclosed practices of classroom organization by social groups. The placement of Black and Latino students into lower-track classes created ecologically dissimilar school experiences and led to uninviting perceptions about what classes would prepare them to fully realize their aspirations for college and professional lives beyond. These practices may also conveyed messages that are interpreted and symbolized as the turf of one racial/ethnic group or another's. From both parental and policy standpoints, tracking is a practice loaded with political tension, especially when it leads to internal friction among parents in schools, the flight of White and middle-class students, or if it adversely affects the pace of students with advanced academic abilities. Nevertheless, as tracked classes in desegregated schools are perceived as de facto ethnically and racially segregated spaces, many Black and Latino students, especially, may come to view the advanced placement, honors, and international baccalaureate classes as the ones for Asian and White students or the "smart kids."[20]

Tracking is also a practice found at majority-minority schools like South City Honors and North City Tech. Their school practices were not without their critics, either, especially among students who are not enrolled in those classes and experience a status competition between those students enrolled in the premier and in the regular, comprehensive high school courses. When we interviewed a group of African American girls at South City Honors, for example, we heard views about favoritism—which featured in at least three of our group interviews at this school— toward those in an elite academic program, APEX (Academic Performance of Excellence). Janeen remarked explicitly about her discontent:

> I get offended sometimes by some cliques. We have an APEX clique…APEX versus regular and honors. That's the biggest clique here. I used to be an APEX student and I understand…like we [are] better than them regular students. But, when you come to high school, it's some teachers that actually tell some APEX students, "You are above everybody else." It's still going on because it's some people in APEX that do tell you like, "We're better than y'all. Regular classes

suck." People don't understand. [W]e're on the same level, just about. Just about. I'm like, how can you say that? I think that's real mean. I take some regular classes, and I don't like it like that.

What I learned from students is that status differences can produce tensions among students with different academic identities, especially if little is done to defuse the messages about one group being "superior" to the other. An additional layer of competition, stereotyping, and potential denigration exists, nonetheless, when race and ethnicity become highly correlated with which students are considered the academic who's who and which are not. When educational practices produce patterns that either preclude or impede the full incorporation of specific groups into school, then those practices signify some form of closure, a semiclosed state of school integration.

Comparatively, educational practices in terms of student organization and curriculum vary between the United States and South Africa. While the United States system can be characterized more as "semiopen" or "semiclosed" (depending on from whose perspective) because of the racialized patterns of ability grouping in its mixed-race schools, South Africa's schools are required by law to practice a relatively more open form of student organization. Educational officials have been tinkering with the national curriculum since 1994 to create an open system and have implemented numerous policies to attempt to equalize opportunities for students across the country. In 2008, the first graduating class (those who were in grade eight when I first began this research) sat for the National Senior Certificate (NSC), the last implementation of policy regarding the restructuring of South African curriculum postapartheid, which began in 1998.[21] For the first time, the exam tested learners on an outcomes-based national curriculum rather than the exams developed individually by each province for previous graduating classes.

Educational researchers, other social scientists, and policy makers now await the long-term outcomes of this type of "open" academic environment in South African multiracial schools. What we do know is that national pass rates declined by nearly 3 percent in 2008, but the percentage of students who earned eligibility for university entrance increased by four percentage points. The results from the first NSC exam also indicated that the well-resourced schools like Williston and Palmer adapted to the new curriculum significantly better than the poorer schools, such as Groveland and Montjane.[22]

Although observations and research on the effects of tracking is virtually nonexistent in the body of South African educational research, American researchers have thoroughly evaluated how tracking and ability grouping correlate to racial and ethnic boundaries. The consequence, as some argue, is a closed opportunity structure *within* schools. [23] Such organizational practices may impede the school's ability to more fully incorporate different groups of learners. Further, the formation of an unambiguous hierarchy of the social and cultural meanings attached to these practices may neutralize the effects of resourceful schools as a conduit for equal educational opportunities.

## From Within: Is the School's Sociocultural Context Closed or Open?

Jennifer Benson described Palmer's early years, saying that even her own kids had issues with "opening" (desegregation). One of her sons was happy with the idea because then his cricket team could have the Black kids from Loni, the nearest township to Palmer, who had beaten them prior, on the team. Meanwhile, her then six-year-old daughter feared that she would be the only White kid in her class and "not have anyone to eat her sandwich with." Ms. Benson had taken a group of Palmer students to a party in Loni the year prior to bridge the social chasm between students from Palmer's neighborhood and the township. "Though it's in Palmer's backyard, not many [students] know of reality beyond the boundaries of their own homes or streets," Ms. Benson commented and continued as follows:

> One of the Diversity Tripper alums [a Black student] was having a party, and I took a group of [White] kids after assuring their parents that they would be safe. One parent refused to allow his son to go, and on the day when they were supposed to leave, he came up to the school and taunted the kids for going, telling them horror stories about what would happen to them. It turned out to be, in contrast, one of the most moving experiences for my students, who had never seen living conditions as such or realized that these families loved and lived, too. Some cried, having never known what lay beyond them across the tracks.

Undoubtedly, students at Palmer High School attended many celebrations and parties with select friends, building and reinforcing strong connections among themselves in the process. But less often, they would move across social, cultural, and geographic boundaries to engage. As an educator who intentionally aimed to create a deeply inclusive atmosphere for all of Palmer's students, Ms. Benson was willing to go so far as to push her privileged White students beyond their comfort zones to learn something about the realities of their classmates from the townships. Through her influence and the support of the principal and other educators, she was an active agent for radical inclusion at Palmer, although I cannot say unequivocally whether Palmer was there 100 percent, especially since many teachers and school staff differ in their beliefs and attitudes and further in how they practice inclusion. Palmer's organizational-racial habitus was evolving, nonetheless, and any new visitor would be immediately struck by some of its programmatic emphasis on inclusion.

When sociocultural practices in schools take either semiopen or closed approaches, generally they attend to social and cultural differences at a superficial level. In such instances, educators might have students share some aspect of their cultural heritage—such as sponsoring a cultural fair or having a day when students either wear ethnic garb or bring tasty ethnic foods to school as "show-and-tell"; this is what some would describe as either "symbolic multiculturalism," or even what Peter McLaren refers to as left-liberal multiculturalism, which tends to exoticize "otherness" in a manner that locates difference in numerous forms of cultural authenticity.[24]

Williston High School held an annual "I'm Proud to be a South African Day" in April. I arrived to school one morning observing students who showed up representing multiple ethnoracial groups: Xhosa, Zulu, Pedi, Swazi, Venda, Sotho, Indian, Muslim, Afrikaner, Scottish, Canadian, and Portuguese, to name a few. Principal Billups had asked the teachers to send three of the "best-dressed" kids to the front of the school for pictures, and she asked for variety. I heard several teachers comment beforehand that they felt the Indian girls would be the most beautiful in the saris; still they sent a diverse group of students to the front to represent their class. I watched as the teachers arranged the kids for one mixed-group photo and then broke them down by ethnicity. It was a beautiful array of colors, beadwork, textiles, and weaving, and the kids seemed proud. "We don't get to see them outside of school, so this is nice," commented a teacher, suggesting that this was how she perceived that students may have dressed when not in uniform.

Noticeably, the White learners were all put into one group for a photo, while the African students were allowed to divide into ethnic groups for their picture. Welcome, the son of a major government spokesperson, was dressed as a Zulu warrior in skins, ankle chains, and beads, with a leopard head wrap. Except for the occasional male whom I spotted dressed in khaki short pants, a white shirt, suspenders, and a safari hat—reminiscent of the one that the popular film character Indiana Jones wears atop his head—imitating a conventional costume of an Afrikaner boer (farmer), many White students felt "cultureless." Lindsay, whom I was shadowing that morning, was wearing a Chinese dress, because she believed that she had no "culture." Lindsay's father is of German heritage, and her mother is Afrikaner, but Lindsay said that her father was an orphan who knows little of his German origins.

Unlike Indian students who wore salwar kameez's, kurtis, and elegant, colorful saris or African students of various ethnic groups whose males regaled themselves in furry Zulu warrior costumes and females in richly textured prints and textiles adorned with intricate beadwork, many mixed-race students and the overwhelming majority of Coloureds (especially those who did not identify as Muslim, some who wore religious attire) could not figure out what garb would accurately capture their ethnoracial identities. Later that afternoon, I sat next to Kai in Mrs. Alicia Silver's eighth-grade biology class. He was dressed in his school uniform. I asked Kai why he chose not to participate, and he said that he wouldn't know what to wear. "I am Indian and White, and I asked them [the teachers] if I could wear a suit, they told me, 'No.'" (When I asked a teacher, Mr. Brad Jefferts, about this later, he denied it and said that he was sure a student would not have been sent home if he wore a suit.)

After school, I met Samaura, who was talking to one of the English and business economics teachers, Mr. Joseph Addy, a Ghanaian. Samaura, the daughter of the head of the school governing body, was in her school uniform, too. She said that Coloureds have no culture and queried what she would wear as a Coloured. Samaura's mother had some Indian in her background, but she knew nothing of her father. Mr. Addy added, "I think that mixed students should have investigated their backgrounds and gone with one of the heritages or have chosen *one* to represent." I asked him how that would have compromised the students' identities to make them choose and if there were another way to express cultural heritage other than through dress. Mr. Addy responded, "This is something to think about." For now, Williston relied on dress as symbols of identity, when a number of students seemed at a loss about what dress would symbolize their ethnicity.

Creating fully open and integrative school contexts is a challenge for many educators. American schools also demonstrate limited knowledge in how to respond to the diversity of their student body. North Village Prep ventured into the practice of multiculturalism, which, at one point, translated into a practice of vulgar cultural tourism. One Saturday morning, in an attempt to grasp an understanding of their students' lives in one day, teachers and administrators hopped aboard a chartered bus and headed into the central areas of North Capital City, where the Black and Latino students in the VDP lived. This "cultural tour" included a vehicular stroll through the neighborhoods, a lunch stop at a soul food restaurant, a quick visit to the local African American museum with, perhaps, some purchases for souvenirs, and even what a few teachers claimed to have been a sighting of a drug deal on one of the street corners. There was a buzz in the air among the staff about the alleged sighting that following week when our research team arrived, much to the chagrin of a few embarrassed and relatively more enlightened administrators. The latter felt that this claim further reproduced already deeply entrenched stereotypes about the VDP students and their lives.

For this very reason, many thinkers criticize such symbolic multicultural practices. Peter McLaren, for example, argues that an emphasis on difference in this manner as the basis of collective identity makes it appear as if all members who share an identity possess the same experience or traits and consequently ignores the variation within groups.[25] Accordingly, not all of the VDP students lived in the type of neighborhood toured; their communities varied in terms of social composition and socioeconomic makeup. Additionally, not all of the Black or Latino students at North Village were participants in the VDP, and on several occasions, such students mentioned how they were frequently mistaken for VDP participants. It was assumed that students of color did not reside in North Village.

## Opening Up Resources

No educational policy or practice is devoid of a particular value or values. Schools have functioned as one of the main sites of socialization for individuals and development in modern society. Schools assist in developing the "glue" that holds a society together, promoting a common agenda of citizenship and patriotism.[26] The great "dilemma" in racialized societies, where discrimination and prejudice have run rampant, however, is how to cultivate a democracy that not only enables the will of the majority but also ensures that those in the minority do not become so deeply dispossessed such that their lifetime realities belie just what a democracy stands for.

At various points in history, especially prior to 1954 and 1994, the moral cores of U.S. and South African societies, respectively, have been in jeopardy, threatened by political values of exclusion to their educational and economic opportunities. The practice of intentional racial and socioeconomic segregation in schools is inherently a morally corrupt and "closed" system, since it violates a democratic society's fundamental values of equality and justice for all. In 1954, the U.S. Supreme Court began to realize this when it ruled that racial segregation in schooling was unconstitutional because it inherently violated the rights of its non-White citizens. Forty years later, a new democratic

South African government emerged from its previous incarnation as a morally bankrupt state when it laid the foundation for the realization of equal opportunity. While the courts have considered various material and psychological rationales for *why* school integration is necessary for historically disadvantaged groups, researchers, lawyers, and policy makers have done little to frame the issue more holistically in terms of its benefits all-around for a national society, for its potential for augmenting the "collective spirit" and social cohesion, and for keeping a nation on the track of sustained productivity and innovation from representative segments of its entire population.[27]

"Openness" in schools is a complex, multilayered and multidimensional process. Given the ecological dissimilarities between very poor black schools and middle-class, white-dominant, multiracial schools, the requisite moral conditions needed to attain a greater level of equality of opportunity is one that engenders a deeper concern for the stability and overall well-being of all of their students. And even if schools with predominantly low-income students of color were to spend similar dollars per capita, the power of "intangible" factors—as sociologist Amy Stuart Wells refers to them—such as status, rank, and vast networking resources that follow affluent and/or white communities cannot be underestimated.[28] So, despite what anyone says, "separate can never be fully equal."

If we use the percentage of poor students in a school as a proxy of the type of parental, material support that can be provided for a school, then African American and Latino students in the United States are at a much bigger disadvantage than their White and Asian peers. Based on national data from 2006–2007, the average Black and Latino student attended a school where nearly 60 percent of the students were poor, while White and Asian students attended a school where 31 percent and 36 percent, respectively, were poor.[29] Schools with the greatest concentrations of poor students have the lowest test scores, send the fewest students to college, and are instead affronted by high dropout rates.

Although South Africa's economic, educational, and political structures are different from the United States, limited material resource contexts in schools work similarly. I came to know Montjane Secondary School's highest achieving student in the matric class the year I was there. I'll call him "Sipho," a young man who assisted me with administering my surveys at his school on several afternoons. I compensated Sipho like I would any undergraduate research assistant back at my university, and I recall the day he ran up to me, breathless, smiling, eager to show off his new multifunction calculator. Sipho had wanted the calculator for his math class and had bought it with his

research assistance funds. Until that point, he did not have the money to purchase one, which I know was not an issue for the average student at Williston.
Sipho was very bright, so smart that a teacher informed me matter-of-factly
that he knew about as much or more than some of his teachers. He had defied
the odds and scored well enough on his matric exams to gain admittance to
one of South Africa's premier universities, the University of Pretoria (UP). I
recall his pride, and even my own, when I learned that he would go to study
engineering. We kept in touch via e-mail over the months, and I was kept
apprised of his academic and personal comings and goings. Much to my sor-
row, however, Sipho, ever desirous to become a chemical engineer, struggled
at UP and eventually was dismissed from the chemical engineering program.
He was not sufficiently prepared. He could not keep up with his peers who
had been exposed to more rigorous teaching and preparation at the former-
white schools like Palmer or Williston. Although Sipho has landed on his feet
somewhat, having acquired a job, which will help him to continue supporting
his family—which he did even on his meager student stipend at UP—he had
not regained admittance to the engineering program that he strongly desired
the last time I was in touch with him.

   For South Africa, the implication is that the socioeconomic integration
of schools is a must-do, if the nation is to save a critical mass of its youths
from succumbing to a cycle of poverty and limited economic productivity. Realistically, a proliferation of integrated schools with critical masses of
White students is not the answer in a black-dominant nation where Whites
comprise only 10 percent of the population. Cases like Sipho's, nonetheless,
expose the urgency with which South Africa must address the unequal contexts of schooling in that society. The overwhelming majority of non-White
students remains segregated in poor township schools, where basic academic
equipment such as chalk for teachers to write on boards, paper for printing,
wired computers for advancement into this sophisticated technological age,
and even a supply of well-trained teachers who can adequately prepare students for university life, are limited.

   Furthermore, because of the curricular changes, most likely a township
school has already "skimmed the cream" of its brightest students by grade
10, since a very high percentage of students drop out by the end of grade
nine, the last year before students' transition into a more difficult secondary
curriculum nationally and right around the time where the compulsory age
of school attendance is reached. At Groveland and Montjane, only about
one-quarter of the students who entered the school in eighth grade made it
to twelfth grade as matrics. This turned out to average about one hundred

students in the senior class per school. Even fewer, perhaps less than one-tenth of these students, will actually attend a university. Fewer of those will actually graduate because they were not fully prepared, like Sipho. Why? Three chief explanations arise: poverty, the lack of affordability of higher education and the students' inability to attain the university exemptions, or the requisite scores on the national exam to attain admission to a university due to multiple factors, from limited English abilities, insufficient teacher preparation, and limited human capital among parents, which impeded their ability to assist their children with schoolwork. In short, Groveland and Montjane are schools threatened by the specter of extreme poverty and limited economic resources. Decades of accumulated economic and academic disadvantages for the majority of African and Coloured students in the country limit the pipeline to higher social mobility via the engine of higher education.

## *Broadening the Moral Core*

While we can believe that most people residing in a democratic society believe in a just, open society, if those beliefs are not either deeply wedded to a commitment in *practice* to both protect and insure educational equality, then all we have in our society is another "attitude-behavioral" paradox or values stretch.[30] My survey data of 1,558 students enrolled at the eight schools in the United States and South Africa reveal that the majority subscribe wholly to values of equality of opportunity and the eradication of poverty (see Table 6.2). Mean percentages of those who agreed that a "good education is the key to ending poverty" ranged from 53 percent to 85 percent of the students. However, there is a significant difference among the schools by nation, school type, and race, while some difference in responses appears to exist *within* schools across race and gender. First, South African students were more likely to believe that a good education would lead to the reduction of poverty than U.S. students. Perhaps, because of the recent advent of democracy and opening of educational opportunity, more students steeped in poverty view schooling as the pathway out. American students, though, appear to be more cynical, and it is likely that an awareness of an enduring inequality gap in the United States reinforces that cynicism.

Second, in terms of racial differences, White students in general were more pessimistic and less likely to agree (61 percent) than Black (70 percent), mixed race, including Latinos, (78 percent), and Asian (65 percent) students. American White students were significantly less optimistic about education's potential as a solution to poverty than South African White students, also.

Regarding differences by school types, students in the majority-black and coloured schools in South Africa were more likely to believe in education as a solution to poverty than those attending the mixed-race, white-dominant schools. In the United States, students at majority-minority North City Tech were more likely to believe this than students at the other three schools. Table 6.2 shows that students at North City Tech were significantly more likely than their peers at the other U.S. schools to believe that a good education and the eradication of poverty are positively associated, and it is possible that at a school with a critical mass of first- and second-generation immigrant and low-income students—like township schools with disproportionately very poor students—a quality education is a main source of hope of breaking away from the cycle of poverty and moving to the next rung of the mobility ladder.

Sociologists and social psychologists have found over time that part of our human nature is to aspire to the highest abstract value, but when it comes right down to the consideration of how to practice those values vis-à-vis our respective material reality, social location, and self-interests, then we tend to teeter on the fringes of duplicity or insincerity. Yet, "for many people, "including judges," as Kevin Welner writes, the foundation for a just society lies in a set of values that supplant racial (and even class) equality.[31]

From a values standpoint, the road ahead is a bumpy one in the United States. First, liberal values of individualism, choice, and competition—what I refer to as either "semiopen" or "semiclosed" moral values—undermine the goals of equality of opportunity as affluent parents now jockey for position and advantage for their children in elite public schools and elite tracked courses within those schools.[32] Of course, these families are not acting out of any pure malevolence or disregard for the "other." Rather they are responding to an opportunity system that favors graduates of elite and competitive colleges, which in turn favors students from highly regarded public (and private) schools where students' chances for admission are strongly linked to their test scores and to how well they participate in the high-status classes offered. Then, of course, students' performances on those tests (the proxies for intelligence and ability) and enrollment in honors, advanced placement, and international baccalaureate classes are not completely independent of who attends those schools.[33] Thus, while it may be enticing for a critic (like me) to attribute the looming demise of diverse schooling to individualistic goals that collude in undermining equality of opportunity in schools, the explanation is not that

Table 6.2 Percent of students who agree that there is a link between a "good education" and the eradication of poverty

| Percent Who Agree among | South African Schools | | | | U.S. Schools | | | |
|---|---|---|---|---|---|---|---|---|
| | Groveland Majority-Coloured | Montjane Majority-Black | Palmer Mixed Race-White Dominant | Williston Mixed Race-White Dominant | N. City Tech Majority-Minority | N. Village Prep Mixed Race-White Dominant | S. City Honors Majority-Black | S. County Prep Mixed Race White-Dominant |
| All students | 85[a] | 81[a] | 72 | 73 | 65[a] | 55 | 53 | 56 |
| Female | 88[bc] | 81[c] | 65[c] | 77[c] | 63 | 55 | 59 | 54 |
| Male | 79[c] | 81[c] | 78[c] | 70[c] | 66[b] | 54 | 42 | 59 |
| Asian | — | — | 83 | 79 | 58[c] | 54[c] | — | — |
| Black | 76[c] | 81[c] | 74[c] | 78[c] | 62 | 48 | 54 | 52 |
| Mixed-race (US)\ Coloured (SA) | 89[c] | — | 75[c] | 67 | 68 | 60 | — | — |
| White | — | — | 65[c] | 67[c] | 62 | 55 | 47 | 44 |
| Number of students responding | 198 | 239 | 227 | 245 | 205 | 146 | 102 | 196 |

[a] Significant difference within nation between majority-minority and white-dominant schools, $p <= .01$
[b] Significant difference within school by race or gender, $p < .05$
[c] Significant difference between schools by nation, $p <= .01$

simple. Parents and students want good schools to improve their chances for good jobs and advancement up the mobility ladders. Paradoxically, the social institutions involved in the steps to making it conspire in the reproduction of both racial and class privilege.

Furthermore, either the U.S. Supreme Court or a lower court has dismantled one of the main redistributive and justice-oriented educational policies of the twentieth century case by case, most recently in Seattle and Louisville in the "PICS" cases.[34] In the 2007 decision, the justices decided this case highlighting an "American dilemma"—a term coined by the social scientist Gunnar Myrdal and revived later by political scientist Jennifer Hochschild, which signals the contradictions between American democratic ideals, including equality and justice for all, and the reality of the determination of a white and middle-class majority that acts in its own best interests.[35] U.S. national data, for instance, reveal a regression in the efforts made by the nation in the 1970s and 1980s in response to the *Brown v. Board of Education* decision.[36] For this reason, many scholars and researchers—alongside activist educators, parents, and community members—continue to struggle to ensure that the battles fought by Charles Hamilton Houston, Thurgood Marshall, Charles Thompson (quoted in the epigraph), and other historic figures to equalize educational opportunity across races have not been in vain. We now seek anxiously to figure out how to minimize the powerful impacts of both accumulated disadvantages accrued from attending lower quality schools and the feeblest implementations of desegregated schools, which will keep many historically unequal and poor groups of students wedged at the bottom of the opportunity ladders.

## What Comes with Cultural Flexibility: The Ethos of Caring for Another

Without proactive and explicit attention to the sociocultural and sociopolitical domains of schooling, then the attendant results of gross achievement and attainment disparities by race and class can easily be used as evidence that school integration does not work or that people no longer care about it, as my esteemed colleague declared. Few schools have truly attained racial integration, and second, few educators and privileged parent communities either accept or comprehend that either *radical inclusion* or *egalitarianism*, a goal of the South African state, is a requisite condition for it to work.

Open school *types* engage in *practices* that support and sustain *moral con-
'tions* of equity, caring, and sharing. Their organizational-racial and -class

habitus inhibit the reproduction of social boundaries. Open schools do not perpetuate beliefs of the deserving "us" versus the undeserving "them" through their everyday educational practices. Instead, open schools fully incorporate all groups of students academically and socially. They also promote cultural flexibility among students and educators.

Palmer High School (multiracial and white-dominant) in Coast City and North City Tech (multiracial and majority-minority) in North Capital City are the two schools in this study that came closest to this ideal-type, although self-admittedly, they still have a ways to go. Both of these schools offered substantive classes and a retreat (in the case of Palmer) to allow their students to deconstruct the meanings of diversity, power, privilege, difference, and inequality—all of those social forces that further entrenched social boundaries and separated the "us" from the "them." This is likely one explanation for why Palmer and North City Tech students reported the highest levels of cultural flexibility and a high propensity to cross social boundaries, relative to all other students in the study.[37]

Finally, a disregard for how racial and economic divides in schools undermine the realization of a truly open society make it clear that the discussion *and* practice of integration has to go beyond principles of equity and fairness in simple material and academic terms. Other values that need to be instilled are those that regard the integrated school as an environment of citizenship building, that not only cultivates respect for a shared national identity but also promotes common understandings and an appreciation of social differences through teaching, interacting, and learning. In schools and classrooms, such practices foster a "sharing" and "caring" society,[38] students and educators do not fear the messiness of disagreement but rather seek to cultivate their abilities to gain consensus and build diverse coalitions. These practices also help to diminish their fears of each other as neighbors, coworkers, and potential family members.

But what do we do about the dilemma of people's demanding their rights to be on their own, to choose where they want to send their children to school? Political theorist Danielle Allen has argued, "The only way to stabilize the idea of 'the people' is to shift its source of authority from the individual wills of a multitude to an institutional will. Institutions [like an educational system] stand in for a consensus that is impossible to achieve."[39] In other words, Allen is arguing that many of our nation's political and educational institutions have the power to achieve equity, in spite of the limitations of human self-interest. Allen also contends that democratic societies should rework the notion of citizenship to mean a combination of a developed conversation about reciprocity and power sharing. This notion of citizen-ship bolsters equity, cultivates habits of attention "by which citizens are attuned to the balances and imbalances in what [they] are giving up for each other."[40] Thus, closing the empathy gap that Judah mentioned entails massive departures from an ethos of self-involvement, according to Allen. After all, empathy comes with knowing, being familiar with, sharing experiences, and caring if our societies will be better for all, not just ourselves and our loved ones. Empathy is not merely about increasing the civility of one social group toward another. Allen also argues that people may negotiate loss and reciprocity without feeling that they are losing their political agency and will when institutions, embodied in judicial and educational systems, step in to equalize resources and opportunity.

Schools whose programs, policies, and practices engender cultural flexibility can help us to achieve the kind of boundary spanning that moves members toward a comprehension of equity beyond self-interests. When practiced wholly, school integration as an educational practice may conflict with other liberal social values, including beliefs in the right to choose where one wants to attend school or to attend a neighborhood school. Certainly, in demo-cratic societies, citizens have freedom of choice. But choice without consideration of the material consequences on less fortunate communities in society is fodder for the reproduction of inequality. To paraphrase a rhetorical question proffered by Allen, "Can we devise an educational system that, rather than unwittingly encouraging citizens not to cross social boundaries or to talk to strangers or out-group members, instead teaches them how to interact with others self-confidently and equitably?[41] Can we devise an educational system that promotes cultural flexibility among educators and students? I think so.

# 7

## *Stubborn Roots*

### WEEDING OUT EDUCATIONAL INEQUALITY

*The Negro needs neither segregated nor mixed schools.
What he needs is education. What he must remember is
that there is no magic, either in mixed or in segregated
schools. A mixed school with poor and unsympathetic teachers, with hostile opinion, and no teaching concerning Black
folk, is bad. A segregated school with ignorant placeholders,
inadequate equipment, poor salaries, and wretched housing, is equally bad. Other things being equal, the mixed
school is the broader, more natural basis for the education
of all youth. It gives wider contacts; it inspires greater self-
confidence; and it suppresses the inferiority complex. But
other things are seldom equal...*[1]

THE CURRENT PROVERBIAL Achilles' heel in public education in both
South Africa and the United States is the two nations' inability to eradicate a
problem so complex and so historically rooted—the glaring academic disparities among social groups, particularly based on racial, ethnic, and class identities. The roots of these problems stem deeply into the social and economic
landscapes of these nations, steeped in practices of systemic exclusion and
discrimination based on phenotypic differences among peoples. Given the
longevity of these practices, it is no wonder, then, that the United States and
South Africa are two of the nations with the largest economic inequality gaps
in the world.[2] In the meantime, schools—what some refer to as "the weakest

and most vulnerable of American institutions"—are asked to bear the brunt of social change required in the battle against racial discrimination.[3]

Certainly, much pressure has been put on principals and teachers to create excellent students who perform well on tests. At the same time, many architects of our society have imagined schools as building blocks that embody the raw materials for sustaining healthy, stable democracies by fostering citizens' abilities to tolerate and work together with others who are different and to exercise a sense of justice and commitment to a fair distribution of resources.[4] If that is indeed the case, then we need schools to facilitate the progress of more perfect unions, to realize radical inclusion, and to produce cohesion among peoples of diverse social and cultural backgrounds.

By now, it is apparent that the findings I share in this book have very little to do with the technical aspects of the contemporary high school in the modern world—the agenda of producing students with strong literacy, numeracy, and test-taking abilities. Certainly, a primary focus of public education today is the production of creative, critical, and skilled workers and producers in a twenty-first-century world economy. Yet, if we want to understand why the experiments with equality of opportunity in educational policies have not produced certain anticipated returns, we must comprehend why access alone is not enough and why social and cultural forces matters. As some scholars have argued, sociocultural approaches have been used to understand how all students learn and develop; and thus, educational practice and policy must take culture as a core, operative social phenomenon.[5] Schools and classrooms are not only active spaces for developing the mastery of scholastic or content knowledge but also are settings encompassing variable systems of meanings, tastes, appreciations, and understandings.

Some shortsightedness, nevertheless, has arisen, as the objectives to reduce resource inequality in schooling supplant an awareness of how symbolic boundaries often remain stable in various aspects of the school experience. Boundaries around student participation in extracurricular activities and academics, language, and the physical presentation of self, to name a few, cloak the specter of cultural inequality in contemporary mixed-race South African and U. S. schools. On the one hand, some of these schools' codes and their students' behaviors encourage the permeability of boundaries and consequently the diffusion of cultural practices. On the other hand, some boundaries operate in ways that disproportionately and adversely impact particular groups of learners. Therefore, educator and policy makers need to consider how nonmaterial factors may undermine the efficacy of their educational reforms.

The power to diminish social and symbolic boundaries, particularly within schools and communities, is often within the hands of adults: parents and educators who control the school's resources and power.[6] Educational leaders in the focal schools in this study varied in their approaches to equity, and this variation corresponds to significant differences in the overall educational well-beings of groups of students who were thought to be included. Still, we forget that "habits of the hearts"[7] and minds are difficult to change, as Du Bois so shrewdly foreshadowed nearly a century ago, and those habits can remain fixed—even unwittingly or unintentionally—in the collective consciousness for an indefinite amount of time. As DuBois understood, forces of cultural inequality, dominance, and perceived superiority may permeate the walls of socially diverse schools. The existence of closed, salient, racial and class boundaries in both U.S. and South African schools undermines the attainment of a truly open society and makes it clear that the discussions *and* practices of mixed schooling must move beyond principles of equity and fairness in simple material and academic terms.

## Remembering the Sociocultural Sphere

Scholars Michelle Fine, Lois Weiss, and Linda Powell argue that although the conditions of equal status contact generally improve for interracial relations, attitudes, and networks, there is still a tendency to bracket various groups' social experiences under the ideal of "we are all the same," which frequently tend to reproduce white, middle-class ways of being as normative and to ignore the disparate economic, political, and social realities of these diverse groups. Instead, they propose the following:

> ...[I]n order for multiracial youth relations to flourish, three political and social conditions—none natural or automatic—must be intentionally set in place: a sense of community, a commitment to creative analysis of difference, power, and privilege; and an enduring investment in democratic practice with youth. In the absence of these three conditions, settings that are technically desegregated will corrode into sites of oppositional identities, racial tensions, and fractured group relations, which simply mirror the larger society...[8]

The implication here is whether contemporary educational leaders are willing to go deeper and assess all of their school practices for any evidence of either overt or latent group inequality. Some questions that I would offer and encourage to be asked follow:

- Does this practice or policy engender an inequitable pattern by social grouping or identity, for example, race, ethnicity, class, and/or gender?
- When should social and cultural identities matter and when should they not matter when it comes to a specific educational practice?
- Are there disadvantages to having this practice only affect a certain subgroup(s) in the school?
- Can this particular educational practice be deemed egalitarian? Can it be deemed balanced or imbalanced? Can it be deemed (dis)favoring some and not others?

## Flexible Students, Schools, and Boundaries

Schooling also entails the cultivation of dense webs of social relationships. Yet, students' and educators' behaviors are not detached from the wider level of social relations that affect them when they leave school daily. Many return home to their racially and economically segregated neighborhoods and communities. Consequently, the strength of interracial ties formed at school is undermined. Or even within schools, as students are tracked, a process that is highly correlated with race and ethnicity,[9] meanings become attached to particular activities or classes, and consequently, the inclination to seek out cross-racial or cross-ethnic friendships gets diminished.[10] Meanwhile, many view these ties as critical because they hold some promise for the socioeconomic advancement of those generally less privileged.[11]

Furthermore, schooling and learning are multidirectional exchange processes between educators and learners and learners and learners. Although the relative gains of mixed-race schools appear greater than segregated schools (namely, minority-dominant ones), further investigation into some of the positive outcomes of the latter might provide more direction for the former. In this study, for example, findings show that African American students in majority-minority schools, even after controlling for parents' educational levels, possess a higher propensity to cross social and cultural boundaries and maintain higher levels of global self-esteem than their peers in affluent, white-dominant schools. Students from minority-dominant schools in the United States may perceive that they can achieve highly because affirming messages are embedded within their schools' ethos,[12] even if their schools' resources are not as great.

Psychological research shows that individuals who cross assorted social boundaries daily and persist in their endeavors are likely to thrive.[13] What is notable about students in this study is that those who were actively encouraged to navigate across multiple cultural, academic, and extracurricular lines reported high levels of cultural flexibility. I observed that the movement of Black and Latino students in the mixed-race, white-dominant schools across academic boundaries was more constrained than it was for their counterparts attending majority-minority schools. Moreover, although I found no significant differences in higher educational aspirations and expectations among the American sample of students, the widest achievement disparities (based on test scores) among racial groups of students existed within the two affluent, white-dominant, and high achieving (for White students) U.S. schools. Certainly, some of this may owe to some selection bias in the case studies chosen. Yet, I would not wager on sample selection as the only cause. Materially, these "good" schools are representative of the other types of solidly performing schools in the surrounding areas. The larger point is that while a school's resource context is necessary for academic achievement, it is not the only requisite condition.

This study has also yielded insights into how, for African American and Latino students, critical identity issues emerge in contexts where their social and cultural realities are either muted or invisible. Many students of color, especially in high school during a developmental period when identity markers mean much to them, ascribe meanings to how classrooms and school activities are organized.[14] When (American) students of color witness more evidence that their coethnic peers cross the spectrum of ability levels and smartness, athleticism, and leadership potential, their reference group for achievement expands and includes some representations of others who share similar social backgrounds as theirs. Such situations should create flexible students who are likely to persist on a long-term educational trajectory, even in the face of, perhaps, lower conventional academic indicators like high test scores. Thus, the social factors for minority students' higher cultural flexibility in majority-minority schools may have as much to do with positive feedback, affirmation, and social support as with experienced teachers highly competent in their subject matter and adequate educational resources.[15]

Additionally, schools that demonstrate a wider distribution of representation across the spectrum of educational activities
their own organizational flexibility. A school organizatic
necessarily encompass attention to practice, as well as a
building a culturally flexible faculty. That is, principals ar

to be culturally flexible, too. After all, if they are not, how can they enable the cultural flexibility of their students? Most of us are somewhat culturally flexible anyway. In this case, I mean a specific type of cultural flexibility, one that supports a deeper comprehension and experience with social identity diversity, as well as cognitive and experiential diversity. Elsewhere I write about the need for the development of "multicultural navigators" among both educators and students.[16] A key trait of a multicultural navigator, someone who can move seamlessly across several social and cultural boundaries and cross-fertilize diverse messages and perspectives, is cultural flexibility.

Over the years, as I have discussed the sociocultural and power dynamics infused throughout schools, frequently the immediate defensive retort that I receive is how can teachers be expected to utilize the cultural toolkits of all children in a diverse classroom. Such responses, one could argue, illuminate the limited vision that we have about learning and even knowledge. Cultural flexibility is about the possession of the skills of adaptability. Although we cannot expect schools to fully supplement or reduce the gaps in socioeconomic resources that its various student populations have, we can expect them to educate more expansively and less selectively. Now, whenever I conduct workshops with educators working in diverse schools, I ask them to consider the following points:

- How aware are you of the limitations of your own (cultural) knowledge base?
- To what extent do you understand how past and present social, economic, and political dynamics inform how we have gotten to this particular historical moment in education?
- Why might it be important for you as an educator to be a multicultural navigator?
- How do you create "community" in your classrooms?

The development of flexible organizational and group boundaries could very well enable educators and learners to commit themselves cognitively to an altogether different mindset and foster an academic environment that allows for both social change and academic rigor for all of its students. Instead of an either-or mentality regarding students' cultural backgrounds, a flexible mind subscribes to both and to approaches that cultivate multicultural, cosmopolitan learners and staff.

## *The Problem of Letting Bygones Be Bygones*

As I pen these words, I am listening to National Public Radio (NPR) and the discussions about a growing segment of the U.S. population's beliefs that U.S. President Barack Obama is Muslim, despite a clear fact on record that he is Christian. Most disturbing to me is not the question of whether he is a Christian, but rather why the American public would find it so problematic that he is of another faith—whether Buddhism, Hinduism, Islam, or any other major religion, or even a nonobserver. The implication here is that a significant percentage of the American public (based on an opinion poll) is uncomfortable with religious diversity, and one cannot help but wonder how this intolerance of religious diversity masks other forms of social intolerance.

These forms of discomfort crop up everywhere, even in our schools. As cultural gatekeepers, policy makers and educators must ask themselves critically and honestly just how comfortable they are dealing with various types of social differences in education. Right now, we continue to slap Band-Aid solutions on the implications of difference. Meanwhile, I have never experienced as much animation in the classroom with learners in both the United States and South Africa as when I have engaged them in debates about how we address disparities in these two societies where racial and class stratification have marked just about every major outcome pertaining to well-being. I have observed that students are bursting to be engaged critically about these issues, and I suspect that critical engagement would disperse to the conventional academic work that so many of them find "boring," if only our curricula would either retool or augment itself to include innovative and creative ways to address vital national questions in the processes of building knowledge.

I recall contacting a school in Coast City early in the development of this study to seek its participation, and the faculty and headmaster declined participation because I asked questions about race in my questionnaire. This school's philosophy was that "race" is a social construction and a fiction, which should not be reified by utilizing it in everyday language. After rejecting my request, the school's headmaster, nonetheless, invited me to come and speak a few days later to the graduating matrics that year, since, as a professor at a prestigious American university, I was viewed as a resource. Surprisingly, while chatting with two of my student escorts after I gave my talk to the crowd of over one hundred students, they mentioned how their school denied the existence of race and racialized phenomenon. "So, do you talk about race?" I asked. "Of course, we do—just not with our educators!" the students, two of South

Africa's best, responded. Indeed, nonracialist discourse in schools cannot fully become what anthropologist Mica Pollock refers to as "colormute"[17] or fully avoidant of race talk, since as these students declared, once they left school and headed for their respective communities in Coast City, race was everywhere, in the patterns of living, in social network compositions, in employment and unemployment rates, in the clientele at particular restaurants—everywhere.

Some argue that the abstract ideal of nonracialism that has served postapartheid South Africa has run up against the imperatives of *transformation*, leading to a more messy terrain, where race has been constitutionally outlawed as a moral basis for citizenship and inclusion in the political sphere. Yet legislatively, race is inscribed for strategic purposes of redress.[18] Critics who espouse an orthodox nonracial society argue that the ANC government in South Africa itself has been operating with race categories in trying to redress the inequalities of the past, and for them, as long as it does, racial differentiation will persist in schools and in the wider community. But we cannot ignore that South African (as well as American) youth are the inheritors of a specific racial formation[19]— historically and socially constructed processes that circumscribe their material realities and that have real consequences for their well-being, whether or not they participate in debates about what is "Black," "Coloured," "Indian," or "White." Often, we find members of certain school-communities expressing concrete beliefs and professing aspirations for equity among students; yet they may resist actual policies and practices that would diminish or eradicate structures of inequity.[20] Therefore, the dominant "we" will allow "them" in (especially when either the law or social pressure mandates this), but "we" do not have to treat them as equals socially and culturally. Frequently, I found students and educators expressing concrete beliefs that exposed a type of "laissez-faire" approach to the reduction of inequality.[21] "The government should not do anything to specifically redress past inequality. Rather, let the past rest," they might say. In this vein, White South African students and educators, for example, often maintained general notions that contradicted their abstract beliefs about success and educational change. Their attitudes were not only borne from but also bred distrust, skepticism, and a resistance to the broader norms of egalitarianism facilitated through macrolevel educational policies and pervasive public discourse. Perceiving themselves to no longer inhabit a solidly dominant, privileged, and secure position in society, they did not trust the social order engendered by the current norms to respect what felt like a new vulnerability.

Labelle argued that dominant groups are likely to permit some change in schools and other social institutions to reflect greater cultural diversity, as long as it does not shift the balance of power among the groups.[22] When that balance of power is threatened, then the alternative is flight to another school where the actual and symbolic reins of power are less contested. As in the case for people of color, being the social and political minority in school or community can be an emotionally challenging state for White students and their families, if social boundaries are characterized by a stronger state of social closure. Meanwhile, when schools and communities are constructed within the culture and interests of Whites, although Blacks and other subordinate groups are included within those institutions, their academic incorporation and performances may suffer compared to the dominant group.

Danielle Allen argues that "fossilized distrust" among citizens and the failure to recognize the common stakes and benefits of citizenship within a society contribute to the failure of democratic ideals like equality and justice and efforts at cultural diversity.[23] That type of fossilized distrust can also fuel the pervasive phenomenon of white flight from desegregated, de-tracked, or other potentially equalized educational contexts.[24] If we accept that integration serves a moral and equitable function in our society, as we enter the sixth decade of *Brown v. Board of Education* and the second decade of South African democracy, the question then becomes how can we improve multiracial schools to feasibly, efficiently, and effectively school all students, no matter what their socioeconomic and/or ethnic and racial backgrounds. Of course, they cannot do it alone. Schools share the responsibility of education with parents and their respective communities. Still, educators must find the highest common denominator, check their own skepticism and leveled expectations at the door, and challenge themselves to engage with all their students.

As the debate in the opening chapter reveals, many disagree about the multifold purposes of education. I continue to believe that the purposes are multidimensional. Educators should continue to work with the knowledge that schools serve both academic and sociocultural functions. First, in an increasingly technological and knowledge-based global economy, modern societies require graduates of myriad social backgrounds to possess a knowledge base of strong math, science, and literacy skills. Second, core values embedded in judicial, social, and educational policies formulated in the United States and South Africa indicate the importance of vital democratic ideals, the maintenance of social harmony and balance and the building of civic community and capacity are critical goals of education, too. Focusing attention on all of these goals in discourse, policy, and practice, no doubt, would lead us closer to the fulfillment of *equal opportunity, equity, and the social integration* of two nations' peoples.

# Appendix

## A Few Notes on Methodology

I am a great believer in embodying the experiences of my research as much as I can, so I chose to go back to high school for a year over the course of the two studies. One of the best ways for a researcher to become familiar with the school culture is to immerse herself in the context. In South Africa, I attended classes daily, documenting the sights, sounds, and experiences encountered in the schools, as well as the social makeup of different academic classes, student social spaces, and extracurricular activities, to develop "thick" descriptions of the sociocultural milieu of the schools.[1] Immediately, I heard about the social and cultural issues those students struggled with immediately—even on my first day in their school. Despite my being (African) American, a foreigner, I was fortunate to build a rapport with numerous students, and thus openly they shared their concerns with me about certain social, cultural, and political aspects of their schooling.

Three years after I completed the first part of this study in South Africa, I returned to the hallways, break rooms, and classrooms of another four schools. This time I remained on American shores. The U. S. component of the study followed similar data collections procedures. Some wonderful student research assistants and I visited the four schools daily for six months from January to June 2007. The research team comprised three African Americans, one Egyptian American, and three European Americans; all except one were female. Again, we relied greatly on ethnography, interviews, and surveys. Except at South City Honors, which was visited mainly by two African American researchers, a mixed-race pair of researchers attended an array of academic classes and extracurricular and lunchroom activities four to five days a week, spending anywhere from three to seven hours at the schools.

## Ethnography

I took a quasi-inductive approach to conducting this research. By that, I mean that I began this project with some ideas already in mind about what transpires within schools and their sociocultural climates. Still, reasonably influenced by the approach of "grounded theory,"[2] I allowed the main conceptual and theoretical underpinnings of the project to emerge from the data, that is, from the voices of my respondents and from the themes and patterns recurrent in the observations. I expected that understandings about the school's *sociocultural context* and its ability to promote *cultural flexibility* would be implicit in interactions between and among students and teachers; in the language that they used to describe themselves and other identity-based groups; in how students were physically organized and distributed across different environments of learning and extracurricular activities; in the schools' written mission statements, rules, norms, and policies; and in how principals, teachers, and students discuss sanctions against students. Our methods enabled us to come to understand both material and cultural elements, which leave an imprint on students and influence how they develop, reproduce, or reconfigure meanings about different groups' statuses within education and their respective schools.

## Individual and Group Interviews

Both formal and informal interviews took place at various points throughout our time visiting the schools. Formal, semistructured interviews with school personnel (namely, the school principal, assistant principals, and a random selection of teachers from each grade) were conducted as a means to gather other information about the schools' organizational and cultural contexts. Questions focused on the schools' formal rules and policies, the educators' mission both academically and culturally, and their assessments of students by different social categories (or the intersections of these social identities). Interviews also occurred informally in the ethnographic context, generally as we sat with students and teachers in the classrooms or spoke with them casually in the hallways or over their lunch breaks and in other social spaces at the school.

Semistructured group interviews with students helped shed light on the schools' *sociocultural context* by exploring how students discuss physical and social *boundaries* at both the group and school levels. We asked students about different meanings, beliefs, attitudes, and expressive actions pertaining to racial, ethnic, and gender identities; about their perceptions and attitudes about interracial and gender dynamics among students and teachers; about their peer cultures and the perceptions of "appropriate" ethnic or cultural behavior among their peers (for example, dress, music, language, friendship circles, etc.); about their perceptions and responses to the school climate, its explicit and hidden curricular policies, about their observable academic patterns across different social groups; and about their attitudes regarding the wider opportunity structure, race relations, and the means to success and achievement in this society.

In South Africa, I conducted about two dozen group interviews, and they ranged in social composition from monoracial to mixed race, and single sex to coed. In the United States, my research assistants and I conducted fifty-seven in-depth one- to two-hour group interviews—also a combination of a different social compositions—with students about their experiences regarding racial, ethnic, gender and class dynamics. Group interviews have emerged as a popular technique for gathering qualitative data among social scientists,[3] and they are especially effective among youth to ascertain specific consensus beliefs, to obtain greater depth and breadth in responses than what occurs in individual interviews (whether formal or informal), and to verify claims made about the school or groups of individuals by a particular person.[4] Having used group interviews with adolescents in past research, let me note two particular strengths of using group interviews with them: 1) When one participant is speaking, other youth have moments to think or ample time for greater reflection of responses that may have already been provided; and 2) youths' responses to one another's comments may well prevent the routine, and perhaps even timid, responses sometimes obtained in interviews between youth and adults.[5] While it is important to stress that group interviews are never intended to provide results that are either representative or generalizable to the entire school population, they are used to indicate the possible range of experiences and attitudes and to ascertain the points of convergence in shared meanings about different facets of student life within the schools. These tape-recorded group interviews were transcribed, and along with the hundreds of pages of field notes, they were systematically coded by another team of research assistants using Atlas.ti. Research assistants and I generated analytic memos highlighting emergent codes and themes pertaining to the research foci, which were then discussed, compared, and reconciled for intercoder reliability purposes.

## Surveys for Individual-Level Data

Surveys constituted another principal component of the research study. The surveys were used to ascertain how student academic incorporation varied on a wider scale across the eight school contexts by measuring between- and within-school differences by ethnicity, race, gender, and ideology. I conducted a half-hour survey with a random, stratified sample (by grade, class section, ethnicity/race, and gender) from the entire student population at each school. Nine hundred seventeen surveys were collected in South Africa the first time. When I returned to the schools again four years later, I resurveyed about ninety-seven students who had been eighth graders but were who were then matrics or graduating seniors. All of the surveys asked questions about students' school experiences, classroom and extracurricular activities, beliefs and perceptions about education, jobs, and race relations, as well as a host of personal questions about their self-esteem, self-efficacy, family makeup, educational and job aspirations, expectations, and self-reported grades and grade point averages, along with a battery of social background characteristics.

The response rate at all four South African schools was on average over 95 percent. In the United States, response rates averaged 40 percent. Although within the larger scheme of survey research this response rate may appear modest, I am confident that we gathered data from significantly wider and representative percentages of the various student populations over the hundreds of hours of school observations and interviews. In both South Africa and the United States, the surveys were conducted to assess within- and between-school levels, as well as cross-national differences, in terms of the connections among individual students' identities, racial, class, and gender ideology, cultural flexibility, and feelings of attachment and engagement to school.

# Notes

## PREFACE

1   *Brown v. Board of Education*, 347 U.S. 483 (1954): "We conclude that the doctrine of 'separate but equal' has no place. Separate educational facilities are inherently unequal" (Chief Justice Earl Warren in the U.S. Supreme Court's majority opinion).

2   For a discussion on "decoupling," see John W. Meyer and Brian Rowan, "The Structure of Educational Organizations," in *Schools and Society: A Sociological Approach to Education*, ed. J. H. Ballantine and J. Z. Spade (Thousand Oaks, CA: Sage, 1978 [2007]), 217–225.

3   Pseudonyms are used throughout this book to protect the identities and confidentiality of students and educators. For these reasons, I have also chosen to mask the identities of the schools and their locales.

4   See Clifford Geertz, "Thick Description: Toward an Interpretive Theory of Culture," in *Contemporary Field Research: A Collection of Readings*, ed. R. M. Emerson (Prospect Heights, IL: Waveland Press, 1983), 37–59.

5   Martin Carnoy, "Rethinking the Comparative and the International," *Comparative Education Review* 50: (2006): 568.

6   Charles C. Ragin, *The Comparative Method: Moving Beyond Qualitative and Quantitative Strategies* (Berkeley: University of California Press, 1987).

7   In the NCLB preamble, the U.S. Congress stated that the express goal of the act is to "close the achievement gap with accountability, flexibility, and choice, so that no child is left behind. NCLB represents one of the U.S. federal government's main efforts at standards-based educational reforms with the aim of raising the bar for the education of all American learners through annual testing and teacher accountability measures.

8   See Jacklyn Cock and Alison Bernstein, *Melting Pots & Rainbow Nations: Conversations about Difference in the United States and South Africa* (Urbana:

University of Illinois Press, 2002); Howard Winant, *The Whole World is a Ghetto: Race and Democracy Since World War II*, New York: Basic Books, 2002).

9 See Salim Vally and Yolisa Dalamba, Racism, 'Racial Integration' and Desegregation in South African Public Secondary Schools: A Report on a Study by the South African Human Rights Commission (SAHRC) (SAHRC, Johannesburg, 1999).

10 Nazir Carrim and Crain Soudien, "Critical Antiracism in South Africa," in *Critical Multiculturalism: Rethinking Multicultural and Antiracist Education*, ed. by S. May, London: Falmer Press, 1999), 153–172; Crain Soudien, "We Know Why We Are Here: The Experiences of African Children in a 'Coloured' School in Cape Town," *Race, Ethnicity and Education* 1 (1998): 7–31.

11 Vally and Dalamba, 1999.

## INTRODUCTION

1 Throughout the text, I capitalize racial categories and treat them as proper nouns when they specifically refer to a particular ethnoracial group or an individual of that social group. In instances when a racially coded term is used to modify or describe either a particular place, thing, context, or object related to that group, then I use the lower case.

2 TheaRenda Abu El-Haj, *Elusive: Wrestling with Difference and Educational Equity in Everyday Practice* (New York: Routledge, 2006).

3 Leah N. Gordon, "The Individual and 'the General Situation': The Tension Barometer and the Race Problem at the University of Chicago, 1947–1954," *Journal of the History of the Behavioral Sciences* 46 (2010): 27–51.

4 Charles Tilly, *Identities, Boundaries, and Social Ties* (Boulder, CO: Paradigm Publishers, 2006).

5 Robert L. Crain and Rita E. Mahard, "The Effect of Research Methodology on Desegregation-Achievement Studies: A Meta-Analysis," *American Journal of Sociology* 88 (1983): 839–54; Ronald G. McIntire, Larry W. Hughes, and Michael W. Say, "Houston's Successful Desegregation Plan," *Phi Delta Kappan* 63 (1982): 536–8; Gary Orfield, *Schools More Separate: Consequences of a Decade of Resegregation* (Cambridge, MA: The Civil Rights Project, Harvard University, 2001).

6 Pat Antonio Goldsmith, "Schools' Role in Shaping Race Relations: Evidence on Friendliness and Conflict," *Social Problems* 51 (2004): 587–612; James Moody, "Race, School Integration, and Friendship in America," *American Journal of Sociology* 107 (2002): 679–701.

7 Roslyn Arlin Mickelson, "Subverting Swann: First- and Second-Generation Segregation in the Charlotte-Mecklenburg Schools," *American Educational Research Journal* 38 (2001): 215–52; Chandra Muller, Catherine Riegle-Crumb, Kathryn S. Schiller, Lindsey Wilkinson, and Kenneth A. Frank, "Race and Academic Achievement in Racially Diverse High Schools: Opportunity and Stratification," *Teach-*

ers *College Record* 112 (2010): 1038–63; Karolyn Tyson, *Integration Interrupted* (New York: Oxford University Press, 2011).

8  Sharon Hays, "Structure and Agency and the Sticky Problem of Culture," *Sociological Theory* 12 (1994): 57–71.

9  Anthony Giddens, *New Rules of Sociological Method: A Positive Critique of Interpretative Sociologies* (London: Hutchinson 1976); William H. Sewell, Jr., "A Theory of Structure: Duality, Agency, and Transformation," *The American Journal of Sociology* 98 (1992): 1–29.

10  Although these social theorists do not maintain an overly rigid conceptualization of structure as untouchable representations of social reality beyond the reach of individuals, they still regard structures as constraining, as well as enabling. That is, various constraints might inhibit individuals from making certain choices, which consequently could either hinder or enhance the reproduction of particular social patterns.

11  Hays 1994.

12  I borrow this concept from sociologists of immigration and ethnic identity formations, who use "incorporation" to refer to the social processes by which "newcomers" (or immigrants) establish relationships with the host society. In this literature, it encompasses the degrees of access that newcomer social groups have to institutional power and legitimization.

13  Pantsula culture stems from both a dance and youth dress styles that were born in the townships of the 1970s. The name is believed to have been taken from a traditional Tsonga dance. Pantsula dance is also said to have evolved from the gumboot dance and other dances popular in townships. Currently in South Africa, the pantsula dance and its accompanying music (known as kwaito) have slowly migrated out of the townships and emerged in the commercial arena. Like American hip-hop culture, pantsula culture has specific clothing styles associated with it, and it is particularly marked by the wearing of Converse All-Stars. Source: Rhodes University New Media Lab, http://cue.ru.ac.za/dance/2008/forever-pantsula.html.

14  See also John Ogbu, *Minority Education and Caste* (New York: Academic Press, 1978); John U. Ogbu and Herbert D. Simons, "Voluntary and Involuntary Minorities: A Cultural-Ecological Theory of School Performance with Some Implications for Education," *Anthropology and Education Quarterly* 29 (1998): 155–188.

15  Prudence L. Carter, *Keepin' It Real: School Success beyond Black and White* (New York: Oxford University Press, 2005).

16  For exceptions, see Mark Granovetter, "The Micro-Structure of School Desegregation," in *School Desegregation Research: New Directions in Situational Analysis*, ed. J. Prager, D. Longshore, and M. Seeman (New York: Plenum. 1985), 81–110; Maureen T. Hallinan and Richard A. Williams, "Interracial Friendship Choices in Secondary Schools," *American Sociological Review* 54 (1989): 67–78; Janet W. Schofield, "Promoting Positive Peer Relations in Desegregated Schools," *Educational Policy*

7 (1993): 297–318; Janet Ward Schofield, "School Desegregation and Intergroup Relations: A Review of the Literature," *Review of Research in Education* 17 (1991): 335–409.

17 See Eviatar Zerubavel, *The Fine Line: Making Distinctions in Everyday Life* (New York: Free Press, 1991), 120–22.

18 Ibid.

19 Kwame Anthony Appiah, "Cosmopolitans Patriots," *Critical Inquiry* 23 (1997): 617–39.

20 Sociologist Elijah Anderson writes about another concept that is related, the "cosmopolitan canopy" (drawing from Robert Merton). See Elijah Anderson, "The Cosmopolitan Canopy," *Annals of the American of Political and Social Science* 595 (2004): 14–31. Anderson's and philosopher Kwame Anthony Appiah's (1997) conceptualization of "cosmopolitanism" have some apparent differences. The cosmopolitan canopy describes public places which diverse groups patronize and interact or exchange information while behaving as businesspersons and consumers. Anderson writes that the cosmopolitan canopy enables patrons to engage in "cultural tourism," a symbolic cross-cultural exchange and consumption of food, music, wares, and so on. The cosmopolitan canopy is a social space that may provide an opportunity for diverse individuals to engage, though it may not necessarily change their a priori stereotypes or viewpoints about other social groups. Appiah, in contrast, writes about a sensibility that runs deeper than symbolic multiculturalism and urges individuals to take pleasure not only in cultural tourism but in the presence, communities, and homes of other, different peoples.

21 The study of boundary making, pioneered by the investigations of the anthropologist Fredrik Barth, constitutes an important and critical area of social science research. For a thorough review of the study of boundary making in the social sciences, see Michèle Lamont and Virág Molnár, "The Study of Boundaries in the Social Sciences," *Annual Review of Sociology* 28 (2002): 167–95. For a recent review of the state of the field of studies about boundaries, see Mark Pachucki, Sabrina Pendergrass, and Michèle Lamont, "Boundary Processes: Recent Theoretical Developments and New Contributions," *Poetics* 35 (2007): 331–51.

22 Lamont and Molnár 2002, 168.

23 Ibid.

24 Pierre Bourdieu and J. C. Passeron, *Reproduction in Education, Society and Culture* (Beverly Hills, CA: Sage, 1977); see also Michele Lamont, *Money, Morals & Manners: The Culture of the French and the American Upper-Middle Class* (Chicago: University of Chicago Press, 1992); Lamont and Molnár 2002.

25 Tom F. Gieryn, "Boundary-work and the Demarcation of Science from Non-Science: Strains and Interests in Professional Interests of Scientists." *American Sociological Review* 48 (1983): 781–95.

26 Jason Kaufman and Orlando Patterson, "Cross-National Cultural Diffusion: The Global Spread of Cricket," *American Sociological Review* 70 (2005): 82–110.

27 Bethany Bryson, "Anything But Heavy Metal": Symbolic Exclusion and Musical Dislikes," *American Sociological Review* 61 (1996): 884–99; Bonnie H. Erikson, "Culture, Class and Connections," *American Journal of Sociology* 102 (1996): 217–51; Richard A. Peterson and Roger M. Kern, "Changing Highbrow Taste: From Snob to Omnivore," *American Sociological Review* 61 (1996): 900–07.

28 Lamont and Molnár 2002; see also Andreas Wimmer, "The Making and Unmaking of Ethnic Boundaries: A Multi-Level Process Theory," *American Journal of Sociology* 113 (2008): 970–1022.

29 john a. powell, "A New Theory of Integrated Education: *True* Integration," in *School Resegregation: Must the South Turn Back?* ed. J. C. Boger and G. Orfield (Chapel Hill: University of North Carolina Press, 2005), 281–304; Crain Soudien, "Constituting the Class": An Analysis of the Process of 'Integration' in South African Schools," in *Education and Social Change in South Africa*, ed. L. Chisholm (Cape Town: HSRC Press, 2004), 89–114; Vally and Dalamba 1999.

30 Kim Kyong-Dong, "Modernization as a Politico-Cultural Response and Modernity as a Cultural Mixture: An Alternative View of Korean Modernization," *Development and Society* 34 (2005): 1–24.

31 Bourdieu theorized that sometimes domination cannot be exercised in an elementary form, or directly, and therefore it must be disguised. Often to the mere observer, domination is not recognized because it is euphemized. Euphemistic and censored forms of domination represent "symbolic violence," according to Bourdieu (1977a: 190–97). Following Bourdieu, I suggest here that symbolic violence may exist in schools with better mobility prospects but where sociocultural relations conflict with the objectives of equalizing opportunity for historically unequal groups.

32 In this text, "nondominant" with reference to the South African context refers to the groups of Africans, Coloureds, and Indians, who in the aggregate remain in an economic subordinate position as a result of decades of exclusion from equal opportunities and oppression under apartheid.

33 Ann Arnett Ferguson, *Bad Boys: Public Schools in the Making of Black Masculinity*, (Ann Arbor: University of Michigan Press, 2000).

34 Amanda E. Lewis, *Race in the Schoolyard: Reproducing the Color Line in School* (New Brunswick, NJ: Rutgers University Press, 2003).

35 Lamont and Molnár 2002.

36 Lamont's work, for example, demonstrates that upper-class and working-class men in France and the United States use cultural objects and practices to distinguish themselves from others around what it means to be worthy and valued. Affluent men in France who Lamont interviewed favored elite cultural knowledge, for instance, as the arbiter of taste, while affluent men in the United States favored financial success. This research validated how symbolic and social boundaries vary by nation, region, class, and race, especially as they pertain to ideas about morality and worthiness. See Lamont 1992; Michèle Lamont, *The Dignity of Working Men: Morality and the*

*Boundaries of Race, Class, and Immigration* (Cambridge and New York: Harvard University Press and Russell Sage Foundation, 2000).

37 For some exceptions, see Amy Binder, *Contentious Curricula: Afrocentrism and Creationism in American Public Schools* (Princeton, NJ: Princeton University Press, 2002); Bethany Bryson, *Making Multiculturalism: Boundaries and Meaning in U.S. English Departments* (Stanford, CA: Stanford University Press, 2005).

38 Pierre Bourdieu, "Cultural Reproduction and Social Reproduction," in *Power and Ideology in Education*, ed. J. Karabel and A. H. Halsey (New York: Oxford University Press, 1977a); Pierre Bourdieu, *Outline to a Theory of Practice* (London: Cambridge University Press, 1977b); Pierre Bourdieu, *Distinction: A Social Critique of the Judgment of Taste*, trans. R. Nice (London: Routledge & Kegan Paul, 1986).

39 McDonough, like Bourdieu, concentrates on the class-specific logic of the habitus, although again her concept applies to the social organization. See Patricia McDonough, "Structuring College Opportunities: A Cross-Case Analysis of Organizational Cultures, Climates, and Habituses," in *Sociology of Education: Emerging Perspectives*, ed. C. A. Torres and T. R. Mitchell (Albany: State University of New York Press, 1998), 181–210.

40 Erin M. Horvat and Anthony L. Antonio, "Hey, Those Shoes Are Out of Uniform: African American Girls in an Elite High School and the Importance of Habitus," *Anthropology and Education Quarterly* 3 (1999): 317–42.

41 Patricia Gurin, Timothy Peng, Gretchen Lopez, and Biren A. Nagda, "Context, Identity, and Intergroup Relations," in *Culture Divides: Understanding and Overcoming Group Conflict*, ed. D. A. Prentice and D. T. Miller, New York: Russell Sage Foundation, 1999), 133–77; Pamela Perry, *Shades of White: White Kids and Racial Identities in High Schools* (Durham, NC: Duke University Press, 2002); Mary C. Waters, *Black Identities: West Indian Immigrant Dreams and American Realities* (New York, NY & Cambridge, MA: Russell Sage Foundation and Harvard University Press, 1999); Sarah Susannah Willie, *Acting Black: College, Identity, and the Performance of Race* (New York: Routledge, 2003).

42 Pierre Bourdieu 1977a, 1977b; Annette Lareau, *Unequal Childhoods: Class, Race, and Family Life* (Berkeley: University of California Press, 2003).

43 Sociologists David Strang and Sarah Soule inform us that those cultural practices that are deemed as appropriate and effective diffuse more quickly. See David Strang and Sarah Soule, "Diffusion in Organizations and Social Movements: From Hybrid Corn to Poison Pills," *American Review of Sociology* 24 (1998): 265–90.

44 See Claude Steele, "A Threat in the Air: How Stereotypes Shape Intellectual Identity and Performance." *American Psychologist* 52 (1997): 613–29; Claude Steele, *Whistling Vivaldi: And Other Clues to How Stereotypes Affect Us* New York: Norton, 2010); Gregory M. Walton and Geoffrey L. Cohen, "A Question of Belonging: Race, Social Fit, and Achievement," *Journal of Personality and Social Psychology* 92 (2007): 82–96.

45 Robert Crosnoe, "Low-Income Students and the Socioeconomic Composition of Public High Schools," *American Sociological Review* 74 (2009): 709–30.

## CHAPTER 1

1 See, for example, Richard Kluger, *Simple Justice: The History of Brown v. Board of Education and Black America's Struggle for Equality* (New York: Vintage Books, 1975).

2 George Frederickson, *White Supremacy: A Comparative Study in American and South African History* (New York: Oxford University Press, 1981); Bernard Makhosezwe Magubane, *The Political Economy of Race and Class in South Africa* (Camden, NJ: Africa New World Press, 1979).

3 Ibid.

4 Bernard Makhosezwe Magubane, "Reflections on the Challenges Confronting Post-Apartheid South Africa," in *Conference on Struggles against Poverty, Unemployment and Social Exclusion: Public Policies, Popular Action and Social Development* (Bologna, Italy, organized by UNESCO in collaboration with the University of Bologna and the City of Bologna, December 2–3, 1994).

5 My first introduction to the notion of the "chameleon," or an individual living under one racial category and then officially changing his or her racial status, was at the Apartheid Museum in Gold Reef City, Gauteng, where I took a photograph of a newspaper article entitled "1985 Had at Least 1000 'Chameleons.'" This article had been published in the *Johannesburg Star* on March 21, 1985.

6 Segregated Indian-majority schools are more prevalent in the eastern region of South Africa. Because Indians are a very small percentage of the populations in the regions I studied, I did not include such schools in this study.

7 Originally filed as *Jane Doe v. State of Louisiana*, the series of cases on the one-drop rule (spanning the period from 1983 to 1986) demonstrates the adherence of the Louisiana Supreme Court and the U.S. Supreme Court—the highest U.S. court—to the rule of hypodescent. The plaintiff and her siblings brought suit after being denied a passport on the basis that she had indicated that her race was White, because her birth certificate indicated that she and her parents were Black. Despite the fact that the plaintiff could clearly establish that she only had one Black ancestor of a slave, back in 1770 (being the great, great, great, great granddaughter), which made her 1/256 Black, the courts refused to classify her as White. The statute in 1983 did not abolish the "traceable amount rule" (the one-drop rule), as demonstrated by the outcomes when the Phipps decision was appealed to higher courts in 1985 and 1986. See Brewton Berry and Henry L. Tischler, "Race and Ethnic Relations" (Boston, MA: Houghton Mifflin, 1978); Kimberlé Williams Crenshaw, "Race, Reform, and Retrenchment: Transformation and Legitimation in Antidiscrimination Law," *Harvard Law Review* 101 (1988); Cheryl I. Harris, "Whiteness as Property," *Harvard Law Review* 106 (1993): 1707–38; Gunnar Myrdal, *The American Dilemma: The*

*Negro Problem and Modern Democracy* (New York: Harper & Row, 1944); Calvin Trillin, "Black or White," *New Yorker*, April 14, 1986. Although the court chose not to address the issue there, the question of hypodescent even appears in *Plessy v. Ferguson*, 163 U.S. 537, the landmark case which established the "separate but equal doctrine." Plessy, the plaintiff, brought suit to challenge Jim Crow laws that prohibited him from sitting in train seats reserved for Whites on the basis that he was one-eighth Black—and could phenotypically pass as White.

8 Anthony Marx, *Making Race and Nation: A Comparison of South Africa, the United States and Brazil* (Cambridge: Cambridge University Press, 1988).

9 James Anderson, *The Education of Blacks in the South, 1860–1935,* (Chapel Hill: The University of North Carolina Press, 1988). See also James Loewen, *The Mississippi Chinese: Between Black and White* (Cambridge: Harvard University Press, 1971).

10 For example, W.E.B. Du Bois, renowned sociologist and activist, and the first African American to receive a doctorate from Harvard University, attended school with White children in Great Barrington, Massachusetts. See David Levering Lewis, *W. E. B. Du Bois, 1868–1919: Biography of a Race* (New York: Henry Holt and Co, 1994) and Kathryn Neckerman, *Schools Betrayed: Roots of Failure in Inner-City Education* (Chicago: University of Chicago Press, 2007).

11 Neckerman 2007.

12 Kluger 1975.

13 See, for instance, subsequent cases such as *Green v. County School Board of New Kent County* (1968), in which the U.S. Supreme Court identified the guidance known as the "Green factors" for formulating school desegregation plans and defined a standard for determining when a school is fully integrated (or achieves unitary status); *Swann v. Charlotte-Mecklenburg Board of Education* (1971), in which the court ruled that desegregation must be achieved by each local district school to the fullest extent possible and approved the use of busing to achieve these ends; *Keyes v. School District No. 1, Denver, Colorado* (1973), in which the court held that even in the absence of explicit statutes requiring segregation, in cases where a school board was found to have participated in intentional segregation (in any portion of the district), the entire district would be presumed segregated—including segregation of Latino learners—and would be subject to the rulings in *Brown I* and *II*; and *Milliken v. Bradley* (1974), in which the court's ruling basically prohibited integrating inner city district schools that have large Black, Latino, Asian, Native American, or other minority school populations by busing in students from the majority white, surrounding suburbs. Milliken is widely viewed as a turning point in the U.S. Supreme Court's efforts at school desegregation.

14 Howard Schuman, Charlotte Steeh, Lawrence Bobo, and Maria Krysan, *Racial Attitudes in America: Trends and Interpretations* (Cambridge, MA: Harvard University Press, 1998).

15 Gary Orfield and Chungmei Lei, "Brown at 50: King's Dream or Plessy's Nightmare," The Civil Rights Project, 2004, http://civilrightsproject.ucla.edu/research/k-12-ed-

ucation/integration-and-diversity/brown-at-50-king2019s-dream-or-plessy2019s-nightmare/orfield-brown-50-2004.pdf.

16 John R. Logan, Brian J. Stults, and Reynolds Farley, "Segregation of Minorities in the Metropolis: Two Decades of Change, "*Demography* 41 (2004): 1–22; Douglas Massey and Nancy Denton, American *Apartheid* (Cambridge: Harvard University Press, 1993).

17 Michael Cross and Linda Chisholm, "The Roots of Segregated Schooling in Twentieth-Century South Africa," in *Pedagogy of Domination*, ed. M. Nkomo (Trenton, NJ: Africa World Press, 1990), 43–76.

18 Ibid.

19 Ibid., p. 56.

20 Under apartheid, nineteen different departments of education existed nationwide and were divided in terms of administration along the lines of "race" and province.

21 Cross and Chisholm 1990.

22 Edward B. Fiske and Helen F. Ladd, Elusive *Equity: Education Reform in Post-Apartheid South Africa* (Washington, DC: Brookings Institution, 2004).

23 Ibid.

24 In 1976, hundreds of students marched through the streets of Soweto in protest of the forced school curriculum that centered on Afrikaner culture. An uprising with police ensued, and a fourteen-year-old boy named Hector Pieterson, now considered a youth martyr for the anti-apartheid resistance movement, was killed. Pieterson's limp and bullet-ridden body being carried by a male schoolmate alongside a distraught and crying female schoolmate is one of the most vivid and iconic images that captured the world's attention during the now infamous Soweto uprising.

25 Vally and Dalamba 1999; Servaas van der Berg, "Resource Shifts in South African Schools after the Political Transition," *Development Southern Africa* 18 (2001): 405–21.

26 Gay Seidman, "Is South Africa Different? Sociological Comparisons and Theoretical Contributions from the Land of Apartheid," *Annual Review of Sociology* 25 (1999): 419.

27 Ibid.

28 Linda Darling-Hammond, "Securing the Right to Learn: Policy and Practice for Powerful Teaching and Learning," *Educational Researcher* 35 (2006): 13–24.

29 Jonathan Kozol, *Savage Inequalities: Children in America's Schools* (New York: Crown Publishers, 1991); Jonathan Kozol, *Shame of the Nation* (New York: Random House, 2005).

30 Krisztina Tihanyi, "Racial Integration in the USA and South Africa: Lessons in a Comparative Perspective," *International Journal of Inclusive Education* 11 (2007): 177–97.

31 South African Institute of Race Relations, "Race Relations Survey 1988/89," South African Institute of Race Relations, Johannesburg, 1990.

32 Pam Christie, *Open Schools: Racially Mixed Catholic schools in South Africa, 1976–1986* (Johannesburg: Ravan Press, 1990).

33 South African Schools Act, p. 1

34 Emphasis added by Language in Education Policy, 1997

35 Ibid.

36 Tihanyi 2007, 191.

37 Amy Stuart Wells, Bianca J. Baldridge, Jacquelyn Durán, Courtney Grzesikowski, Richard Lofton, Allison Roda, Miya Warner, and Terrenda White, "Interdistrict Desegregation Plans and the Struggle for Equal Educational Opportunity," in *Passing the Torch: The Past, Present, and Future of Interdistrict School Desegregation* (Cambridge, MA: Charles Hamilton Houston Institute, Harvard Law School, 2009).

CHAPTER 2

1 Reynolds Farley and William Frey, "Changes in the Segregation of Whites from Blacks during the 1980s: Small Steps toward a More Integrated Society," *American Sociological Review* 59 (1994): 23–45.

2 Upper schools in townships, which run from grades eight through twelve, generally are called "secondary schools," while the schools with the same grade structure in the former white schools in the cities and suburbs are referred to as "high schools."

3 For a more detailed history of apartheid schooling, see Peter Kallaway, *The Doors of Culture and Learning Shall Be Open: The History of Education Under Apartheid (1948–1994)* (New York and Cape Town: Peter Lang and MML, 2002).

4 In Xhosa, nouns have stems that mostly serve a grammatical function, and language names always begin with the stem "isi-." For this reason, many people refer to the language as "isiXhosa," as opposed to simply "Xhosa."

5 These estimates are rough since many South African schools do not collect racial data in keeping with the nonracial ideology that pervades there.

6 South African educational policy requires that all students graduate with proficiency in at least two of its eleven national languages.

7 I should note that neither of the Black teachers in this school were native-born South Africans. Rather they were both male immigrants from Ghana and Zimbabwe.

8 Grant Saff, "Residential Segregation in Postapartheid South Africa: What Can Be Learned from the United States Experience," *Urban Affairs Review* 30 (1995): 782–808; Tihanyi, 2007.

9 Organization for Economic Co-operation and Development (OECD), "Reviews of National Policies for Education: South Africa-978–92-64–05348-9," Paris, France, 2008. http://www.fedusa.org.za/pdfdocs/Reviews%20of%20National%20Policies%20for%20Education_South%20Africa.pdf.

10 Source: National Center for Education Statistics, Common Core Public School Data, 2005–2006 academic year.

11 Ibid.

12 VDP is a state-funded program designed to eliminate racial imbalance through the busing of children of color from North Capital City to public school systems in surrounding suburban communities.

13 Sources: Census Data, http://factfinder.census.gov and http://www.statssa.gov.za.

14 World Bank, 2008, World Bank List of Economies (country classification), http:// go.worldbank.org/K2CKM78CC0.

## CHAPTER 3

1 Beverly Daniel Tatum, *"Why Are All the Black Kids Sitting at the Cafeteria Table?" and Other Conversations about Race* (New York: Basic Books, 1997).

2 Ibid.

3 Hazel Markus, Claude Steele, and Dorothy Steele, "Colorblindness as a Barrier to Inclusion: Assimilation and Nonimmigrant Minorities," *Daedalus* 129 (2002): 233–59.

4 Nadine Dolby, *Constructing Race: Youth, Identity and Popular Culture in South Africa* (Albany: State University of New York, 2001).

5 Ibid., p. 17.

6 In 2004, South African high schools varied greatly in the degree to which they offer this level of courses, either for lack of resources or for a dearth of educators experienced in teaching these more advanced classes.

7 For the survey, White students were slightly oversampled (based on either the Anglicized or Afrikaaner-sound of the surname), since at the time, the schools in the study did not include precise racial data on their student populations.

8 Organization for Economic Co-operation and Development (OECD), "Reviews of National Policies for Education: South Africa-978–92-64–05348-9," Paris, France, 2008. http://www.fedusa.org.za/pdfdocs/Reviews%20of%20National%20Policies% 20for%20Education_South%20Africa.pdf; see also Chisholm 2005, as quoted in OECD report, 2008.

9 Verashni Pillay, "Matric Pupils Receive Results," *Mail & Guardian Online* (Johannesburg, SA, 2010), http://www.mg.co.za/article/2010-01-07-matric-pupils-receive-results.

10 Zimitri Erasmus and Edgar Pieterse, "Conceptualising Coloured Identities in the Western Cape Province of South Africa," in *National Identity and Democracy in Africa*, ed. M. Palmberg (South Africa: Human Sciences Research Council and Mayibuye Centre of the University of the Western Cape, 1999), 167–87.

11 For more discussion of the history of coloured identity and the history of black-coloured relations, see Zimitri Erasmus, "Coloured by History, Shaped by Place: New Perspectives on Coloured Identities in Cape Town" (Cape Town: Kwela, 2001).

12 William Trent as quoted in Mitchell Chang, "Beyond Artificial Integration: Reimagining Cross-Racial Interactions among Undergraduates," *New Directions for Student Services* 120 (2007): 25–36.

13 Psychologist Beverly Tatum wrote a book with this very title to explore the psychosocial reasons for why racial minorities seek each other out when they are the minority in a school. Tatum argues that these out-group members (i.e., Black students) generally find psychological safety, belonging, and cohesion among one another and seek to mitigate the psychological toll of racism, stereotyping, and social alienation in their self-segregated spaces. See Tatum, 1997.

14 There were only a handful of Asian and Latino students attending this school.

15 Some studies show that students are more attached to schools when they attend them with proportionately more students of their own race, ethnicity, or class. See Crosnoe 2009; Jeremy D. Finn and Kristin Voelkl, "School Characteristics Related to Student Engagement," *Journal of Negro Education* 62 (1993): 249–68; Monica K. Johnson, Robert Crosnoe, and Glen H. Elder, Jr., "Students' Attachment and Academic Engagement: The Role of Race and Ethnicity," *Sociology of Education* 74 (2001): 318–40.

16 The school maintained some restrictions on all students in terms of length and adornments. Williston also forbade the use of hair gels and mousse.

17 Alison Dundes Renteln, "Visual Religious Symbols and the Law," *American Behavioral Scientist* 47 (2004): 1573–96.

18 Gabriele Vom Bruck, "Naturalising, Neutralising Women's Bodies: The 'Headscarf Affair' and the Politics of Representation," *Identities* 15 (2008): 51–79.

19 Bourdieu and Passeron 1977; Erin M. Horvat and Anthony L. Antonio, "Hey, Those Shoes Are Out of Uniform: African American Girls in an Elite High School and the Importance of Habitus," *Anthropology and Education Quarterly* 30 (1999): 317–42; Michèle Lamont and Annette Lareau, "Cultural Capital: Allusions, Gaps and Glissandos in Recent Theoretical Developments," *Sociological Theory* 6 (1988): 153–68; Jay MacLeod, *Ain't No Makin' It: Aspirations and Attainment in a Low-Income Neighborhood* (Boulder, CO: Westview Press, 1995).

20 Being sent to a confined punishment space for talking in class or talking back to teachers or misbehaving in other ways is not a new issue, especially in the United States. For studies of race and punishment in school, see Ann Arnett Ferguson, *Bad Boys: Public Schools in the Making of Black Masculinity* (Ann Arbor: University of Michigan, 2000); Edward Morris Press, *An Unexpected Minority: White Kids in an Urban School* (New Brunswick, NJ: Rutgers University Press, 2006).

21 Kevin Welner and colleagues developed this concept in the context of research on various school communities' responses to the politically sensitive practice of de-tracking. See Jeannie Oakes, Kevin Welner, Susan Yonezawa, and Ricky Lee Allen, "Norms and Politics of Equity-Minded Change: Researching the "Zone of Mediation," in *Fundamental Change: International Handbook of Educational Change*, ed. M. Fullan (Netherlands: Springer, 1998), 282–305.

22 Linda Chisholm, "Change and Continuity in South African Education: The Impact of Policy," *African Studies* 58 (1999): 87–103.

23 Chisholm, 1999; Kevin Welner, Legal *Rights, Local Wrongs: When Community Control Collides with Educational Equity* (Albany: State University of New York Press, 2001).

24 *Johannesburg Sunday Times*, "Posh School Says Girl's Braids Are 'Unacceptable,'" December 4, 2005.

25 A methodological note is due here. Although I encountered this practice at Palmer years before the graduate student visitor arrived, I chose to remain neutral, to not disrupt the "natural setting" of my research field and to not express my disfavor of the policy for a few reasons: First, because my orthodox research methods training had mandated neutrality, and second, because my position as an African American woman and foreigner in a "white"-dominant school trying to establish rapport and the trust of its staff members was already delicate and tenuous. In the spirit of full reflexivity, I admit my relief that a White person raised the specter of inequality embedded in the school's hair policy, since I believed that the school personnel could and would hear it better from a member of their own racial group than from me.

26 Fiske and Ladd 2004; Yusuf Sayed and Crain Soudien, "Decentralisation and the Construction of Inclusion Education Policy in South Africa," *Compare*, 35(2005): 115–125; Thobeka V. Mda, "Issues in the Making of South Africa's Language in Education Policy," *The Journal of Negro Education* 66 (1997): 366–75.

27 I invoke the broader, inclusive, political connotation of "Black" here to include Africans, Coloureds, and Indians.

28 Chisholm 1999; Glenda Kruss, "Towards Human Rights in South African Schools: An Agenda for Research and Practice," *Race, Ethnicity and Education* 4 (2001): 45–62.

29 For a more in-depth discussion of racialized tracking patterns in American high schools, see Roslyn Mickelson, "The Academic Consequences of Desegregation and Segregation: Evidence from the Charlotte-Mecklenburg Schools," *North Carolina Law Review* 51 (2003): 1513–62; Oakes 2005; Tyson 2011.

30 Founded in 1987, "Challenge Day," a program that is a part of the "Be the Change Movement"—which promotes kind and compassionate acts for others and the infusion of humanist tendencies throughout society—was developed by a husband-wife team of motivational speakers. The founders travel to high schools and had students and teachers spend time in one-day retreats discussing and breaking across social boundaries, from Black versus White, poor versus middle class, popular versus non-popular, overweight versus slim, bully versus nerd, and so on.

31 Tyson 2011.

32 As the opportunity structure opened, various sectors of U.S. society also struggled with the physical presentation of African Americans, for instance, as they were being included into the fold economically. American legal scholar Kenji Yoshino discusses such past pervasive forms of cultural inequality in the United States, focusing specifically on the district court decision in *Rogers v. American Airlines* in which judges ruled that an African American female airport operations agent had to abide by her

company's hair policy that forbade all-braided hairstyles. The court ruled that Rogers could not invoke Title VI and claim that she was being discriminated against because a hairstyle did not constitute an immutable racial trait. Meanwhile, the court did posit that an "Afro/bush" style could be protected "because banning a natural hairstyle would implicate the policies underlying the prohibition of discrimination on the basis of immutable characteristics." See Kenji Yoshino, *Covering: The Hidden Assault on Our Civil Rights* (New York: Random House, 2006), 132. Also, various camps in the United States continue to debate the virtues of either bilingualism or multilingualism in a dominant English-speaking nation with immense social diversity; see Kenji Hakuta, *Mirror Language: The Debate on Bilingualism* (New York: Basic Books, 1986); John Rhee, "Theories of Citizenship and Their Role in the Bilingual Education Debate," *Columbia Journal of Law and Social Problems* 33 (1999): 33–83.

33 Meyer and Rowan, "The Structure of Educational Organizations," in *Schools and Society: A Sociological Approach to Education*, ed. J. H. Ballantine and J. Z. Spade (Thousand Oaks, CA: Sage, 2007), 217–25.

34 Diane Reay, "It's All Becoming a Habitus": Beyond the Habitual Use of Habitus in Educational Research." *British Journal of Sociology of Education* 25 (2004): 431–44.

CHAPTER 4

1 Samuel Bowles and Herbert Gintis, *Schooling in Capitalist America: Educational Reform and the Contradictions of Economic Life* (New York: Basic Books, 1976); MacLeod 1995; Paul Willis, *Learning to Labor: How Working Class Kids Get Working Class Jobs* (New York: Columbia University Press, 1977).

2 Roslyn Arlin Mickelson and Anne E. Velasco, "Bring It On! Diverse Responses to 'Acting White' among Academically Able Black Adolescents," in *Beyond Acting White: Reassessments and New Directions in Research on Black Students and School Success*, ed. E. Horvat and C. O'Connor (New York: Rowman & Littlefield, 2006), 27–56; Karolyn Tyson, William Darity, and Domini Castellino, "It's Not a Black Thing: Understanding the Burden of Acting White and Other Dilemmas of High Achievement," *American Sociological Review* 70 (2005): 582–605.

3 Maureen T. Hallinan and Richard A. Williams, "Interracial Friendship Choices in Secondary Schools," *American Sociological Review* 54 (1989): 67–78; Moody 2002.

4 Carter 2005; Signithia Fordham and John Ogbu, "Black Students' School Success: Coping with the 'Burden of Acting White'," *Urban Review* 18 (1986): 176–206; Margaret Gibson, *Accommodation without Assimilation* (Ithaca, NY: Cornell University Press, 1988); Carla O'Connor, "Making Sense of the Complexity of Social Identity in Relation to Achievement: A Sociological Challenge in the New Millennium," *Sociology of Education* Extra Issue (2001): 159–68; Ogbu 1978.

5 Angela Valenzuela, *Subtractive Schooling: Issues of Caring in Education of U.S.-Mexican Youth* (Albany: State University of New York Press, 1999).

6 Gibson 1988.

7 Donna Deyhle, "Navajo Youth and Anglo Racism: Cultural Integrity and Resistance," *Harvard Educational Review* 65 (1995): 403–44.

8 See Antonia Darder, *Culture and Power in the Classroom: A Critical Foundation for Bicultural Education* (New York: Bergin & Garvey, 1991); Gibson 1988; Teresa LaFramboise, Hardin L. K. Coleman, and Jennifer Gerton, "Psychological Impact of Biculturalism: Evidence and Theory," *Psychological Bulletin* 114 (1993): 395–412; Hugh Mehan, Lea Hubbard, and Irene Villanueva, "Forming Academic Identities: Accommodation without Assimilation among Involuntary Minorities," *Anthropology & Education Quarterly* 25 (1994): 91–117; Jean Phinney and Mona Devich-Navarro, "Variations in Bicultural Identification among African American and Mexican American adolescents," *Journal of Research on Adolescence* 7 (1997): 3–32; Henry T. Trueba, "Multiple Ethnic, Racial, and Cultural Identities in Action: From Marginality to a New Cultural Capital in Modern Society," *Journal of Latinos and Education* 1 (2002): 7–28.

9 Nan Sussman, "The Dynamic Nature of Cultural Identity throughout Cultural Transitions: Why is Home Not So Sweet," *Personality and Social Psychology Review* 4 (2000): 355–73.

10 Ibid., p. 368.

11 While social and organizational psychologists use the term "interculturalism," sociologists have developed the idea of a cultural "omnivore," traits capturing individuals' capacity to be eclectic and multicultural in their tastes, knowledge, or cultural appreciation. Studies of omnivorous individuals have pertained to cultural studies of musical tastes, however. See, for example, Bryson 1996; Peterson and Kern, 1996.

12 In 2008, I returned to South Africa and followed up with ninety-seven high school matrics (seniors) who were initially eighth graders when I met them four years prior; these ninety-seven students also completed a new survey including the cultural flexibility measure. However, the sample is too small to conduct the type of analysis I report here with the U.S. students.

13 I took a grounded theory approach (Glaser and Strauss 1967) to the development of these questions. Based on my group interviews and prior research (Carter 2005), I used items that students discussed mostly when describing themselves as cultural actors and boundary crossers.

14 Both factor and scale analyses reveal that these items constitute a highly reliable construct of one unique factor (with an eigenvalue greater than 5.0). Also, analyses yielded a separate reliability coefficient of .91 for both Black and White groups. Moreover, the high-scale reliability coefficients maintained across the four multiracial high schools, ranging from .88 to .92.

15 See also Maureen Hallinan and Ruy Teixeira, "Students' Interracial Friendships: Individual Characteristics, Structural Effects, and Racial Differences," *American Journal of Education* 95 (1987): 563–83.

16 Jomills Henry Braddock II and Amaryllis Del Carmen Gonzalez, "Social Isolation and Social Cohesion: The Effects of K–12 Neighborhood and School Segregation on Intergroup Orientations," *Teachers College Record* 112 (2010): 1631–53.

17 Contrary to popular perceptions, multiple studies find that African Americans report significantly higher rates of individualism and similar rates of collectivism compared to European Americans, although the effects are small. For more discussion of these concepts and findings, see Daphna Oyserman, Heather M. Coon, and Markus Kemmelmeier, "Rethinking Individualism and Collectivism: Evaluation of Theoretical Assumptions and Meta-Analyses," *Psychological Bulletin* 128 (2002): 3–72.

18 Morris Rosenberg, "Self-Esteem Research: A Phenomenological Corrective," in *School Desegregation Research: New Directions in Situational Analysis*, ed. J. Prager, D. Longshore, and M. Seeman (New York: Plenum, 1985), 175–203.

19 Some researchers question the patterns of high self-esteem among Blacks in research results and suggest that Blacks have a propensity for using the "extreme" answer categories in their response to self-esteem questions by arguing that no differences would ensue if answer categories were collapsed (Bachman & O'Malley 1984). Such research, however, has provided little to no theoretical account for why Black respondents have a tendency to be more "extreme" than other groups. Meanwhile, hundreds of studies have shown consistently that Blacks maintain higher self-esteem than their White counterparts. Also, Whites maintain higher self-esteem than other racial groups in the United States (Gray-Little and Hafdahl 2000; Twenge and Crocker 2002), although, to our knowledge, no study has attributed Whites' higher self-esteem—compared to American Indians, Hispanics, and Asian Americans—to answering in the extreme. Meta-analyses of self-esteem studies show that such race-difference patterns are consistently strong, and social psychologists attribute these differences to cultural differences, levels of individualism (as opposed to collectivism), and protective mechanisms to stigma and location (ibid.).

20 Glenn Firebaugh and Kenneth Davis, "Trends in Antiblack Prejudice: 1972–1984, Region and Cohort Efforts," *American Journal of Sociology* 94 (1988): 251–72; Lincoln Quillian, "Group Threat and Regional Change in Attitudes Towards African Americans," *American Journal of Sociology* 102 (1996): 816–60.

21 cf. Braddock and Gonzalez 2010.

22 William Edward Burghardt Du Bois, "Does the Negro Need Separate Schools?" *Journal of Negro Education* 4 (1935): 328–35; powell 2005.

23 Jean Anyon, "Social Class and the Hidden Curriculum of Work," in *Education and Society*, ed. K. J. Dougherty and F. M. Hammack (Orlando, FL: Harcourt Brace Jovanovich, 1990); Bowles and Gintis 1976; Adam Gamoran, "The Stratification of High School Learning Opportunities," *Sociology of Education* 60 (1987): 135–55; Oakes 2005.

24 Robin M. Kyburg, Holly Hertberg-Davis, and Carolyn M. Callahan, "Advanced Placement and International Baccalaureate Programs: Optimal Learning Envi-

ronments for Talented Minorities?" *Journal of Advanced Academics* 18 (2007): 172–215.

25 Oakes 2005; Amy Stuart Wells and Irene Serna, "The Politics of Culture: Understanding Local Political Resistance to Detracking in Racially Mixed Schools," *Harvard Educational Review* 66 (1996): 93–118.

26 Robert L. Crain, Rita E. Mahard, and Ruth Narot, *Making Desegregation Work* Cambridge: Ballinger, 1982); Amy Stuart Wells and Robert L. Crain, "Perpetuation Theory and the Long-Term Effects of School Desegregation," *Review of Educational Research* 64 (1994): 531–55.

27 Rosenberg 1985.

28 Title 1 is the nation's oldest and largest federally funded, educationally related program. Annually, it provides billions of dollars in supplementary funds to school systems across the country for students at risk of failure and living at or near poverty. At least 40 percent of students must qualify for either free or reduced lunch. Originally, the idea of Title 1 was enacted in 1965 under the Elementary and Secondary Education Act. This policy committed to closing the achievement gap between low-income students and other students. The policy was rewritten in 1994 to improve fundamental goals of helping at-risk students. With the implementation of the No Child Left Behind legislation, schools must make adequate yearly progress on state testing and focus on best teaching practices in order to continue receiving funds.

29 "Girbaud" refers to French designer wear, especially blue jeans, which were popularized by rappers and hip-hop artists and have acquired a strong following among urban minority youth, especially among Black youth. The cultural appropriation of "Girbaud" as "black" in the United States marks another striking moment of how styles and tastes become racialized (see Dolby 2001).

30 Hallinan and Williams 1989; Hallinan and Teixeira 1987; Moody 2002; Janet W. Schofield, "Promoting Positive Peer Relations in Desegregated Schools," *Educational Policy* 7 (1993): 297–318; Janet Ward Schofield, "School Desegregation and Intergroup Relations: A Review of the Literature," *Review of Research in Education* 17 (1991): 335–409.

31 Maria Glod, "Fairfax Success Masks Gap for Black Students: Test Scores in County Lag Behind State's Poorer Areas," *Washington Post*, April 14, 2006, A01.

32 Mark Winerup, "How a Cleveland Suburb Spurs Black Achievement," *New York Times*, December 14, 2005, 8; Kathryn Borman, Tamela M. Eitle, Deanne Michael, David J. Eitle, Reginald Lee, Larry Johnson, Deidre Cobb-Roberts, Sherman Dorn, and Barbara Shircliffe, "Accountability in a Postdesegregation Era: The Continuing Significance of Racial Segregation in Florida's Schools," *American Educational Research Journal* 41 (2004): 605–31; Crain and Mahard 1983; Eric Hanushek, John F. Kain, and Steven Rivkin, "New Evidence about *Brown v. Board of Education*: The Complex Effects of School Racial Composition on Achievement," *Journal of Labor Economics* 27 (2009): 349–83; Roslyn Mickelson, "The Academic Consequences of Desegregation and Segregation: Evidence from the Charlotte-Mecklenburg

Schools," *North Carolina Law Review* 51 (2003): 1513–62; Roberta G. Simmons, Leslie Brown, Diane Mitsch Bush, and Dale A. Blyth, "Self-Esteem and Achievement of Black and White Adolescents," *Social Problems* 26 (1978): 86–96.

33 Robert L. Crain, "School Integration and Occupational Achievement of Negroes," *American Journal of Sociology* 75 (1970): 593–606; Crain and Mahard 1983; McIntire et al. 1982; Gary Orfield, *Schools More Separate: Consequences of a Decade of Resegregation* (Cambridge, MA: The Civil Rights Project, Harvard University, 2001); Wells and Crain 1994.

34 Goldsmith 2004; Moody 2002.

35 Hallinan and Williams 1989.

36 For another discussion of this, see Amy Stuart Wells, Jennifer Jellison Holme, Anita Tijerina Rivilla, and Awo Korantemaa Atanda, *Both Sides Now* (Berkeley: University of California Press, 2009).

37 Johnson et al. 2001.

38 Donald O. Leake and Christine J. Faltz, "Do We Need to Desegregate All of Our Black Schools?" *Educational Policy* 7 (1993): 370–88.

39 Douglas Massey, Camille Charles, Garvey F. Lundy, and Mary Fischer, *The Source of the River: The Social Origins of Freshmen at America's Selective Colleges and Universities* (Princeton, NJ: Princeton University Press, 2003).

40 Tatum 1997.

41 The outcomes of intergroup experiences are very much dependent on the structure of the contact situation, however. Hence, I would caution any reader from essentializing and reading all schools with similar social compositions as the same. Research informs us that variation in experiences exists even within schools with similar social, racial, and ethnic compositions (Schofield 1991).

42 Linda Darling-Hammond, "Race, Inequality and Educational Accountability: The Irony of 'No Child Left Behind'" *Race, Ethnicity and Education* 10(2007): 245–60; Jacqueline Irvine, *Black Students and School Failure: Policies, Practices, and Prescriptions* (New York: Praeger Publications, 1990); Gloria Ladson-Billings, *The Dreamkeepers: Successful Teachers of African-American Children* (San Francisco, CA: Jossey-Bass, 1994).

43 Jean Phinney and Mona Devich-Navarro, "Variations in bicultural identification among African American and Mexican American adolescents," *Journal of Research on Adolescence* 7 (1997): 3–32.

44 Mickelson 2001; Oakes 2005; Sayed and Soudien 2005; Tyson et al. 2005; Wells et al. 2009.

## CHAPTER 5

1 Mark Gevisser, *A Legacy of Liberation: Thabo Mbeki and the Future of the South African Dream* (New York: Palgrave Macmillan, 2009); Nelson Mandela, *Long Walk to Freedom: An Autobiography of Nelson Mandela* (Boston, MA: Back Bay Books, 1995).

2 Herbert Blumer, "Race Prejudice as a Sense of Group Position," *Pacific Sociological Review* 1 (1958): 3–7; Lawrence Bobo and Vincent L. Hutchings, "Perceptions of Racial Group Competition: Extending Blumer's Theory of Group Position to a Multiracial Social Context," *American Sociological Review* 61 (1996): 951–72; Schuman et al. 1998.

3 Susan Dumais, "Cultural Capital, Gender and School Success: The Role of Habitus," *Sociology of Education* 75 (2002): 44–68; Reay 2004.

4 Haroon Bhorat and S. M. Ravi Kanbur, "Poverty and Policy in Post-Apartheid South Africa" (Cape Town: Human Sciences Research Council Press, 2006).

5 Report retrieved at http://www.labour.gov.za/documents/annual-reports/Commission%20for%20Employment%20Equity%20Report/2009–2010/commission-for-employment-equity-report-2009–2010 on December 21, 2010.

6 See Ali A. Abdi, "Integrated Education and Black Development in Post-Apartheid South Africa: Critical Analyses," *Compare: A Journal of Comparative Education* 31 (2001): 229–35; George Subotzky, "South Africa," in *African Higher Education: An International Handbook*, ed. D. Teferra and P. G. Altbach (Bloomington: Indiana University Press, 2003).

7 Although Asian American students attending majority-minority schools appeared three times as likely as Asian American students attending majority-white schools to prefer schools where their group was in the majority, this difference is not significant, which is possibly due to the small cell sizes.

8 Lawrence Bobo, James Kluegel, and Ryan Smith, "Laissez-Faire Racism: The Crystallization of Kinder, Gentler, Anti-Black Ideology," in *Racial Attitudes in the 1990s: Continuity and Change*, ed. S. A. Tuch and J. K. Martin (New York: Russell Sage, 1997), 15–44.

9 In writing about dominant group ethnic identity in the United States, sociologist Ashley Doane defines the "dominant group" as "the ethnic group in a society that exercises power to create and maintain a pattern of economic, political, and institutional advantage, which in turn results in the unequal (disproportionately beneficial to the dominant group) distribution of resources" (1999: 73). Doane continues that a key element of dominance is the disproportionate ability to shape the sociocultural understandings of society. In the United States, the dominant group is defined as White Americans.

10 For a empirical analyses of whiteness in the twenty-first century, see Charles A. Gallagher, "White Racial Formation: Into the Twenty-First century," in *Rethinking the Color Line: Readings in Race and Ethnicity*, ed. C. A. Gallagher (Mountain View, CA: Mayfield, 1999), 503–08; Mary Waters, *Ethnic Options: Choosing Identities in America* (Berkeley: University of California Press, 1990).

11 Another condition that Wimmer (2008) discusses is stability (or the propensity of an ethnic group to either remain the same or change its nature over time). The stability of an ethnic group's identity and practices is often dependent on a host of economic, political, and social factors.

12 Black students at South County High, a minority group, agreed with this statement the most. The reader might recall from chapter 4 that this is the group that appeared to have the most difficult time based on social, cultural, and psychological indicators such as cultural flexibility and self-esteem.

13 Gans defined "symbolic" ethnicity as "a nostalgic allegiance to culture of the immigrant generation, or that of the old country: a love for and a pride in a tradition that can be felt without having to be incorporated in everyday behavior" (1999: 422).

14 For a more incisive analysis of this racial "fatigue," see John Jackson, *Racial Paranoia: The Unintended Consequences of Political Correctness* (New York: Basic Civitas Books, 2008); Jonathan Jansen, *Knowledge in the Blood: Confronting Race and the Apartheid Past* (Stanford, CA: Stanford University Press, 2009).

15 South Africa's Black Economic Empowerment (BEE) policy is a strategy implemented by the national government to redress past inequality and systematic exclusions of Asian, Black, and Coloured South Africans from the economy. It is often dubbed as an "affirmative action" mandate. An integral part of the BEE Act of 2003 is a sector-wide generic scorecard, which measures companies' empowerment progress in four areas: direct empowerment of previously disenfranchised groups through ownership and control of enterprises and assets; access to management jobs at senior level; human resource development and employment equity; and indirect empowerment through channels such as preferential procurement and business development (source: http://www.southafrica.info/business/trends/empowerment/bee.htm).

16 Robert Merton, *Social Theory and Structure* (New York: Free Press, 1968); Hyman Rodman, "The Lower-Class Value Stretch," *Social Forces* 42 (1963): 205–15.

17 Gloria Ladson-Billings, "From the Achievement Gap to the Education Debt: Understanding Achievement in U.S. Schools," *Educational Researcher* 35 (2006): 3–12.

18 Ira Katznelson, "When Is Affirmative Action Fair? On Grievous Harms and Public Remedies," *Social Research* 73 (2006): 541–68.

19 Roslyn Mickelson, "The Attitude-Achievement Paradox among Black Adolescents," *Sociology of Education* 63 (1990): 44–61.

20 Similar processes occur in the United States where immigrant Blacks appear to have higher social status than native African Americans (Waters 1990).

21 Jansen (2009) recounts a poignant experience that occurred during his time as dean of the School of Education at the University of Pretoria when he ran into a colleague at the mall who refused to acknowledge his presence and wave in public.

22 Blumer 1958.

23 Silva, Graziella Moraes Dias da, "Re-Making Race, Class, and Nation: Black Professionals in Brazil and South Africa," PhD Dissertation, Sociology, Harvard University, Cambridge, MA, 2010.

24 Jansen, 2009, p. 261.

25 See John Hartigan, *Racial Situations: Class Predicaments of Whiteness in Detroit* (Princeton, NJ: Princeton University Press, 1999); Lewis 2003; Morris 2006.

26 Pamela Perry, *Shades of White: White Kids and Racial Identities in High Schools* (Durham, NC: Duke University Press, 2002).

27 James A. Banks, "Multicultural Education: Characteristics and Goals," in *Multicultural Education: Issues and Perspectives*, ed. J. Banks and C. McGee Banks (New York: John Wiley and Sons, 2001), 3–30; Cameron McCarthy, *Race and Curriculum: Social Inequality and the Theories and Politics of Difference in Contemporary Research on Schooling* (London: Falmer, 1990).

28 Orfield and Lei 2004

29 See Thomas J. LaBelle, "Schooling and Intergroup Relations: A Comparative Analysis," *Anthropology and Education Quarterly* 10 (1979): 43–60.

30 Tyrone Forman, "Color-Blind Racism and Racial Indifference: The Role of Racial Apathy in Facilitating Inequalities," in *The Changing Terrain of Race and Ethnicity*, ed. M. Krysan and A. E. Lewis (New York: Russell Sage Foundation, 2006).

31 Nina Eliasoph and Paul Lichterman, "'We Begin with Our Favorite Theory…': Reconstructing the Extended Case Method," *Sociological Theory* 17 (1999): 228–34.

32 Robert L. Linn and Kevin G. Welner, eds., "Race-Conscious Policies for Assigning Students to Schools: Social Science Research and the Supreme Court Cases" (Washington, DC: National Academy of Education, 2007).

33 Blumer 1958; Bobo and Hutchings 1996.

## CHAPTER 6

1 Charles H. Thompson, "Race and Equality of Educational Opportunity: Defining the Problem," *Journal of Negro Education* 37 (1968): 191–203.

2 National Academy of Education, "Race-Conscious Policies for Assigning Students to Schools: Social Science Research and the Supreme Court Cases" (Washington, DC, 2007)

3 Schuman et al. 1998.

4 Reynolds Farley and William Frey, "Changes in the Segregation of Whites from Blacks during the 1980s: Small Steps toward a More Integrated Society," *American Sociological Review* 59 (1994): 23–45; Schuman et al. 1998.

5 David Laberee, *How to Succeed in School without Really Learning: The Credentials Race in American Education* (New Haven, CT: Yale University Press, 1997).

6 Paul Attewell, "The Winner-Take-All High School: Organizational Adaptations to Educational Stratification," *Sociology of Education* 74 (2001): 267–95.

7 Thomas J. Espenshade, Lauren E. Hale, and Chang Y. Chung, "The Frog Pond Revisited: High School Academic Context, Class Rank, and Elite College Admission," *Sociology of Education* 78 (2005): 269–93; Lareau 2003.

8 Elizabeth Anderson, *The Imperative of Integration* (Princeton, NJ: Princeton University Press, 2010); John Dewey, *Democracy and Education* (New York: Macmillan, 1916).

9 For example, an evaluation of a "treatment" program to facilitate multicultural relations in a university setting, Gurin et al. (1999) found that those students who actively participated in a program facilitating intergroup relations were more likely to participate in campus cross-cultural events, to take specific courses on inequality, and to maintain intergroup dialogues and discussions.

10 john powell 2005.

11 An ideal type is not regarded as a perfect representation of a given social phenomenon. Rather, social theorists utilize the concept for heuristic purposes, and that is the goal in this section, to elucidate a typology of what school integration may aspire to if we listen and learn from the current struggles of students attending socially diverse schools today.

12 powell 2005; Derrick Bell, *And We Are Not Saved: The Elusive Quest for Racial Justice* (New York: Basic Books, 1989).

13 Gary Orfield, "Reviving the Goal of an Integrated Society: A 21st Century Challenge," The Civil Rights Project, 2009, http://civilrightsproject.ucla.edu/research/k-12-education/integration-and-diversity/reviving-the-goal-of-an-integrated-society-a-21st-century-challenge/orfield-reviving-the-goal-mlk-2009.pdf..

14 See also Van der Berg 2001.

15 Harris Seloda and Yves Zenoub, "Private versus Public Schools in Post-Apartheid South African Cities: Theory and Policy Implications," *Journal of Development Economics* 71 (2003): 351–94; Wells and Serna 1996.

16 Logan et al. 2004; Schuman et al. 1998.

17 In analyzing racial differences in crime in urban neighborhoods, Sampson and Wilson question whether it is even possible to reproduce in communities of color the (material) structural circumstances under which many Whites live. See Robert Sampson and William J. Wilson, "Toward a Theory of Race, Crime, and Urban Inequality," in *Crime and Inequality*, ed. J. Hagan and R. D. Peterson (Stanford, CA: Stanford University Press, 1995), 37–54.

18 Wells and Serna 1996.

19 Tyson 2011; Oakes 2005; Mickelson 2001.

20 Mickelson and Velasco 2006; Tyson et al. 2005.

21 Prior to 2006, the Senior Certificate curriculum consisted of 124 subjects that expanded to 264 subject offerings after taking into consideration the three grades of subjects that were being offered: higher, standard, and lower. Of these 224 subjects, only 10 were offered by 90 percent of the candidates at any single sitting of the Senior Certificate (Department of Education Republic of South Africa, 2003). The new National Curriculum Statement offers twenty-nine subjects that can only be studied and tested at a general grade level for all learners.

22 Emsie Ferreira, "Matric Results Lay Bare Inequalities," *Mail & Guardian Online,* December 30, 2008.

23 Oakes 2005; Tyson et al. 2005; Mickelson 2001.

208 NOTES

24 Peter McLaren, "White Terror and Oppositional Agency: Towards a Critical Multiculturalism," in *Multiculturalism: A Critical Reader*, ed. D. T. Goldberg (Cambridge,
MA: Blackwell, 1994), 45–74.

25 Ibid.

26 Kymlicka 2001; see also Durkheim 2008; Parsons 2008.

27 Kymlicka 2001; Anderson 2010.

28 Wells 2000.

29 Orfield 2009

30 Welner 2001; Mickelson 1990; Rodman 1963

31 Welner 2001.

32 Ibid.

33 Wells et al. 2009; Welner 2001.

34 In the 5–4 decision of the *Parents Involved in Community Schools v. Seattle School
District No. 1* and *Meredith v. Jefferson County Board of Education* ("*PICS*"), by the
U.S. Supreme Court, June 28, 2007, two justices concurred with Chief Justice John
Roberts's majority opinion against the race-based practices for admissions to school
and provided further nuance to their decisions by writing separate opinions about
the United States' inclination for creating social diversity in schools. Justice Anthony
Kennedy, referring to the spirit of the precedent set by *Brown v. the Board of Education* and writing ostensibly the controlling opinion for the PICS case, argued that
racial diversity remains a compelling state goal, although narrow state-based racial
classification schema that have adverse effects on individuals but are used to achieve
racial balance are unconstitutional. In contrast, Justice Clarence Thomas, a consistent conservative voice on the court, argued that students of color could succeed in
schools when there exist high educational expectations and that their proclivity to
learn is not affected by whether they have proximity to Whites. He also argued that
there is no authoritative evidence to suggest that physical proximity among different races guarantees improved interracial contact and other social outcomes across
the races. Ironically, some progressive-minded academics agree with him, albeit for
divergent reasons. Justice Thomas's rationale evinces a position that White students
should not be forced to sacrifice access to scarce educational positions and resources
to which they feel entitled. In contrast, critical race theorists are more likely to offer
arguments about how systemic inequalities that are pervasive within many white-
majority desegregated schools can maintain noxious educational environments for
historically excluded groups (Bell 1989; Ladson-Billings 2004; powell 2005).

35 Jennifer L. Hochschild, *The New American Dilemma: Liberal Democracy and School
Desegregation* (New Haven, CT: Yale University Press, 1984); Myrdal 1944.

36 Orfield 2009.

37 The subsample of Palmer students was too small compared to the groups of students
who responded in the United States to attain statistical significance. Nonetheless,
their average mean score was 4.39 (out of 5) compared to North City Tech's average
of 4.10, which is the highest average among all of the U.S. schools.

38 Nel Noddings, *The Challenge to Care in Schools: An Alternative Approach to Educa-tion* (New York: Teachers College Press, 1992).

39 Danielle S. Allen, *Talking to Strangers: Anxieties of Citizenship since Brown v. Board of Education* (Chicago, IL: University of Chicago Press, 2004a).

40 Ibid., p. 134.

41 Ibid., p. 165.

CHAPTER 7

1 Du Bois 1935.

2 Source: CIA World Factbook, https://www.cia.gov/library/publications/the-world-factbook/rankorder/2172rank.html.

3 Legal scholar, Morton J. Horwitz, as quoted in Waldo E. Martin, *Brown vs. Board of Education: A Brief History with Documents* (Boston, MA: St. Martin's Press, 1998), 35.

4 Kymlicka 2001.

5 Na'ilah Nasir and Victoria Hand, "Exploring Sociocultural Perspectives on Race, Culture, and Learning," *Review of Educational Research* 76 (2006): 449–475.

6 Oakes et al. 1998; Wells et al. 2009.

7 Robert N. Bellah, Richard Madsen, William Sullivan, Ann Swidler, and Stephen M. Tipton, *Habits of the Heart: Individualism and Commitment in American Life* (Berkeley: University of California Press, 2008).

8 Fine, Weiss, and Powell 1997, 249.

9 Tyson 2011; Mickelson 2001; Oakes 2005; Robert E. England, Kenneth J. Meier, and Luis Ricardo Fraga, "Barriers to Equal Opportunity: Educational Practices and Minority Students," *Urban Affairs Review* 23 (1988): 635–46.

10 Mark Granovetter, "The Micro-Structure of School Desegregation," in *School Desegregation Research: New Directions in Situational Analysis*, ed. J. Prager, D. Longshore, and M. Seeman (New York: Plenum, 1985), 81–110.

11 Jomills Braddock and James M. McPartland, "Social Psychological Processes That Perpetuate Racial Segregation: The Relationship between School and Employment Desegregation," *Journal of Black Studies* 19 (1989): 267–89.

12 Donald O. Leake and Christine J. Faltz, "Do We Need to Desegregate All of Our Black Schools?" *Educational Policy* 7 (1993): 370–88.

13 See Sussman 2000; Phinney and Devich-Navarro 1997; LaFramboise et al. 1993.

14 See Tyson 2011 for a more detailed discussion of this social phenomenon.

15 Darling-Hammond 2007; Irvine 1990; Ladson-Billings 1994.

16 Carter 2005.

17 Mica Pollock, *Colormute: Race Talk Dilemmas in an American School* (Princeton, NJ: Princeton University Press, 2004).

18 Amy Ansell, "Two Nations of Discourse: Mapping Racial Ideologies in Post-Apartheid South Africa," *Politikon: South African Journal of Political Studies* 31 (2004): 3–26.

19 Michael Omi and Howard Winant, *Racial Formations in the United States* (New York: Routledge, 1994).

20 See also Wells and Serna (1996), for example, for a discussion of how White, middle-class parents resisted de-tracking in their schools to maintain their children's advantages and privilege.

21 Bobo et al. (1997) discuss the notion of laissez-faire approach in how white attitudes have changed toward institutional racism. They discuss the historical evolution of the movement from support of explicit forms of de jure discrimination to now a hand-off approach to state intervention in discriminatory housing, job, and educational practices after the implementation of the Civil Rights Acts, which are perceived by many Whites as having sufficiently redressed past exclusions by the state.

22 Labelle 1979; see also Mark Gould, "Race and Theory: Culture, Poverty and Adaptation to Discrimination in Wilson and Ogbu," *Sociological Theory* 17 (1999): 171–200.

23 Danielle S. Allen, "Turning Strangers into Political Friends," In These Times, 2004b, http://www.inthesetimes.com/article/1777/turning_strangers_into_political_friends/.

24 For an analysis of white flight in schools and neighborhoods over the last several decades in the United States, see Logan et al. 2005; Sean F. Reardon and John T. Yun, "Integrating Neighborhoods, Segregating Schools: The Retreat from School Desegregation in the South, 1990–2000," *North Carolina Law Review* 81 (2003): 1563–69.

APPENDIX

1 Geertz 1983.

2 Glaser and Strauss 1967.

3 David L. Morgan, "Focus Groups," *Annual Review of Sociology* 22 (1996): 122–52.

4 Ann Lewis, "Group Child Interviews as a Research Tool," *British Educational Research Journal* 18 (1992): 413–21.

5 Ibid.

# Bibliography

Abdi, Ali A. "Integrated Education and Black Development in Post-Apartheid South Africa: Critical Analyses." *Compare: A Journal of Comparative Education* 31 (2001): 229–35.

Abu El-Haj, and Thea Renda. *Elusive: Wrestling with Difference and Educational Equity in Everyday Practice.* New York: Routledge, 2006.

Allen, Danielle S. *Talking to Strangers: Anxieties of Citizenship since Brown v. Board of Education.* Chicago: University of Chicago Press, 2004a.

———, 2004b. "Turning Strangers into Political Friends." In *These Times,* accessed November 18, 2011. http://www.inthesetimes.com/article/1777/turning_strangers_into_political_friends/.

Anderson, Elijah. "The Cosmopolitan Canopy." *Annals of the American of Political and Social Science* 595 (2004):14–31.

Anderson, Elizabeth. *The Imperative of Integration.* Princeton, NJ: Princeton University Press, 2010.

Anderson, James. *The Education of Blacks in the South, 1860–1935.* Chapel Hill, NC: University of North Carolina Press, 1988.

Ansell, Amy. "Two Nations of Discourse: Mapping Racial Ideologies in Post-Apartheid South Africa." *Politikon: South African Journal of Political Studies* 31 (2004): 3–26.

Anyon, Jean. "Social Class and the Hidden Curriculum of Work." In *Education and Society.* Edited by K. J. Dougherty and F. M. Hammack, 423–437. Orlando, FL: Harcourt Brace Jovanovich, 1990.

Appiah, Kwame Anthony. "Cosmopolitans Patriots." *Critical Inquiry* 23 (1997): 617–39.

Attewell, Paul. "The Winner-Take-All High School: Organizational Adaptations to Educational Stratification "*Sociology of Education* 74 (2001): 267–95.

Bachman, Jerald G., and Patrick M. O'Malley. "Yea-Saying, Nay-Saying, and Going to Extremes: Black-White Differences in Response Styles." *Public Opinion Quarterly* 48 (1984): 491–509.

Banks, James A. "Multicultural Education: Characteristics and Goals." In *Multicultural Education: Issues and Perspectives*. Edited by J. Banks and C. McGee Banks, 3–30. New York: John Wiley and Sons, 2001.

Bell, Derrick. *And We Are Not Saved: The Elusive Quest for Racial Justice*. New York: Basic Books, 1989.

Bellah, Robert N., Richard Madsen, William Sullivan, Ann Swidler, and Stephen M. Tipton. *Habits of the Heart: Individualism and Commitment in American Life*. Berkeley: University of California Press, 2008.

Berry, Brewton, and Henry L. Tischler. "Race and Ethnic Relations." Boston, MA: Houghton Mifflin, 1978.

Bhorat, Haroon, and S. M. Ravi Kanbur. "Poverty and Policy in Post-Apartheid South Africa." Cape Town: Human Sciences Research Council Press, 2006.

Binder, Amy. *Contentious Curricula: Afrocentrism and Creationism in American Public Schools*. Princeton, NJ: Princeton University Press, 2002.

Blumer, Herbert. "Race Prejudice as a Sense of Group Position." *Pacific Sociological Review* 1 (1958): 3–7.

Bobo, Larry, James Kluegel, and Ryan Smith. "Laissez-Faire Racism: The Crystallization of Kinder, Gentler, Anti-Black Ideology." In *Racial Attitudes in the 1990s: Continuity and Change*. Edited by S. A. Tuch and J. K. Martin, 15–44. New York: Russell Sage Foundation, 1997.

Bobo, Lawrence, and Vincent L. Hutchings. "Perceptions of Racial Group Competition: Extending Blumer's Theory of Group Position to a Multiracial Social Context." *American Sociological Review* 61 (1996): 951–72.

Borman, Kathryn, Tamela M. Eitle, Deanne Michael, David J. Eitle, Reginald Lee, Larry Johnson, Deidre Cobb-Roberts, Sherman Dorn, and Barbara Shircliffe. "Accountability in a Postdesegregation Era: The Continuing Significance of Racial Segregation in Florida's Schools." *American Educational Research Journal* 41 (2004): 605–31.

Bourdieu, Pierre. "Cultural Reproduction and Social Reproduction." In *Power and Ideology in Education*. Edited by J. Karabel and A. H. Halsey, 487–510. New York: Oxford University Press, 1977a.

Bourdieu, Pierre. *Outline to a Theory of Practice*. Cambridge: Cambridge University Press, 1977b.

———. *Distinction: A Social Critique of the Judgment of Taste*. Translated by R. Nice. London: Routledge & Kegan Paul, 1986.

Bourdieu, Pierre, and J. C. Passeron. *Reproduction in Education, Society and Culture*. Beverly Hills. CA: Sage, 1977.

Bowles, Samuel, and Herbert Gintis. *Schooling in Capitalist America: Educational Reform and the Contradictions of Economic Life*. New York: Basic Books, 1976.

Braddock, Jomills, and James M. McPartland. "Social Psychological Processes That Perpetuate Racial Segregation: The Relationship between School and Employment Desegregation." *Journal of Black Studies* 19 (1989): 267–89.

Braddock II, Jomills Henry, and Amaryllis Del Carmen Gonzalez. "Social Isolation and Social Cohesion: The Effects of K–12 Neighborhood and School Segregation on Intergroup Orientations." *Teachers College Record* 112 (2010): 1631–53.

Bryson, Bethany. "Anything but Heavy Metal": Symbolic Exclusion and Musical Dislikes." *American Sociological Review* 61 (1996): 884–99.

———. *Making Multiculturalism: Boundaries and Meaning in U.S. English Departments.* Stanford, CA: Stanford University Press, 2005.

Carnoy, Martin. "Rethinking the Comparative-and the International." *Comparative Education Review* 50 (2006): 551–70.

Carrim, Nazir, and Crain Soudien. "Critical Antiracism in South Africa." In *Critical Multiculturalism: Rethinking Multicultural and Antiracist Education.* Edited by S. May, 153–172. London: Falmer Press, 1999.

Carter, Prudence L. *Keepin' It Real: School Success beyond Black and White.* New York: Oxford University Press, 2005.

———. "Opportunities & Paradoxes: An Examination of Culture, Race & Group Incorporation in Post-Apartheid South African Schools." In *Thinking Diversity, Building Cohesion: A Transnational Dialogue on Education.* Edited by M. Nkomo and S. Vandeyar, 109–132. Amsterdam: Rozenberg, 2009.

———. "Race and Cultural Flexibility among Students in Different Multiracial Schools." *Teachers College Record* 112 (2010): 1529–74.

Chang, Mitchell. "Beyond Artificial Integration: Reimagining Cross-Racial Interactions among Undergraduates." *New Directions for Student Services* 120 (2007): 25–36.

Chisholm, Linda. "Change and Continuity in South African Education: The Impact of Policy." *African Studies* 58 (1999): 87–103.

———. "The Politics of Curriculum Review and Revision in South Africa in Regional Context." *Compare: A Journal of Comparative Education* 35 (2005): 79–100.

Christie, Pam. *Open Schools: Racially Mixed Catholic schools in South Africa, 1976–1986.* Johannesburg: Ravan Press, 1990.

Cock, Jacklyn, and Alison Bernstein. *Melting Pots & Rainbow Nations: Conversations about Difference in the United States and South Africa.* Urbana: University of Illinois Press, 2002.

Crain, Robert L. "School Integration and Occupational Achievement of Negroes." *American Journal of Sociology* 75 (1970): 593–606.

Crain, Robert L., and Rita E. Mahard. "The Effect of Research Methodology on Desegregation-Achievement Studies: A Meta-Analysis." *American Journal of Sociology* 88 (1983): 839–54.

Crain, Robert L., Rita E. Mahard, and R. Narot. *Making Desegregation Work.* Cambridge: Ballinger, 1982.

Crenshaw, Kimberlé Williams. "Race, Reform, and Retrenchment: Transformation and Legitimation in Antidiscrimination Law." *Harvard Law Review* 101 (1988):-1331–87.

Crosnoe, Robert. "Low-Income Students and the Socioeconomic Composition of Public High Schools." *American Sociological Review* 74 (2009): 709–30.

Cross, Michael and Linda Chisholm. "The Roots of Segregated Schooling in Twentieth-Century South Africa." In *Pedagogy of Domination*. Edited by Mokubung Nkomo, 43–76. Trenton, NJ: Africa World Press, 1990.

Darder, Antonia. *Culture and Power in the Classroom: A Critical Foundation for Bicultural Education*. New York: Bergin & Garvey, 1991.

Darling-Hammond, Linda. "Securing the Right to Learn: Policy and Practice for Powerful Teaching and Learning." *Educational Researcher* 35 (2006): 13–24.

———. "Race, Inequality and Educational Accountability: The Irony of 'No Child Left Behind.'" *Race, Ethnicity and Education* 10 (2007): 245–60.

Department of Education, Republic of South Africa. National Curriculum Statements, Grades 10–12 (General): Overview. Pretoria, 2003.

Dewey, John. *Democracy and Education*. New York: Macmillan, 1916.

Deyhle, Donna. "Navajo Youth and Anglo Racism: Cultural Integrity and Resistance." *Harvard Educational Review* 65 (1995): 403–44.

DiMaggio, Paul. "Classification in Art." *American Sociological Review* 52 (1987): 440–55.

Doane, Ashley W. "Dominant Group Ethnic Identity in the United States: The Role of 'Hidden' Ethnicity in Intergroup Relations." In *Majority and Minority: The Dynamics of Race and Ethnicity in American Life*. Edited by N. R. Yetman, 375–397. Boston, MA: Allyn & Bacon, 1999.

Dolby, Nadine. *Constructing Race: Youth, Identity and Popular Culture in South Africa*. Albany: State University of New York, 2001.

Du Bois, William Edward Burghardt. "Does the Negro Need Separate Schools?" *Journal of Negro Education* 4 (1935): 328–35.

Dumais, Susan. "Cultural Capital, Gender and School Success: The Role of Habitus." *Sociology of Education* 75 (2002): 44–68.

Durkheim, Emile. "Moral Education." In *Schools and Society: A Sociological Approach to Education*. Edited by J. H. Ballantine and J. Z. Spade, 29–33. Thousand Oaks, CA: Sage, 2008.

Eliasoph, Nina, and Paul Lichterman. "'We Begin with Our Favorite Theory...': Reconstructing the Extended Case Method." *Sociological Theory* 17 (1999): 228–34.

England, Robert E., Kenneth J. Meier, and Luis Ricardo Fraga. "Barriers to Equal Opportunity: Educational Practices and Minority Students." *Urban Affairs Review* 23 (1988): 635–46.

Erasmus, Zimitri. "Coloured by History, Shaped by Place: New Perspectives on Coloured Identities in Cape Town." Cape Town: Kwela, 2001.

Erasmus, Zimitri, and Edgar Pieterse. "Conceptualising Coloured Identities in the Western Cape Province of South Africa." In *National Identity and Democracy in Africa*. Edited by M. Palmberg, 167–187. South Africa: Human Sciences Research Council and Mayibuye Centre of the University of the Western Cape, 1999.

Erikson, Bonnie H. "Culture, Class and Connections." *American Journal of Sociology* 102 (1996): 217–51.

Espenshade, Thomas J., Lauren E. Hale, and Chang Y. Chung. "The Frog Pond Revisited: High School Academic Context, Class Rank, and Elite College Admission." *Sociology of Education* 78 (2005): 269–93.

Farley, Reynolds, and William Frey. "Changes in the Segregation of Whites from Blacks during the 1980s: Small Steps toward a More Integrated Society." *American Sociological Review* 59 (1994): 23–45.

Ferguson, Ann Arnett. *Bad Boys: Public Schools in the Making of Black Masculinity.* Ann Arbor: University of Michigan Press, 2000.

Ferreira, Emsie "Matric Results Lay Bare Inequalities," *Mail & Guardian Online,* December 30, 2008. http://mg.co.za/article/2008–12-30-matric-results-lay-bare-inequalities-in-sa.

Fine, Michelle, Lois Weis, and Linda Powell. "Communities of Difference: A Critical Look at Desegregated Spaces Created for and by Youth." *Harvard Educational Review* 67 (1997): 247–84.

Finn, Jeremy D., and Kristin Voelkl. "School Characteristics Related to Student Engagement." *Journal of Negro Education* 62 (1993): 249–68.

Firebaugh, Glenn, and Kenneth Davis. "Trends in Antiblack Prejudice: 1972–1984, Region and Cohort Efforts." *American Journal of Sociology* 94 (1988): 251–72.

Fiske, Edward B., and Helen F. Ladd. *Elusive Equity: Education Reform in Post-Apartheid South Africa.* Washington, DC: Brookings Institution, 2004.

Fordham, Signithia, and John Ogbu. "Black Students' School Success: Coping with the 'Burden of Acting White.'" *Urban Review* 18 (1986): 176–206.

Forman, Tyrone. "Color-blind Racism and Racial Indifference: The Role of Racial Apathy in Facilitating Inequalities." In *The Changing Terrain of Race and Ethnicity.* Edited by M. Krysan and A. E. Lewis, 43–66. New York: Russell Sage, 2006.

Frederickson, George. 1981. *White Supremacy: A Comparative Study in American and South African History.* New York: Oxford University Press.

Gallagher, Charles A. "White Racial Formation: Into the Twenty-First century." In *Rethinking the Color Line: Readings in Race and Ethnicity.* Edited by C. A. Gallagher, 503–508. Mountain View, CA: Mayfield, 1999.

Gamoran, Adam. "The Stratification of High School Learning Opportunities." *Sociology of Education* 60 (1987): 135–55.

Gans, Herbert J. "Symbolic Ethnicity: The Future of Ethnic Groups and Cultures in America." *Ethnic and Racial Studies* 2, no. 1 (1979): 1–20.

Geertz, Clifford. "Thick Description: Toward an Interpretive Theory of Culture." In *Contemporary Field Research: A Collection of Readings.* Edited by R. M. Emerson, 37–59. Prospect Heights, IL: Waveland Press, 1983.

Gevisser, Mark. *A Legacy of Liberation: Thabo Mbeki and the Future of the South African Dream.* New York: Palgrave Macmillan, 2009.

Gibson, Margaret. *Accommodation without Assimilation*. Ithaca, NY: Cornell University Press, 1988.

Giddens, Anthony. *New Rules of Sociological Method: A Positive Critique of Interpretative Sociologies*. London: Hutchinson, 1976.

Gieryn, Tom F. "Boundary-work and the Demarcation of Science from Non-Science: Strains and Interests in Professional Interests of Scientists." *American Sociological Review* 48 (1983): 781–95.

Glaser, Barney G., and Anselm L. Strauss. *The Discovery of Grounded Theory: Strategies for Qualitative Research*. New York: Aldine de Gruyter, 1967.

Glod, Maria. "Fairfax Success Masks Gap for Black Students: Test Scores in County Lag Behind State's Poorer Areas." *Washington Post,* April 14, 2006, A01.

Goldsmith, Pat Antonio. "Schools' Role in Shaping Race Relations: Evidence on Friendliness and Conflict." *Social Problems* 51 (2004): 587–612.

Gordon, Leah N. "The Individual and 'the General Situation:' The Tension Barometer and the Race Problem at the University of Chicago, 1947–1954." *Journal of the History of the Behavioral Sciences* 46 (2010): 27–51.

Gould, Mark. "Race and Theory: Culture, Poverty and Adaptation to Discrimination in Wilson and Ogbu." *Sociological Theory* 17 (1999): 171–200.

Granovetter, Mark. "The Micro-Structure of School Desegregation." In *School Desegregation Research: New Directions in Situational Analysis*. Edited by J. Prager, D. Longshore, and M. Seeman, 81–110. New York: Plenum, 1985.

Gray-Little, Bernadette, and Adam Hafdahl. "Factors Influencing Racial Comparisons of Self-Esteem: A Quantitative Review." *Psychological Bulletin* 126 (2000): 26–54.

Gurin, Patricia, Timothy Peng, Gretchen Lopez, and Biren A. Nagda. "Context, Identity, and Intergroup Relations." In *Culture Divides: Understanding and Overcoming Group Conflict*. Edited by D. A. Prentice and D. T. Miller, 133–177. New York: Russell Sage, 1999.

Hakuta, Kenji. *Mirror Language: The Debate on Bilingualism*. New York: Basic Books, 1986.

Hallinan, Maureen T., and Richard A. Williams. "Interracial Friendship Choices in Secondary Schools." *American Sociological Review* 54 (1989): 67–78.

Hallinan, Maureen, and Ruy Teixeira. "Students' Interracial Friendships: Individual Characteristics, Structural Effects, and Racial Differences." *American Journal of Education* 95 (1987): 563–83.

Hanushek, Eric, John F. Kain, and Steven Rivkin. "New Evidence about *Brown v. Board of Education*: The Complex Effects of School Racial Composition on Achievement." *Journal of Labor Economics* 27 (2009): 349–83.

Harris, Cheryl I. "Whiteness as Property." *Harvard Law Review* 106 (1993): 1707–38.

Hartigan, John. *Racial Situations: Class Predicaments of Whiteness in Detroit*. Princeton, NJ: Princeton University Press, 1999.

Hays, Sharon. "Structure and Agency and the Sticky Problem of Culture." *Sociological Theory* 12 (1994): 57–71.

Hochschild, Jennifer L. *The New American Dilemma: Liberal Democracy and School Desegregation*. New Haven, CT: Yale University Press, 1984.

Horvat, Erin M., and Anthony L. Antonio. "Hey, Those Shoes Are Out of Uniform: African American Girls in an Elite High School and the Importance of Habitus." *Anthropology and Education Quarterly* 30 (1999): 317–42.

Irvine, Jacqueline. *Black Students and School Failure: Policies, Practices, and Prescriptions*. New York: Praeger Publications, 1990.

Jackson, John. *Racial Paranoia: The Unintended Consequences of Political Correctness*. New York: Basic Civitas Books, 2008.

Jansen, Jonathan. *Knowledge in the Blood: Confronting Race and the Apartheid Past*. Stanford, CA: Stanford University Press, 2009.

Johnson, Monica K., Robert Crosnoe, and Glen H. Elder, Jr. "Students' Attachment and Academic Engagement: The Role of Race and Ethnicity." *Sociology of Education* 74 (2001): 318–40.

Kallaway, Peter. *The Doors of Culture and Learning Shall Be Open: The History of Education Under Apartheid (1948–1994)*. New York and Cape Town: Peter Lang and MML, 2002.

Katznelson, Ira. "When Is Affirmative Action Fair? On Grievous Harms and Public Remedies." *Social Research* 73 (2006): 541–68.

Kaufman, Jason, and Orlando Patterson. "Cross-National Cultural Diffusion: The Global Spread of Cricket." *American Sociological Review* 70 (2005): 82–110.

Kluger, Richard. *Simple Justice: The History of Brown v. Board of Education and Black America's Struggle for Equality*. New York: Vintage Books, 1975.

Kozol, Jonathan. *Savage Inequalities: Children in America's Schools*. New York: Crown, 1991.

———. *Shame of the Nation*. New York: Random House, 2005.

Kruss, Glenda. "Towards Human Rights in South African Schools: An Agenda for Research and Practice." *Race, Ethnicity and Education* 4 (2001): 45–62.

Kyburg, Robin M., Holly Hertberg-Davis, and Carolyn M. Callahan. "Advanced Placement and International Baccalaureate Programs: Optimal Learning Environments for Talented Minorities?" *Journal of Advanced Academics* 18 (2007): 172–215.

Kymlicka, Will. *Politics in the Vernacular: Nationalism, Multiculturalism and Citizenship*. New York: Oxford University Press, 2001.

Kyong-Dong, Kim. "Modernization as a Politico-Cultural Response and Modernity as a Cultural Mixture: An Alternative View of Korean Modernization." *Development and Society* 34 (2005): 1–24.

LaBelle, Thomas J. "Schooling and Intergroup Relations: A Comparative Analysis." *Anthropology and Education Quarterly* 10 (1979): 43–60.

Laberee, David. *How to Succeed in School without Really Learning: The Credentials Race in American Education*. New Haven, CT: Yale University Press, 1997.

Ladson-Billings, Gloria. *The Dreamkeepers: Successful Teachers of African-American Children*. San Francisco, CA: Jossey-Bass, 1994.

————. "Landing on the Wrong Note: The Price We Paid for *Brown*." *Educational Researcher* 33 (2004): 3–13.

————. "From the Achievement Gap to the Education Debt: Understanding Achievement in U.S. Schools." *Educational Researcher* 35 (2006): 3–12.

LaFramboise, Teresa, Hardin L. K. Coleman, and Jennifer Gerton. "Psychological Impact of Biculturalism: Evidence and Theory." *Psychological Bulletin* 114 (1993): 395–412.

Lamont, Michele. *Money, Morals & Manners: The Culture of the French and the American Upper-Middle Class*. Chicago, IL: University of Chicago Press, 1993.

————. *The Dignity of Working Men: Morality and the Boundaries of Race, Class, and Immigration*. Cambridge and New York: Harvard University Press and Russell Sage, 2000.

Lamont, Michele, and Annette Lareau. "Cultural Capital: Allusions, Gaps and Glissandos in Recent Theoretical Developments." *Sociological Theory* 6 (1988): 153–68.

Lamont, Michèle, and Virág Molnár. "The Study of Boundaries in the Social Sciences." *Annual Review of Sociology* 28 (2002): 167–95.

Lareau, Annette. *Unequal Childhoods: Class, Race, and Family Life*. Berkeley: University of California Press, 2003.

Leake, Donald O., and Christine J. Faltz. "Do We Need to Desegregate All of Our Black Schools?" *Educational Policy* 7 (1993): 370–88.

Lewis, Amanda E. *Race in the Schoolyard: Reproducing the Color Line in School*. New Brunswick, NJ: Rutgers University Press, 2003.

Lewis, Ann. "Group Child Interviews as a Research Tool." *British Educational Research Journal* 18 (1992): 413–21.

Lewis, David Levering, *W. E. B. Du Bois, 1868–1919: Biography of a Race*. New York: Henry Holt and Co, 1994.

Linn, Robert L., and Kevin G. Welner. Eds. "Race-Conscious Policies for Assigning Students to Schools: Social Science Research and the Supreme Court Cases." Washington, DC: National Academy of Education, 2007.

Loewen, James. *The Mississippi Chinese: Between Black and White*. Cambridge, MA: Harvard University Press, 1971.

Logan, John R., Brian J. Stults, and Reynolds Farley. "Segregation of Minorities in the Metropolis: Two Decades of Change." *Demography* 41 (2004): 1–22.

MacLeod, Jay. *Ain't No Makin' It: Aspirations and Attainment in a Low-income Neighborhood*. Boulder, CO: Westview Press, 1995.

Magubane, Bernard Makhosezwe. *The Political Economy of Race and Class in South Africa*. Camden, NJ: Africa New World Press, 1979.

————. "Reflections on the Challenges Confronting Post-Apartheid South Africa." In *Conference on Struggles against Poverty, Unemployment and Social Exclusion: Public Policies, Popular Action and Social Development*. Bologna, Italy. Organized by UNESCO in collaboration with the University of Bologna and the City of Bologna, December 2–3, 1994.

Mandela, Nelson. *Long Walk to Freedom: An Autobiography of Nelson Mandela.* Boston, MA: Back Bay Books, 1995.

Markus, Hazel, Claude Steele, and Dorothy Steele. "Colorblindness as a Barrier to Inclusion: Assimilation and Nonimmigrant Minorities." *Daedulus* 129 (2002): 233–59.

Martin, Waldo E. *Brown vs. Board of Education: A Brief History with Documents.* Boston, MA: St. Martin's Press, 1998.

Marx, Anthony. *Making Race and Nation: A Comparison of South Africa, the United States and Brazil.* Cambridge: Cambridge University Press, 1998.

Massey, Douglas, Camille Charles, Garvey F. Lundy, and Mary Fischer. *The Source of the River: The Social Origins of Freshmen at America's Selective Colleges and Universities.* Princeton, NJ: Princeton University Press, 2003.

Massey, Douglas, and Nancy Denton. *American Apartheid.* Cambridge, MA: Harvard University Press, 1993.

McCarthy, Cameron. *Race and Curriculum: Social Inequality and the Theories and Politics of Difference in Contemporary Research on Schooling.* London: Falmer, 1990.

McDonough, Patricia. "Structuring College Opportunities: A Cross-Case Analysis of Organizational Cultures, Climates, and Habituses." In *Sociology of Education: Emerging Perspectives.* Edited by C. A. Torres and T. R. Mitchell, 181–210. Albany: State University of New York Press, 1998.

McIntire, Ronald G., Larry W. Hughes, and Michael W. Say. "Houston's Successful Desegregation Plan." *Phi Delta Kappan* 63 (1982): 536–8.

McLaren, Peter. "White Terror and Oppositional Agency: Towards a Critical Multiculturalism." In *Multiculturalism: A Critical Reader.* Edited by D. T. Goldberg, 45–74. Cambridge, MA: Blackwell, 1994.

Mda, Thobeka V. "Issues in the Making of South Africa's Language in Education Policy." *The Journal of Negro Education* 66 (1997): 366–75.

Mehan, Hugh, Lea Hubbard, and Irene Villanueva. "Forming Academic Identities: Accommodation without Assimilation among Involuntary Minorities." *Anthropology & Education Quarterly* 25 (1994): 91–117.

Merton, Robert. *Social Theory and Structure.* New York: Free Press, 1968.

Meyer, John W., and Brian Rowan. "The Structure of Educational Organizations." In *Schools and Society: A Sociological Approach to Education.* Edited by J. H. Ballantine and J. Z. Spade, 217–225. Thousand Oaks, CA: Sage, 2007. First published 1978.

Mickelson, Roslyn. "The Attitude-Achievement Paradox among Black Adolescents." *Sociology of Education* 63 (1990): 44–61.

———. "The Academic Consequences of Desegregation and Segregation: Evidence from the Charlotte-Mecklenburg Schools." *North Carolina Law Review* 51 (2003): 1513–62.

Mickelson, Roslyn Arlin. "Subverting Swann: First- and Second-Generation Segregation in the Charlotte-Mecklenburg Schools." *American Educational Research Journal* 38 (2001): 215–52.

Mickelson, Roslyn Arlin, and Anne E. Velasco. "Bring it On! Diverse Responses to 'Acting White' Among Academically Able Black Adolescents." In *Beyond Acting White: Reassessments and New Directions in Research on Black Students and School Success*. Edited by E. Horvat and C. O'Connor, 27–56. New York: Rowman & Littlefield, 2006.

Moody, James. "Race, School Integration, and Friendship in America." *American Journal of Sociology* 107 (2002): 679–701.

Morgan, David L. "Focus Groups." *Annual Review of Sociology* 22 (1996): 122–52.

Morris, Edward. *An Unexpected Minority: White Kids in an Urban School*. New Brunswick, NJ: Rutgers University Press, 2006.

Muller, Chandra, Catherine Riegle-Crumb, Kathryn S. Schiller, Lindsey Wilkinson, and Kenneth A. Frank. "Race and Academic Achievement in Racially Diverse High Schools: Opportunity and Stratification." *Teachers College Record* 112 (2010): 1038–63.

Myrdal, Gunnar. *The American Dilemma: The Negro Problem and Modern Democracy*. New York: Harper & Row, 1944.

Nasir, Na'ilah, and Victoria Hand. "Exploring Sociocultural Perspectives on Race, Culture, and Learning." *Review of Educational Research* 76 (2006): 449–75.

National Academy of Education. "Race-Conscious Policies for Assigning Students to Schools: Social Science Research and the Supreme Court Cases." Washington, DC: Author, 2007.

Neckerman, Kathryn M. *Schools Betrayed: Roots of Failure in Inner-City Education*. hicago: University of Chicago Press, 2007).

Noddings, Nel. *The Challenge to Care in Schools: An Alternative Approach to Education*. New York: Teachers College Press, 1992.

O'Connor, Carla. "Making Sense of the Complexity of Social Identity in Relation to Achievement: A Sociological Challenge in the New Millenium." *Sociology of Education* Extra Issue (2001): 159–68.

Oakes, Jeannie. *Keeping Track: How Schools Structure Inequality*. New Haven, CT: Yale University Press, 1985.

Oakes, Jeannie, Kevin Welner, Susan Yonezawa, and Ricky Lee Allen. "Norms and Politics of Equity-Minded Change: Researching the 'Zone of Mediation.'" In *Fundamental Change: International Handbook of Educational Change*. Edited by M. Fullan, 282–305. Netherlands: Springer, 1998.

Ogbu, John. *Minority Education and Caste*. New York: Academic Press, 1978.

Ogbu, John U., and Herbert D. Simons. "Voluntary and Involuntary Minorities: A Cultural-Ecological Theory of School Performance with Some Implications for Education." *Anthropology and Education Quarterly* 29 (1998): 155–88.

Omi, Michael, and Howard Winant. *Racial Formations in the United States*. New York: Routledge, 1994.

Orfield, Gary. *Schools More Separate: Consequences of a Decade of Resegregation*. Cambridge, MA: The Civil Rights Project, Harvard University, 2001.

———. 2009. "Reviving the Goal of an Integrated Society: A 21st Century Challenge." In UCLA Civil Rights Project, accessed November 18, 2011. http:// civilrightsproject.ucla.edu/research/k-12-education/integration-and-diversity/ reviving-the-goal-of-an-integrated-society-a-21st-century-challenge/orfield-reviv- ing-the-goal-mlk-2009.pdf

Orfield, Gary, and Chungmei Lei. 2004. "Brown at 50: King's Dream or Plessy's Nightmare." The Civil Rights Project, http://civilrightsproject.ucla.edu/research/ k-12-education/integration-and-diversity/brown-at-50-king2019s-dream-or- plessy2019s-nightmare/orfield-brown-50-2004.pdf.

Organization for Economic Co-operation and Development (OECD). 2008. "Reviews of National Policies for Education: South Africa-978–92-64–05348-9." Paris, France. Accessed November 18. 2011. http://www.oecd.org/document/58/0,334 3,en_33873108_39418625_41422650_1_1_1_1,00.html

Oyserman, Daphna, Heather M. Coon, and Markus Kemmelmeier. "Rethinking Individualism and Collectivism: Evaluation of Theoretical Assumptions and Meta- Analyses." *Psychological Bulletin* 128 (2002): 3–72.

Pachucki, Mark, Sabrina Pendergrass, and Michele Lamont. "Boundary Processes: Recent Theoretical Developments and New Contributions." *Poetics* 35 (2007): 331–51.

Parsons, Talcott. "The School Class as a Social System." In *Schools and Society: A Sociological Approach to Education*. Edited by J. H. Ballantine and J. Z. Spade, 80–85. Thousand Oaks, CA: Sage, 2008.

Perry, Pamela. *Shades of White: White Kids and Racial Identities in High Schools*. Durham, NC: Duke University Press, 2002.

Peterson, Richard A., and Roger M. Kern. "Changing Highbrow Taste: From Snob to Omnivore." *American Sociological Review* 61 (1996): 900–07.

Pew Forum on Religion and Public Life Analysis. 2006. "Prospects on Inter-religious Understanding." http://pewforum.org/uploadedfiles/Topics/Religious_Affiliation/ Muslim/Inter-Religious-Understanding.pdf.

Phinney, Jean, and Mona Devich-Navarro. "Variations in bicultural identification among African American and Mexican American adolescents." *Journal of Research on Adolescence* 7 (1997): 3–32.

Pillay, Verashni. 2010. "Matric Pupils Receive Results." In *Mail & Guardian Online*. Accessed November 18, 2011. http://www.mg.co.za/article/2010–01-07-matric- pupils-receive-results.

Pollock, Mica. *Colormute: Race Talk Dilemmas in an American School*. Princeton, NJ: Princeton University Press, 2004.

powell, john a. "A New Theory of Integrated Education: *True* Integration." In *School Resegregation: Must the South Turn Back?* Edited by J. C. Boger and G. Orfield, 281–304. Chapel Hill: University of North Carolina Press, 2005.

Quillian, Lincoln. "Group Threat and Regional Change in Attitudes Towards African Americans." *American Journal of Sociology* 102 (1996): 816–60.

Ragin, Charles C. *The Comparative Method: Moving Beyond Qualitative and Quantitative Strategies*. Berkeley: University of California Press, 1987.

Reardon, Sean F., and John T. Yun. "Integrating Neighborhoods, Segregating Schools: The Retreat from School Desegregation in the South, 1990–2000." *North Carolina Law Review* 81 (2003): 1563–69.

Reay, Diane. "It's All Becoming a Habitus": Beyond the Habitual Use of Habitus in Educational Research. *British Journal of Sociology of Education* 25 (2004): 431–44.

Renteln, Alison Dundes. "Visual Religious Symbols and the Law." *American Behavioral Scientist* 47 (2004): 1573–96.

Rhee, John. "Theories of Citizenship and Their Role in the Bilingual Education Debate." *Columbia Journal of Law and Social Problems* 33 (1999): 33–83.

Rodman, Hyman. "The Lower-Class Value Stretch." *Social Forces* 42 (1963): 205–15.

Rosenberg, Morris. "Self-Esteem Research: A Phenomenological Corrective." In *School Desegregation Research: New Directions in Situational Analysis*. Edited by J. Prager, D. Longshore, and M. Seeman, 175–203. New York: Plenum, 1985.

Saff, Grant. "Residential Segregation in Postapartheid South Africa: What Can Be Learned from the United States Experience." *Urban Affairs Review* 30 (1995): 782–808.

Sampson, Robert, and William J. Wilson. "Toward a Theory of Race, Crime, and Urban Inequality." In *Crime and Inequality*. Edited by J. Hagan and R. D. Peterson, 37–54. Stanford, CA: Stanford University Press, 1995.

Sayed, Yusuf, and Crain Soudien. "Decentralisation and the Construction of Inclusion Education Policy in South Africa." *Compare* 35(2005): 115–125.

Schofield, Janet W. "Promoting Positive Peer Relations in Desegregated Schools." *Educational Policy* 7 (1993): 297–318.

Schofield, Janet Ward. "School Desegregation and Intergroup Relations: A Review of the Literature." *Review of Research in Education* 17 (1991): 335–409.

Schuman, Howard, Charlotte Steeh, Lawrence Bobo, and Maria Krysan. *Racial Attitudes in America: Trends and Interpretations*. Cambridge, MA: Harvard University Press, 1998.

Seidman, Gay. "Is South Africa Different? Sociological Comparisons and Theoretical Contributions from the Land of Apartheid." *Annual Review of Sociology* 25 (1999): 419–40.

Seloda, Harris and Yves Zenoub. "Private versus Public schools in Post-apartheid South African Cities: Theory and Policy Implications." *Journal of Development Economics* 71 (2003): 351–94.

Sewell, Jr., William H. "A Theory of Structure: Duality, Agency, and Transformation." *The American Journal of Sociology* 98 (1992): 1–29.

Silva, Graziella Moraes Dias da. "Re-Making Race, Class, and Nation: Black Professionals in Brazil and South Africa." PhD Dissertation, Sociology, Harvard University, Cambridge, MA, 2010.

Simmons, Roberta G., Leslie Brown, Diane Mitsch Bush, and Dale A. Blyth. "Self-Esteem and Achievement of Black and White Adolescents." *Social Problems* 26 (1978): 86–96.

Soudien, Crain. "We Know Why We Are Here: The Experiences of African Children in a 'Coloured' School in Cape Town." *Race, Ethnicity and Education* 1 (1998): 7–31.

———. "Constituting the Class": An Analysis of the Process of 'Integration' in South African Schools. In *Education and Social Change in South Africa.* Edited by L. Chisholm, 89–114. Cape Town: HSRC Press, 2004.

South African Institute of Race Relations. "Race Relations Survey 1988/89." South African Institute of Race Relations, Johannesburg, 1990.

Steele, Claude. "A Threat in the Air: How Stereotypes Shape Intellectual Identity and Performance." *American Psychologist* 52 (1997): 613–29.

———. *Whistling Vivaldi: And Other Clues to How Stereotypes Affect Us.* New York: W. W. Norton, 2010.

Stevens, Mitchell. *Creating a Class: College Admissions and the Education of Elites.* Cambridge, MA: Harvard University Press, 2009.

Strang, David, and Sarah Soule. "Diffusion in Organizations and Social Movements: From Hybrid Corn to Poison Pills." *American Review of Sociology* 24 (1998): 265–90.

Subotzky, George. "South Africa." In *African Higher Education: An International Handbook.* Edited by D. Teferra and P. G. Altbach, 545–62. Bloomington: Indiana University Press, 2003.

Sussman, Nan. "The Dynamic Nature of Cultural Identity throughout Cultural Transitions: Why Is Home Not So Sweet." *Personality and Social Psychology Review* 4 (2000): 355–73.

Tatum, Beverly Daniel. *"Why Are All the Black Kids Sitting at the Cafeteria Table?" and Other Conversations about Race.* New York: Basic Books, 1997.

Thompson, Charles H. "Race and Equality of Educational Opportunity: Defining the Problem." *Journal of Negro Education* 37 (1968): 191–203.

Tihanyi, Krisztina. "Racial Integration in the USA and South Africa: Lessons in a Comparative Perspective." *International Journal of Inclusive Education* 11 (2007): 177–97.

Trillin, Calvin. "Black or White," *New Yorker,* April 14, 1986, 62.

Trueba, Henry T. "Multiple Ethnic, Racial, and Cultural Identities in Action: From Marginality to a New Cultural Capital in Modern Society." *Journal of Latinos and Education* 1 (2002): 7–28.

Twenge, Jean M., and Jennifer Crocker. "Race and Self-Esteem: Meta-Analyses Comparing Whites, Blacks, Hispanics, Asians, and American Indians and Comment on Gray-Little and Hafdahl (2000)." *Psychological Bulletin* 128 (2002): 371–408.

Tyson, Karolyn. *Integration Interrupted.* New York: Oxford University Press, 2011.

Tyson, Karolyn, William Darity, and Domini Castellino. "It's Not a Black Thing: Understanding the Burden of Acting White and Other Dilemmas of High Achievement." *American Sociological Review* 70 (2005): 582–605.

Valenzuela, Angela. *Subtractive Schooling: Issues of caring in education of U.S.-Mexican youth*. Albany: State University of New York Press, 1999.

Vally, Salim, and Yolisa Dalamba. Racism, "Racial Integration" and Desegregation in South African Public Secondary Schools. A Report on a Study by the South African Human Rights Commission (SAHRC), SAHRC, Johannesburg, 1999.

Van der Berg, Servass. "Resource Shifts in South African Schools after the Political Transition." *Development Southern Africa* 18 (2001): 405–21.

Vom Bruck, Gabriele. "Naturalising, Neutralising Women's Bodies: The 'Headscarf Affair' and the Politics of Representation." *Identities* 15 (2008): 51–79.

Walton, Gregory M., and Geoffrey L. Cohen. "A Question of Belonging: Race, Social Fit, and Achievement." *Journal of Personality and Social Psychology* 92 (2007): 82–96.

Waters, Mary C. *Ethnic Options: Choosing Identities in America*. Berkeley: University of California Press, 1990.

———. *Black Identities: West Indian Immigrant Dreams and American Realities*. New York & Cambridge, MA: Russell Sage and Harvard University Press, 1999.

Wells, Amy Stuart. "The 'Consequences' of School Desegregation: The Mismatch between the Research and the Rationale." *Hastings Constitutional Law Quarterly* 28 (2000): 771–97.

Wells, Amy Stuart, Bianca J. Baldridge, Jacquelyn Durán, Courtney Grzesikowski, Richard Lofton, Allison Roda, Miya Warner, and Terrenda White. "Interdistrict Desegregation Plans and the Struggle for Equal Educational Opportunity." Unpublished report. Cambridge, MA: Charles Hamilton Houston Institute, Harvard Law School, 2009.

Wells, Amy Stuart, and Robert L. Crain. "Perpetuation Theory and the Long-Term Effects of School Desegregation." *Review of Educational Research* 64 (1994): 531–55.

Wells, Amy Stuart, Jennifer Jellison Holme, Anita Tijerina Rivilla, and Awo Korantemaa Atanda. *Both Sides Now*. Berkeley: University of California Press, 2009.

Wells, Amy Stuart, and Irene Serna. "The Politics of Culture: Understanding Local Political Resistance to Detracking in Racially Mixed Schools." *Harvard Educational Review* 66 (1996): 93–118.

Welner, Kevin. *Legal Rights, Local Wrongs: When Community Control Collides with Educational Equity*. Albany, NY: SUNY Press, 2001.

Willie, Sarah Susannah. *Acting Black: College, Identity, and the Performance of Race*. New York: Routledge, 2003.

Willis, Paul. *Learning to Labor: How Working Class Kids Get Working Class Jobs*. New York: Columbia University Press, 1977.

Wimmer, Andreas. "The Making and Unmaking of Ethnic Boundaries: A Multi-Level Process Theory." *American Journal of Sociology* 113 (2008): 970–1022.

Winant, Howard. *The Whole World is a Ghetto: Race and Democracy since World War II*. New York: Basic Books, 2002.

Winerup, Mark. "How a Cleveland Suburb Spurs Black Achievement, *New York Times,* December 14, 2005, 8.

Yoshino, Kenji. *Covering: The Hidden Assault on our Civil Rights.* New York: Random House, 2006.

Zerubavel, Eviatar. *The Fine Line: Making Distinctions in Everyday Life.* New York: Free Press, 1991.

# Index

A student discussed in the text is indexed under her/his first name. Educators (school name) mentioned in the text are listed by their last names. Pseudonyms are used for all students, educators, schools, and their locations. Page numbers in italics refer to tables or figures in the text.